PEARSON CUSTOM
Education

EDSE 662

George Mason University

PEARSON

Custom
Publishing

Sponsoring Editor: Natalie Danner
Development Editor: Abbey Briggs
Editorial Assistant: Jill Johnson
Marketing Manager: Amy Dyer
Operations Manager: Eric M. Kenney
Production Manager: Jennifer M. Berry
Rights Editor: Francesca Marcantonio
Art Director: Renée Sartell
Cover Designers: Kristen Kiley

Cover Art: "Textbooks and apple" used by permission of istock; "Teacher and students" used by permission of istock; "Classroom, globe on desk, US flag hanging from blackboard" Copyright © 1999-2008 Getty Images, Inc. All rights reserved.

Copyright © 2008 by Pearson Custom Publishing.

All rights reserved.

This copyright covers material written expressly for this volume by the editor/s as well as the compilation itself. It does not cover the individual selections herein that first appeared elsewhere. Permission to reprint these has been obtained by Pearson Custom Publishing for this edition only. Further reproduction by any means, electronic or mechanical, including photocopying and recording, or by any information storage or retrieval system, must be arranged with the individual copyright holders noted.

Printed in the United States of America.

Please visit our websites at *www.pearsoncustom.com* and *www.customliterature.com*.
Attention bookstores: For permission to return any unsold stock, contact us at *pe-uscustomreturns@pearsoncustom.com*.

ISBN-13: 978-0-558-09169-9
ISBN-10: 0-558-09169-5

Package ISBN-13: N/A
Package ISBN-10: N/A

PEARSON CUSTOM PUBLISHING
501 Boylston Street, Suite 900, Boston, MA 02116
A Pearson Education Company

Contents

CHAPTER ONE

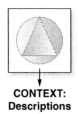

CONTEXT:
Descriptions

Working Together in Collaboration, Consultation, and Co-Teaching

Why do teachers choose education as a career? Some of us over the course of many years have posed that question to experienced teachers, graduate students in education, and undergraduate students in teacher preparation programs. Their responses have been like this:

> "I want to make a difference in children's lives."
> "I want to do my part to make the world better."
> "I want to help kids reach their potential."

Some teachers, especially those at the secondary level, also mention having a fondness for their curricular areas and a desire to share their enthusiasm for content in those areas with students. But other probable incentives such as respect from the public, desire to emulate a favorite teacher, plentiful job opportunities, steady salary, or even the anticipation of an extended summer vacation are farther down on teachers' lists of priorities for wanting to be an educator.

Goals to mold younger generations and make the world into a better place are lofty ones indeed. Such goals have tended in the past to be predicated on expectations of being in "my classroom," with "my students," using "the teaching ideas I have been assembling and now can put into practice." But these goals no longer fit neatly into the environment of twenty-first-century schools and classrooms. Teachers are being called on to work in more collegial ways by consulting and collaborating and often teaching as partners with their colleagues, for "*our* students" in "*our inclusive* classrooms," with "*our* shared plans and ideas."

FOCUSING QUESTIONS

1. What factors influence educators to become collaborative, collegial professionals rather than teachers in more isolated and autonomous roles?

2. How are collaboration, consultation, and team activities such as co-teaching defined?

From Chapter 1 of *Collaboration, Consultation, and Teamwork for Students with Special Needs*, 6/e. Peggy Dettmer. Linda P. Thurston. Ann Knackendoffel. Norma J. Dyck. Copyright © 2009 by Pearson Merrill. All rights reserved.

3

3. What perspectives on collaboration, consultation, and teamwork are appropriate within contemporary educational contexts?

4. What four key elements are necessary for strong collaborative school environments?

5. What benefits can be expected from collaborative school consultation, and what competencies are needed for educators to be effective collaborators and team members?

6. What ethical principles should guide the collaborative, consultative, and team-oriented processes in schools?

KEY TERMS

asynchronous	consultant	role clarification
client	consultation	role delineation
co-educator	consultee	role parity
collaboration	consulting teacher	synchronous
collaborative ethic	co-teaching	teamwork
collaborative school	exceptional learning needs	
consultation	(ELN)	
collaborator	preservice teacher	

SCENARIO 1.A*

The setting is the faculty room of a typical high school where four faculty members are sharing school news and airing their concerns.

English Teacher: I'm getting another special education student next week—with rather severe learning disabilities this time. I guess this is more fallout from the IDEA legislation, or inclusion, or whatever. Anyway, I'll have this student in my composition and literature classes, along with a student with behavior disorders I'm coping with, and state assessments, and our district curriculum standards committee, and on and on.

Math Teacher: (chuckling) Must be because you're doing such a great job. (serious tone) But I know what you mean. Our special ed teachers don't seem to be taking these kids out of our classes like they did when I first started teaching. But that was before we'd ever heard the words "inclusion" or "collaboration" or "co-teaching."

Music Teacher: And before legislators and national committees had come up with things like Goals 2000 and No Child Left Behind.

English Teacher: Well, they say a "consulting teacher" is coming to our next departmental meeting to talk about our roles in helping these students with their special needs. I understand we're going to be asked to collaborate—whatever that involves—along with all the other things we do, of course. We may even be encouraged to co-teach with other teachers.

Physical Education Teacher/Coach: Hmmm, don't those two words cancel each other out? "Consult" and "collaborate," that is. I believe you English teachers call that an oxymoron.

Music Teacher: I guess I'd be inclined to consult a tax accountant for some expert advice and think of collaboration as when everyone works together to accomplish some common goals they've agreed on. As for co-teaching, I can tell you what a difficult process that is when you have a group of independent thinkers and free spirits who like to do things their own way and want to be the star!

English Teacher: Well, frankly I'm not interested in word games right now. I'm more concerned about finding out where the time is going to come from to do one more thing. My schedule is packed, and my few minutes of free time don't jibe with anyone else's except for this brief lunch period. And I want to know who will have the bottom-line responsibility for which students, and when, and where. And how!

Math Teacher: Right. I've had some concerns about including all students in my instruction and testing, not to mention the NCLB-required testing. I think we need more help to do all of this and I hope we get it.

*We recommend that persons using this book with a group read each of the scenarios aloud, having readers contribute their parts in conversational tone and style. In this way the situations will seem relevant and facilitative rather than artificial and contrived.

TEACHER AUTONOMY IN THE PAST

In the past, teachers worked alone in their classrooms for the most part. They marked attendance forms, took lunch counts, completed other daily procedures, and then closed their classroom doors to begin instruction of the required content. They tried to handle each learning situation with minimal outside help. Asking for assistance would have been tantamount to showing insecurity or demonstrating incompetence. After all, hardy and capable teachers in the past had managed eight grades in one-room schoolhouses without help, hadn't they?

In more recent times schools have become multi-dimensional centers of activity and very social places. But the individual teacher with myriad responsibilities and goals for personal as well as professional accomplishment can still feel stranded in a crowded setting devoid of adult interactions and professional stimulation. Paradoxically, teachers are just next door or down the hall from other adults, yet somewhat insulated from each other during the school day. They tend to go about their responsibilities autonomously without much meaningful adult interaction. This can make teaching a lonely occupation in a very public place. (See Figure 1.1.)

As one example, at the secondary level Inger (1993) notes that academic and vocational teachers are expected to work together and make connections between their

FIGURE 1.1   "I feel so alone!"

school-based subjects and the world of work. But the insularity of some subjects and departmental boundaries are barriers for meaningful collaboration where, even if teachers would want to collaborate and co-teach, there is limited opportunity. Nevertheless, they have mutual expectations for students that include development of good work habits, punctuality, ability to follow directions, and most importantly, capacities for complex reasoning and problem solving. These shared goals are grounds for collaborating with each other even though they may be located far from the main buildings along the perimeters of sprawling campuses (Inger, 1993).

Many teachers, particularly those who are just beginning their careers, have been reluctant to discuss their concerns or ask for assistance from support personnel lest their confidence and competency be called into question. This absence of dialogue with peers has been consistently recognized as contributing to teachers' feelings of isolation and even inhibiting their inclination to modify classroom practices (Johnson & Pugach, 1996). In the meantime, resource teachers, related services personnel, and support personnel have waited in the wings until called on for assistance with a student's escalating learning or behavioral problems. Too often these potential co-educators are involved only after situations reach crisis level, rather than when they could have a more participatory and helpful role in problem identification and early intervention.

So as teachers' lists of responsibilities grow and the time available for instructing their class as an intact group becomes shorter, the burden of trying to meet the needs of all students becomes heavier. Chunking of the typical school day can further insulate teachers from sources of ideas beyond their own background of experiences. Here again, this is particularly evident at the high school level where teachers might have up to five classes and several different preparations daily while interacting with more than 100-plus students during the course of the day and sometimes the evening.

Adding to the complexity of the school day with its myriad curricular *and* extracurricular activities is the growing awareness by perceptive teachers that *every* student has special needs requiring special attention. Furthermore every student has unique abilities and talents. The task of developing the potential of all students and preparing them for future careers, more education, and responsibilities as citizens can be overwhelming. That "little red schoolhouse" concept of having one teacher serve a wide range of student needs and abilities and attend to the expanding curricular demands of the twenty-first century just will not do.

WHY WORK TOGETHER AND NOT AUTONOMOUSLY?

Today, in our increasingly interdependent and specialized world, it is unlikely that any one person possesses enough knowledge and ability in any field of endeavor to handle every circumstance. So it is reasonable and prudent to consult, collaborate, and team up, working in partnerships with others to achieve common goals. Consultation and collaboration are routine in fields as varied as medicine, law, industry, fashion, sports, construction, scientific research, journalism, decorating, finance—the list is endless. Some consultants even have their own consultants! Teamwork is emphasized frequently in a wide range of work settings from professions to trades to government to community affairs. In fields that encourage networking with others who have similar yet helpfully different perspectives, the results have been dramatic. Sharing of expertise stimulates productivity and growth as colleagues collaborate and provide consultation for peers in their areas of special abilities.

Teaching is a multidimensional activity. An educator's role has never been easy and it is becoming more challenging each year. School personnel are bombarded with more and more responsibilities, and the legislatures and general public are raising expectations for student achievement and measurable yearly progress. Cosmetic alteration of existing programs and practices will not be enough to address such complex issues and multiple concerns. Responsibilities for instruction, management of the learning environment, assessment of student achievement, professional development activity, and communication with a broad range of school personnel and families have escalated and expanded well beyond the one-room schoolhouse or isolated classroom where the teacher was be-all and end-all for students.

APPLICATION 1.1
IDENTIFYING TEACHER RESPONSIBILITIES

What does a teacher do in the course of a day, a week, a school year? With short phrases list all the specific responsibilities you can think of that a teacher typically performs during the course of a school year. Draw upon recollections of your student days, college coursework, student teaching, and any teaching experiences that you have had. Remember to include, along with instruction and curriculum preparation, responsibilities for things such as assessment, classroom management, extracurricular and supervisory duties, maintenance responsibilities, and professional development and involvement. Expect to come up with dozens and dozens.

If you collaborate with other teachers in various grade levels, content areas, and specialized roles to do this activity, your combined lists could become a colorful and impressive collection of teaching responsibilities. The process itself will be an example of collaborative consultation, with each person adding information from his or her own perspectives and experiences.

DEFINING CONSULTATION, COLLABORATION, AND CO-TEACHING

Practical definitions of collaboration, consultation, and team teaching for school settings must be general enough to apply to a wide range of school structures and circumstances, yet flexible enough for adapting to many types of schools and communities. Defining is difficult due to the challenges of drawing meaningful boundaries and the risks of being too limiting or too broad (John-Steiner, Weber, & Minnis, 1998). *Webster's Third New International Dictionary* (1976), *Webster's New Collegiate Dictionary* (1998), and *World Book Dictionary* (2003) provide several shades of meaning and a number of synonyms for terms relevant to schools and education. The words and synonyms complement each other to form a conceptual foundation for collaboration, consultation, and teamwork in educational environments.

The issue of definitions or descriptions requires careful attention to semantics because meanings can vary from user to user and from context to context. People who say, "Oh, it's just semantics; don't bother," fail to recognize the importance of appropriate word selection for verbal or written communication (or signs for signed communication). Consider the foreign diplomat in a press conference who is striving to communicate complex ideas and delicate nuances of meanings that are critical to matters on the world stage. It is possible that much potential for achieving international understanding is eroded in the translation process, especially in face-to-face, here-and-now discourse. Discussing abstract concepts such as respect, effort, expectations, and fairness with others is oftentimes a land mine that can blow up the best intentions to communicate. Consider concrete words also, such as *chair*. That word might signal time-out to a misbehaving toddler, or a place for a tired teacher to sit. A dentist may see a chair as a special piece of equipment for work, while to a college professor it might mean a coveted position, or to a convicted murderer it might portend imminent death (Sondel, 1958).

> Words make the trip through the nervous system of a human being before they can be referred outward to the real thing—chair, or whatever it is. Don't assume that everyone responds to your words in precisely the same way you do. Make the context in which you use the words clear, and do this through the use of words that refer to specific things. (Sondel, 1958, p. 55)

Perusing synonyms for a particular word can give a sense of the shades of meaning available for diverse settings. Definitions that will be helpful here are

collaborate: To labor together or work jointly in cooperative interaction to attain a shared goal.

collaborative ethic in schools: An educational philosophy encompassing a shared spirit and interdependence practices among co-educators who are working together in the best interests of students and schools.

teamwork, teaming: Joint action in which persons participate cooperatively; also, joining forces or efforts so that each individual contributes a clearly defined portion of the effort and subordinates personal prominence to the effectiveness of the whole.

consult: To advise or seek advice, confer, confab, huddle, parley, counsel, discuss, deliberate, consider, examine, refer to, communicate in order to decide or plan something, take counsel, seek an opinion as a guide to one's own judgment, request information or facts from, talk over a situation or subject with someone.

consultation: Advisement, counsel, conference, or formal deliberation to provide direct services to students or work with co-educators to serve students' special needs.

consulting: Deliberating together, asking for information or opinion, conferring.

consultant: One who gives professional advice or renders professional services in a field of special knowledge and training, or more simply, one who consults with another.

client: Individual, group, agency, or other entity receiving consulting services to enhance abilities for learning (knowing the material) and for doing (applying the learning) in school and beyond. In some instances *target* is used as a synonym. The client is often, but not always, the student.

consultee: As traditionally described in social science literature, a mediator between a consultant and client (Tharp, 1975); one who confers with the consultant to gather and exchange information and advice and then applies it for the client's needs. The consultee is often, but by no means always, the general education or classroom teacher.

co-educator: An educator who collaborates, consults, teams with, co-teaches, or networks with other educator(s) to address students' needs for learning and doing. May be a school educator, a home educator (parent or other family member), or a community resource person.

co-teaching: Two or more teachers planning and implementing instruction, and monitoring and assessing student achievement, typically in an inclusive classroom setting.

network: A system of connections among individuals or groups having similar interests who interact to accomplish shared goals.

Drawing from the words just defined, the following descriptions frame major concepts presented in this book.

The concept of collaborative school consultation and teamwork denotes an interactive process whereby school personnel in general education and special education, related services and support personnel, families of students, and the students themselves are working together and sharing their diversity of knowledge and expertise to define needs, plan, implement, assess, and follow up on ways of helping students develop to their fullest.

Co-educators are persons who collaborate, consult, and work in teams to provide appropriate learning experiences for students' diverse needs. Co-educators can be school-based such as teachers and related services or support personnel, home-based such as family members or caregivers of students, and community-based in support roles.

In Scenario 1.A earlier, the targeted client is the new student who has a learning disability. The learning disabilities consultant in this case will serve that student indirectly for the most part by collaborating with the classroom English teacher who will be consultee and provider of direct services to the student. Some direct service may be given to the student by the learning disabilities consultant, but for the most part, direct service comes to the student from the classroom teacher. Those in the consultant role do not hold claim to all the expertise. Competent consultants also listen and learn. They sometimes help consultees discover what they already know. They help them recognize their own talents and trust their own skills. Johnson and Donaldson (2007) present collaboration as a way of overcoming the triple-threat norms of autonomy, egalitarianism, and deference to authority that have long characterized schools.

Sheridan (1992) characterizes consultation as a form of collaboration. Consultation helps consultees develop skills to solve current problems and generalize those skills to other problems. Consultation is interactive and requires the active participation of the consultee, not an imposition of the relationship. Sheridan calls for consultants to engage in self-reflection and self-evaluation about the impact they will have on the interactive process of consultation. Co-teaching and other team interactions would be examples of collaboration.

A collaborative consultation relationship is characterized by mutual trust and behaviors that facilitate joint exploration of ways to help students. Effective collaborative school consultation and teamwork result in having co-educators who are more capable and have more confidence in their abilities than they did when teaching in autonomous contexts.

WHY COLLABORATION IS SO IMPORTANT FOR EDUCATORS

The word *collaborate* has come a long way from days when it was often construed to mean working in collusion with the enemy. In recent years it has popped up everywhere with a much different meaning. Greer (1989) describes goals for collaboration as sharing resources, fostering and improving institutional cooperation, creating linkages and partnerships, building trust, encouraging accountability, and taking other positive actions for the benefit of students. But Greer also expresses concern that goals can become institutionalized rather than put students' needs first. So the primary question must be, "Collaborate for whom?" Collaborative efforts are meaningful only when they help educators function in ways that promote student learning (Brownell, Adams, Sindelar, Waldron, & Vanhover, 2006).

A vital area of need is that of students with exceptional learning needs (ELN). In categorizing exceptionality, one would like to say, "Labels are for jelly jars, not children." But special education services and goals for Individualized Education Plans (IEPs) are based on definitions of the disability or disabilities. Lists may vary among federal, state, and local agencies, but typical terms include autism, behavioral disorder, communicative disability, cultural and linguistic diversity, deafness or being hard of hearing, developmental disability or mental retardation, dual sensory impairment, emotional disturbance, learning disability, multiple disabilities, physical disability, traumatic brain injury, and visual impairment or blindness. More than half of states in the United States also include gifted and talented as a part of special education because of the students' exceptional learning needs.

In comparison and contrast with practices in business, industry, and numerous other professions, collaboration on a regular basis in school settings tends to be more occasional and happenstance than frequent and planned. Available and congruent time blocks are necessary for productive interaction with colleagues, but these opportunities are few in the course of a busy school day. Then, too, practical structures for working together and training for these less familiar roles have been minimal. It follows that careful assessment of collaborative outcomes has been the exception, rather than the rule. However, the growing complexities of teaching and escalating demands for student achievement and accountability of schools underscore the strong need for working together in many dimensions. Furthermore, the twenty-first century has brought major differences in ways educators can communicate with colleagues as well as with students. Schools are connected electronically with multiple opportunities for collaborating and networking. These opportunities, which undoubtedly will increase in number and function in the decades to come, include:

- Computer-mediated communication, such as instant messaging and text messaging, hypertext, distance learning, Internet forums, bulletin boards, chat rooms, videoconferencing, e-mail, webcasts, podcasts, web logs, wikis, and more
- Technology devices for assistance with special needs in classrooms
- Virtual education

Technology has revolutionized the processes of collaboration and consultation among educational colleagues. School personnel who collaborate must communicate often and coordinate plans. With help from modern technology, communication can take place asynchronously, that is, intermittently without the requirement of a "common clock" for transmission between sender and receiver.

The autonomous teacher in that little red, eight-grade schoolhouse would have been amazed at the kinds and wonders of technological assistance. Information can be retrieved on just about any topic the teacher or student wants. Data can be analyzed and stored efficiently. Students are motivated by the newest methods of social computing and connecting with each other.

A note of caution is in order when highlighting the effects of technology on interactions. Do these tools make us more communicative or less so? More accessible or more isolated? More efficient or less? These questions bear analysis and careful study by educators who want to be effective communicators and successful collaborators and are exploring ways that technology can help them. The best approach is probably to accept the benefits of technology after setting stringent guidelines for use—for example, limiting the times one checks e-mail each day, taking care to make text messages and other electronic mail convey tone and substance so they are not likely to be misinterpreted, foregoing electronic connections when person-to-person interactions are almost as convenient and could be much more effective, monitoring personal attitudes toward technology so we are using it to help and not to intentionally remove ourselves from the fray of human experiences.

A later chapter will describe a number of technological assists that are available. These tools free up time and facilitate ways in which co-educators can locate pertinent information for dealing with topics and issues. They improve teacher efficiency with routine tasks so more time is available for collaborative activities, and importantly, for more direct services to students. Furthermore, technology can improve achievement and feelings of self-esteem for many students with disabilities. Technology tools are powerful motivators for students who have experienced failure and frustration in school. Many electronic communication devices allow students to speak and add their voices to those of their classmates.

Most preservice students today are quite comfortable with technology and many absorb much of their information in electronic contact using asynchronous communication that happens at any time they wish, not just at set intervals. Their book learning and teacher instruction have been enhanced by multifarious opportunities for interconnections with agencies, travel experiences, community involvement, parent partnerships, and mentorships. As one university professor put it, "My students are always connected and always on."

Veteran teachers who completed their teacher preparation programs years ago are less advantaged in the use of technology. But they are learning to learn and to be prepared for their students' high-level skills through self-study, tutorials, professional development activities, and social networking via electronic communication. Sometimes they are disposed to become mentees in technology with students as their mentors. The entire process of planning for use of technology in teaching and learning extends across all disciplines with many opportunities for professional collaboration.

APPLICATION 1.2
CATEGORIZING TEACHER RESPONSIBILITIES

Sort the list of teacher responsibilities you compiled in Application 1.1 into categories of tasks—for example, instructional, curricular, managerial, evaluative, supportive, and professional growth–related. Then decide which tasks might be carried out most productively and enjoyably in collaborative contexts. As an example, if the responsibility for ordering books and supplies is classified as managerial, teams of teachers might collaborate to pool their library allocations and make decisions about materials that could be shared or used for team teaching. Then mark with an asterisk (*) others with collaborative potential. Add some that may have been overlooked such as "organizing cross-grade tutors and study-buddies," or "involving families in preparing a notebook of potential community resources."

Motivation for Working Together

Teachers may wish for more small-group meetings that are focused on mutual interests and more grade-level meetings that address common concerns. They may want more opportunities to observe other teachers and other schools. They may seek richer professional development experiences. But that does not mean they are keen on engaging in collaboration and consultation activities. Some even comment candidly that they did not choose teaching as a career to work all that much with adults. Others feel that teaming up with co-teachers or consulting teachers will be perceived as a flag calling attention to their weaker areas or a no-confidence vote in their abilities. They could argue as well that too little time is available for the careful planning and concentrated effort that productive interaction requires. Opportunities may be rare and hard to arrange for meaningful observation of educators in other school settings. One more aspect that troubles special education teachers is the possibility that collaboration may siphon off time available for direct services to students.

When teachers do have time and opportunity to interact with colleagues for learning new ideas and revitalizing their professional enthusiasm, it is likely to be during professional development sessions. Unfortunately, these activities are often too highly structured and short-lived to allow for productive interaction. Many are scheduled at the end of a hectic day, when teachers are tired and want to reflect a bit on their teaching day, set the stage for the next day, and then turn their attention toward home or community activities. Now and again teachers are visited in their classrooms by other teachers, supervisors, administrators, student teachers, and sometimes parents. However, these occasions tend to trigger feelings of anxiety and defensiveness more than support and collegiality. Some school systems do promote co-teaching as a way of allowing teachers to support each other and broaden their teaching repertoires. But well-intentioned efforts to co-teach can result in turn-teaching—"You teach this part of the lesson and then take a break or make the copies we need for next hour, while I handle the part coming up."

Professionals cannot be coerced into being collegial (Wildman & Niles, 1987). Teachers who are accustomed to being in charge and making virtually all the day-to-day decisions in their classrooms cannot be ordered to just go out and collaborate with each other or co-teach to any significant degree. Along with incentive and time, they need structure, practice, encouragement, and positive feedback about their effectiveness in order to perform these sophisticated and demanding functions successfully.

In laboring together, collaborators do not compromise and cooperate so much as they confer and concur. Compromise often means giving up some part of, or conceding, something, and cooperation may dilute interaction so that it does not fully benefit the student. Collaboration, on the other hand, involves talking and planning, contributing, adding to, and coming to agreement so all can benefit.

DuFour (2004) finds that educators may equate collaboration with congeniality and camaraderie, but a professional learning community must have the right structures to build a culture of collaboration. He asserts that collaborative teachers must not ask what they are expected to teach, but rather how they will know each of their students has learned. Team members should make public such educational matters as goals, strategies, materials, and outcomes, and everyone in the school should belong to a team that focuses on student learning.

Reports from school districts throughout the United States identify collaboration as a key variable in the successful implementation of inclusive education (Villa & Thousand, 2003, p. 22). In collaboration, differentiated tasks can be allocated among individuals having various skills to contribute. Sometimes collaboration means recognizing differences and finding ways to accommodate those differences. The collaborative process is enriched by diversity among collaborators—diversity of experience, perspectives, values, skills, and interests. Individual differences of adults who consult and collaborate are rich ingredients for successful collaborations. The great need to recognize adult differences and use them constructively in collaborative enterprises will be the focus of Chapter 2.

The concept of team teaching is receiving increased attention among school professionals. Teamwork as co-educators means working for the good of the whole—where individual preferences are subtended or set aside for the larger cause. Many heads and hearts are better than one, and the pooled experiences, talents, knowledge, and ideas of a group are even better than the sum of the individual parts. Various forms for team teaching exist, with many different terms used to describe the process, such as team teaching, co-teaching (discussed further in Chapter 7), cooperative teaching, and collaborative teaching (Welch, 1998). Welch and Sheridan (1995) suggest that team-taught instruction can be micro-level staff development when each teacher models instruction for the other. Commercial companies offer activities, games, puzzles, and outdoor gaming equipment for team building. They purport to develop rapport and team spirit by energizing members to work together harmoniously. Some seem glitzy and merely playful, but others have potential for building awareness and trust through cohesion-building activities. Professional development consultants should observe in schools and query school personnel to determine if such techniques would be a turn-on or a turn-off for that group. Simple, straightforward collaborative structures, with explanation of benefits they provide for helping students with their special needs, may be most time efficient and acceptable to busy teachers.

Distinguishing among Consultation, Collaboration, and Working in Teams

All three processes—collaboration, consultation, and teamwork as they occur in the school context—involve interaction among school personnel, families and students, and community in working together to achieve common goals. However, subtle distinctions can be made.

In school consultation, the consultant contributes specialized expertise toward an educational problem, and the consultee delivers direct service utilizing that expertise. Consultants and consultees begin to collaborate when they assume equal ownership of the problem and solutions. Collaboration is a way of working in which power struggles *and* ineffectual politeness are regarded as detrimental to team goals. Friend and Cook (1992) stress that collaborative consultation must be voluntary, with one professional assisting another to address a problem concerning a third party. They further emphasize that successful consultants use different styles of interaction under different circumstances within different situations.

Collaborating as a teaching team fuels group spirit, develops process skills that help teachers interact in more productive ways, and fosters a more intellectual atmosphere (Maeroff, 1993). One of the best examples of working together is a musical ensemble. Whether one is accompanying, performing with a small group, or playing with an orchestra, band, or choir, it is the united effort that creates the musical experience. Musicians of many instruments are not brought together to play the same note. Doing so would make the music only louder, not richer and more harmonious. In similar fashion, co-teachers work in concert, not usually in perfect unison, to create an effective learning experience for all students in the class. Consultation, collaboration, and teaming up to co-teach or partner in learning activities will create many opportunities to engage in a strengths-type interaction so that each person is learning from and building on the strengths of the others.

What Collaborative Consultation *Is*

As illustrated by Pugach and Johnson (2002), collaboration is a way of being, not a set of isolated actions. The collaborative process reframes how educators interact in school contexts, including special education teachers with regular education teachers, public schools with institutions of higher education, and agencies with schools and families.

Welch (1998) deconstructs the term *collaboration* and comes up with a unique concept of working together for mutual benefit. It is different from cooperation in which all come to agreement but perhaps not all are benefiting. He contends that schools tend to be more cooperative than collaborative, explaining it as parallel but sometimes uneasy coexistence of general and special education. He further notes that coordination is more characteristic of interagency involvement such as in the Individualized Family Service Plan (IFSP) than of school-managed IEP. Welch faults the IEP process as often involving little or no collaboration during development and implementation; it tends to be drafted before a meeting using a generalized template, then quickly reviewed and hastily approved by the team, thus "essentially negating the 'I' in the IEP process" (Welch, 1998, p. 128.). One way to improve the process would be for the classroom teacher, who is required by IDEA 2004 to participate, to participate very actively rather than as a relatively passive observer.

Wesley and Buysse (2006) distinguish consultation as operating on two planes simultaneously; that is, consulting co-educators manage consultation components while concentrating on interpersonal aspects of trusting relationships with consultees. These early childhood special educators propose that critical elements in the consultative process are having the best research findings available, using family and professional wisdom, and drawing on family and professional values. The collaborating consultant must first do no harm and then deliver services that are academically and ethically sound (Wesley & Buysse, 2006).

When educators—special education teachers, classroom teachers, school administrators, related services and support personnel, as well as families and community agencies—are consulting and collaborating as members of an educational team, what specific kinds of things are they doing? A summary list typically includes engaging in one or more of these:

- Discussing students' needs and ways of addressing those needs
- Listening to colleagues' concerns about a teaching situation
- Identifying learning and behavior problems
- Assisting families in transition periods—from early childhood education programs to kindergarten, from elementary to middle school, from middle school to high school, and from high school to work or postsecondary education
- Planning for students' needs in the school setting
- Recommending classroom alternatives as first interventions for students with special learning and behavior needs
- Serving as a medium for student referrals
- Demonstrating instructional techniques to help with special needs or abilities
- Providing direct assistance to colleagues in learning and behavioral needs of students
- Leading or participating in professional development activities
- Designing and implementing individual education programs
- Sharing resources, instructional materials, and teaching ideas
- Utilizing technology for efficient and productive interactions among students as well as among co-educators
- Participating in co-teaching or demonstration teaching
- Engaging in observation, assessment, and evaluation activities
- Serving on curriculum committees, textbook committees, extracurricular activities committees, and school advisory councils
- Following through and following up on educational issues and concerns with co-educators, students and their families, and communities
- Networking with other educational professionals and other agencies who can be resources for students' needs

And these are just some of the activities that educators engage in when they are collaborating.

What Collaborative Consultation Is *Not*

School consultation is *not* therapy, counseling, or supervision. West and Idol (1987) and Morsink, Thomas, and Correa (1991) have distinguished consultation as being focused on issues, contrasting with counseling that is focused on individuals. The focus must be on educational concerns relevant to the welfare of the client and not on problems of consultees. Conoley and Conoley (1982) caution that the consultant must collaborate for issues and needs of the client, typically the student, and not on the consultee who tends to be the teacher.

Consulting specialists have to work diligently to shed the "expert" image held by many teachers toward consultants or specialists (Pugach & Johnson, 1989). So it is important for classroom teachers to be recognized as having expertise and resourcefulness to contribute. Collaborative consultation can emanate from any role pertinent to the case if the participants are well-informed. As a professional in the medical field commented, patients collaborate with their doctors because they are so well informed about their own conditions. This approach could be applied legitimately and productively to collaborative school consultation. No consultant is the be-all, end-all expert. Any co-educator can play a consultant role when circumstances dictate.

Collaboration among professional colleagues is *not* talk or discussion for its own sake. Furthermore, collaboration during co-teaching must not be hierarchical or judgmental, but voluntary and entered into with parity among the teaching partners.

It is very important that collaborative services *not* be used as a money-saving strategy in inclusive settings to eliminate or reduce the number of school personnel. Then, too, consultative and collaborative structures that provide indirect service must not be substituted in cases for which there is a strong need for direct services. School administrators and members of local school boards must plan carefully to avoid setting up hierarchical climates and unintentionally encouraging inappropriate consultative practices.

Collaborative school consultation and co-teaching cannot be forced on educators. As stated earlier, the process *must* be voluntary. There will be times when teachers relish having some autonomy in their work. Also, having quality think time is important for busy, multitasking educators. For example, individual brainstorming is an important process, not a frill. To elaborate, the benefits of individual brainstorming as occasional precursor to group brainstorming will be discussed in Chapter 5.

Another important consideration is to protect the rights of teachers to have some ideas that are theirs alone. Most teachers are willing, even eager, to share ideas and lend help to colleagues; however, they should not be asked to give up their specialties any more than chefs should be expected to relinquish their most prized recipes. Such altruistic behavior would result in giving up practices that are individually special and personally satisfying. That is not the purpose of collaboration, nor should it be a presumed condition of co-teaching. Instead, collaborators should help and encourage colleagues to develop their skills and personal strengths to come up with their own teaching specialties.

ROLE RESPONSIBILITIES IN COLLABORATIVE ENDEAVORS

When contemplating collaborative and consultative roles, educators often express their concerns by asking questions such as these:

- Who am I in this role?
- How do I carry out the responsibilities of this role?

■ How will I know whether I am succeeding?
■ How can I prepare for the role?

First, it is essential that central administrators and policy makers such as school boards explain the importance of consultative, collaborative, and co-teaching roles. Then building-level administrators must reiterate the value of these practices to the school, staff, and students. Parity, voluntary participation, and collegial interdependence must be emphasized. A key factor for success is allocating sufficient time and suitable places for interactions to take place.

Teachers will need encouragement to share enthusiastically the responsibilities for all students in collaborative environments. Related services personnel and support personnel will need to be integrated into a collaborative context. Families must receive information about the purposes and benefits of collaborative roles and partnered teaching. They will need to be assured that these services are right for their child. Students should be an integral part of the planning process and have opportunities to participate as young collaborators intensely involved in their own educational process. Ultimately, the community should support the establishment of a collaborative climate and anticipate its potential benefits for all.

SCENARIO 1.B

Now consider another event. This one takes place in the same school district a short time after Scenario 1.A described at the beginning of this chapter. Four special education teachers are talking in the district's main conference room before their special education director arrives for a planning meeting.

Secondary Learning Disabilities Teacher: I understand we're here to decide how we're going to inform staff and parents about the consultation and collaboration and perhaps co-teaching practices we'll be implementing soon. But first, I think we'd better figure out just what it is we *will* be doing in these roles.

Behavioral Disorders Teacher: Definitely. I have a really basic question that I've been thinking about a lot. What am I going to do the first week, even the first day, as a consulting teacher? I understand a few people on our staff have had some training in collaboration and consulting in former positions, but this is new to the rest of us.

Gifted Education Teacher: I agree. I've been thinking about all those different teaching styles and methods of doing things that will surface as we work closely together. Teachers won't all like or want the same things for their classrooms and their students.

Elementary Learning Disabilities Teacher: And remember, we are supposed to say, "*Our* students." Yes, I doubt this is something we can become experts about very quickly. From what little I've had a chance to read about collaborative processes, the key to success is using good communication skills and problem-solving techniques.

Gifted Education Teacher: Yes, and at the same time we have to take into account the wide array of resources it will take to provide the materials and methods each student needs. I'm a bit apprehensive about it all, but I'm willing to try it.

Behavioral Disorders Teacher: I guess I am, too. I've been thinking for some time now that our current methods of dealing with learning and behavior problems are not as effective and efficient as they should be. And I realize really bright kids are being kept on hold in the classroom much of the time. Besides, changing the way we do things can be energizing, you know. I think we have to be optimistic about the possible benefits for both students *and* teachers.

Secondary Learning Disabilities Teacher: Well, I for one happen to feel a sense of urgency because my first experience of consulting and collaborating is coming up soon. I'll be doing some observation and perhaps co-teaching with an English teacher at the high school next week. We'll be organizing a plan for working with a new student with severe learning disabilities who's enrolling in that school. That's why I'd like to talk it over and arrive at some consensus about collaborative consultation and also about co-teaching.

Elementary Learning Disabilities Teacher: I'll be interested both professionally and personally in how you get along with that. As I think you all know, I have a son at the high school who has learning disabilities with severe attention-deficit and behavioral disorders. It's been a struggle for him *and* the teachers in many of his high school classes. In my family we are concerned about his eventual transition either to getting more education or going to the job market. From what I've read and heard about resource consultation and interagency networking, I'm very interested in having more collaborative efforts in our schools.

Interchangeable Roles and Responsibilities

Educators are becoming more and more aware that collaborating to achieve a common goal often produces more beneficial results than do isolated efforts by an individual. The whole of the combined efforts is greater than the sum of its parts (Slavin, 1988). This describes the well-known homily that two heads are better than one, and several heads are better yet. The collaborative consultation process channels each individual's strengths and talents toward serving a client's needs.

Any person who consults in one situation may be a consultee or even a client in another. In each of these instances, consultant and consultee would share responsibility for working out a plan to help the client. As examples, a special education teacher might be a consultant for one situation and a consultee in another. The student is typically a client (as target of the intervention), but in some cases could be a consultee or even a consultant. Consultation might be initiated by a social worker, a special reading teacher, or a general classroom teacher. Consultation in which several educators collaborate could also be requested by a parent or a school counselor. The combinations of "people roles" that might participate in school collaboration and consultation to help students and teachers are virtually limitless. In Figure 1.2, depending on the circumstance, each collaborator could be a consultant, a consultee, or a client. Although roles and responsibilities may vary among individuals and across situations, if there is understanding about the nature of the role and appreciation for its possibilities, a collaborative and facilitative spirit can prevail.

Special education teacher	Student with learning disability
General classroom teacher	Student with behavioral disorder
School psychologist	Preschool student
School counselor	Student with mental retardation
Reading specialist	Student with high aptitude
Building administrator	Student with attention deficit disorder
Gifted program facilitator	Student with physical disabilities
School nurse	Parent of student with disability(ies)
Media specialist	Parent of student with advanced aptitude
Assistive technology specialist	Community-based mentor
Resource room teacher	Student with autism or Asperger's syndrome
School cafeteria staff	Pediatrician
School bus driver	University professor in special education
School custodian	Speech and language pathologist
Special education director	University professor in general education
Early childhood teacher	Probation officer
Curriculum specialist	Head Start personnel
Professional development staff	State Department of Education staff
Health care specialist/School nurse	Textbook publishers

FIGURE 1.2   Potential Collaborators as Consultants, Consultees, or Clients

INITIATING COLLABORATIVE ACTIVITIES

School improvement issues and legislative mandates may have convinced educators that the concept of collaborative school consultation is a promising method for helping students with special needs. But conversion of concepts to practice is not so simple. Questions in Scenario 1.B earlier that were voiced in the school district conference room by four special educators raised practical concerns and hinted at even more issues:

■ Where do I begin as a collaborating school consultant?
■ What do I do the first day on the job? And the first week?
■ Let me see a sample schedule for the first week. And the first month as well.
■ Where am I to be headed by the end of the year?

Other questions and concerns that are likely to surface sooner or later include:

■ Will I have opportunity to work with students? That is why I chose teaching as a career.
■ Where's my room? Will I have office space and supplies?
■ Will I have a space for group work with students?
■ Will I be welcomed and regarded as an important part of the teaching staff?
■ If I need some special preparation for this role, how do I get that?
■ How will I be evaluated in this role, and by whom?
■ As a collaborating consultant who helps consultees meet special needs, will I be working myself out of a job?

Novice teachers may be thinking:

■ Will participating in collaboration and consultation make me appear less competent?
■ How much of my classroom time with students will be needed to provide this service to kids and how do I go about allocating that time?
■ Don't I need to work out a plan for my classroom and get experience with that before I collaborate and certainly before I co-teach?
■ When in the world will I find time and space to interact like this with other teachers anyway?

Participants in consultation and collaboration must voice their concerns and work through their feelings of insecurity as they sort out the dynamics of their new roles. School administrators have the responsibility of initiating open, candid expressions of concerns and encouraging intensive discussions about issues before they escalate into problems.

KEY ELEMENTS IN SUCCESSFUL COLLABORATION

Four essential elements of consultation, collaboration, and teamwork processes are pictured in the clocklike Figure 1.3:

1. Preparation for the roles
2. Delineation of roles
3. Framework for structuring the roles
4. Evaluation of outcomes

Within the four categories, twelve key areas are to be addressed. Each will be introduced and previewed, with references made to the subsequent chapters in which they will be developed more fully.

The sequence of the twelve elements is very important. Note that the recommended starting point for collaborative school consultation is shown at about the 6:30 position in

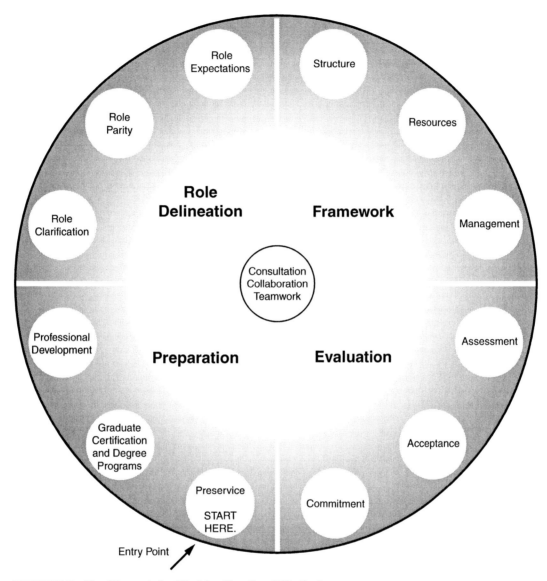

FIGURE 1.3   Key Elements for Working Together Effectively

Figure 1.3. Educators who intend to collaborate must resist the temptation to begin "too late in the day"—for example, at "11:30." with role expectations. Neither should they begin with a call for commitment to the process, shown at "5:30," or development of a structure for interactions, shown at "12:30." The place to begin for best results is at the early-in-the-day preparation position, and then proceed clockwise through the other elements.

Preparation

Educators in every role—administrators, teachers, support staff, and instructors of preservice teachers—will want to prepare mindfully for co-educator participation. Preparation for this should take place at the preservice level before novice teachers step into that first classroom and attend their first faculty meeting or IEP conference. Preparation and practice should continue at the graduate level with more advanced coursework, and then at the professional development level for experienced personnel who want to expand their skills and move into leadership roles.

A collaborative school climate can be developed through well-planned professional growth experiences, careful coaching, and constructive feedback in process areas such as communication, problem finding, and problem solving for example, and in content areas such as co-teaching models. In sum, preparation programs for developing skills of collaboration, consultation, and co-teaching are fundamental for three populations:

1. Preservice students who need orientation and practice in simulated roles as consultees and future consultants
2. Graduate students in advanced degree programs who will be collaborating and co-teaching, and also assisting others as co-educators
3. Veteran teachers who want to be collaborators, co-teachers, mentors, advocates, and school leaders in their school contexts

Preservice Preparation.   New teachers have many pressures that can curb their enthusiasm in those first years of teaching. This is the time when temptation to leave the profession is high. Novice teachers may be very stressed emotionally, physically, and socially. Babinski and Rogers (1998) reported that the two most frequently discussed problems of novice teachers were dealing with the special needs of children such as behavioral problems, learning disabilities, and attention deficits, and working with other adults such as parents, administrators, mentors, teaching assistants, and other teachers. Understandably, new teachers often fear being judged as incapable and failing if they ask for suggestions or outright assistance.

Novice teachers can benefit greatly by observing more experienced colleagues and participating in consultations, by working as part of teaching teams, and by collaborating with a wide range of school personnel. They will need knowledge about resources and strategies for sharing them, practice in interactive situations such as IEP conferences and parent conferences, and experience in showing accountability for their expenditures of time and energy in collaboration with co-educators. A particularly important area of preparation for novice teachers while they are still forming their teaching philosophies and strategies is that of relating to families of students and working with them as valued co-educators (Kerns, 1992).

Two decades ago, Phillips, Allred, Brulle, and Shank (1990) recommended that teacher preparation programs provide introductory education courses in which general and special education preservice teachers participate jointly in practicum experiences that serve a diverse range of children's needs. But this plan requires concerted effort by college and university personnel, many of whom are not prepared themselves to engage in collaboration and consultation functions, let alone to facilitate development of these behaviors in their students. But perhaps it is time to revisit the concept.

Some veteran educators may be nervous about having novice teachers engage in consultation practices before they have had teaching experiences in the real world. Nevertheless, the seeds of awareness can and should be planted early to bear fruit later in important ways. After all, for most new teachers there is not much time to acquire experience between the last day of a teacher education program and the first day of stepping into a bustling school environment and their own inclusive classroom. Preservice teachers will be a major topic in Chapter 10.

Mentoring of preservice and novice teachers in a collaborative atmosphere will benefit mentees and help the students of those mentees. Mentorships can build confidence in the mentee and generate a sense of professional satisfaction in the mentor as well. This type of professional partnership will be addressed in more detail in Chapter 12.

Preparation in Graduate Certification and Degree Programs.   Special education teachers who consult and collaborate with general education colleagues need to understand the scope and sequence of grade-level curriculum content. Kauffman (1994) stresses that they also must have particular expertise in instructional and behavioral techniques for students with disabilities or their input will have little significant import. Universities have far to go to meet these all-encompassing needs.

A source for delineating standards pertaining to collaboration among special educators, families, other educators, related service providers, and community agency personnel is the *NCATE/CEC Program Standards, Programs for the Preparation of Special Education Teachers* (2002). (These standards have been posted online at www.cec.sped.org/ps/perf_based_stds/knowledge_standards.html.)

One of the standards (*Standard 10: Collaboration*) in this document calls for special educators to collaborate with co-educators to ensure that exceptional learning needs (ELN) of students are addressed in schools. The standard refers to special educators as resources for their colleagues in understanding the laws and policies of special education and in facilitating transitions of students across many learning settings and contexts.

Some states require development of consultation skills for teacher certification. Inclusion of this training in standards for accreditation of teacher education programs is one way to encourage more emphasis on ensuring the presence of collaborative teachers and school environments. School administrators would be wise to recruit those who welcome opportunities to work collaboratively with their colleagues.

Every teacher preparation program for collaborative consultation and co-teaching would be unique. However, a basic program should include:

- Ensuring preparation of experienced teachers and preservice teachers, along with school administrators and related services personnel, for working together collegially and productively
- Delineating co-educator roles
- Gaining understanding of frameworks and skills that help educators fulfill those roles
- Evaluating effectiveness of collaborations and co-teaching activities

Graduate and undergraduate degree programs need to provide experiences that extend beyond a "mentioning" mode of superficial exposure to professional interaction.

Course syllabi should include not only the conventional learning strategies of lecture, reading, and discussion but also a strong focus on practical experiences and interactions. Small-group activities, simulations and role plays, interviewing, videotaped consultation practice, reaction and reflection papers, resource searches, practice with tools and strategies of technology, and assessment of outcomes will help educators to be more comfortable and capable in interactive school roles.

Preparation through Professional Development. Friend and Cook (1990) have stressed for a number of years that teachers are being set up to fail when they enter the profession having content expertise and skills in methods but not competencies for working effectively with colleagues. But the lack of preparation for consultation is compounded by absence of empirical studies that could justify such training. However, school improvement movements have begun to stimulate efforts toward accountability such as that reported some two decades ago by Rule, Fodor-Davis, Morgan, Salzberg, and Chen (1990). In their study Rule and colleagues identified the need for administrative support, technical assistance, and follow-up assistance along with professional development. Through inservice and other professional development activities, consultation and collaboration programs can be tailored to each school context. More recent studies have reported the impact of several newly developed models and these will be described in Chapter 3. Professional development techniques will be a major focus in Chapter 12.

Role Delineation

As indicated previously, a school role such as counselor, general classroom teacher, learning disabilities specialist, speech pathologist, or facilitator for gifted education programs does not automatically determine a specific consultative role. Rather, the consultative role emanates from the situation. For example, it might be that of a parent in providing information to the school administrator, or a learning disabilities teacher who helps the coach assess a student athlete's learning problem, or a mentor who gives the gifted program facilitator suggestions for materials to use with a student for enrichment and acceleration.

The consultee collaborates with the consultant to provide direct service to the client. The client is the one with the identified need or problem. This total concept reflects the contemporary approach to special services whereby student *needs,* not student labels, determine the service and delivery method, and an array of services are targeted and made available to address those needs.

Role Clarification. The first requirement of role delineation is to clarify the role as consultative *and* collaborative. Until educators become comfortable with that concept, ambiguous feelings may persist. Teachers and school staff may wonder why there are consulting teachers or what these people are supposed to be doing. Classroom teachers may blame their own heavy responsibilities on the seemingly lighter caseloads of consulting teachers. One high school English teacher told a newly appointed consulting teacher, "If you were back in your classroom teaching five hours of English instead of 'facilitating' for a few high-ability students part of the time, my own student numbers wouldn't be so high." Paradoxically, consulting teachers often have excessively demanding workloads when travel time among schools, conferencing with teachers and students and perhaps parents, preparing IEPs, and constructing or locating special curriculum and materials are taken into account. If their workload is too great, the effectiveness of their services will be diminished severely because little time and energy will remain for the coordination and communication activities that are integral to consultation success.

Seamless, well-coordinated instructional plans for students with special needs require keen awareness of role responsibilities and service possibilities among all who are involved. A classroom teacher and a reading specialist may have information to share in addressing a struggling reader's strengths and deficits, yet they may know relatively little about each other's curriculum, educational priorities, or expectations for the student. They must coordinate their efforts, or those efforts may be counterproductive. In one unfortunate case, a reading specialist was instructing a fifth-grader with reading problems to slow down and read more deliberately, while the learning disabilities specialist was encouraging him to read much more rapidly and was in the process of referring him to the gifted program facilitator. The student, a pleasant and cooperative child, was trying valiantly to please both teachers simultaneously before the situation came to light in the course of that referral process. Nevertheless, classroom teachers who have functioned autonomously for years may question how a process of collaborating with special education personnel or other classroom teachers can help their students. It is a fair and thoughtful question that deserves and will receive careful treatment throughout this book.

Teachers may doubt the ability of a consulting teacher or co-teacher to fit into their classroom structure, especially if that other person is young and inexperienced. As one classroom teacher put it when asked about involving the special education consulting teacher, "I'd never ask *her* for help. What does she know about managing a full classroom of students whose needs are all over the chart? She's never dealt with more than five or six at a time, and she's not yet been responsible for a regular classroom for an entire school year." Collaborative school consultation calls for people to relinquish traditional roles in order to share what they have learned and practiced. But many educators are not prepared for such flexibility and changes in school structure.

Role Parity.   Along with role ambiguity and misunderstanding, special education teachers who travel back and forth among several schools may feel an absence of role parity in that they do not belong exclusively to any one school or faculty. They may feel minimally important to students and the educational system, cut off from general classroom teachers because of differing responsibilities, and isolated from special education colleagues because of distance and schedules.

As an obvious example of nonparity, when consulting teachers are absent, substitutes are not often provided for them. In fact, on occasion they may be taken away from their own assignments to *be* the substitute for absent classroom teachers or to perform other tasks that come up suddenly. Consulting teachers have been asked to guide visitors on a school tour, monitor school events, and perform secretarial tasks. These feelings are accentuated by the misconception that they have no ownership in student welfare and development. Some who travel extensively, usually in their own cars or vans, from school to school have been dubbed "windshield" personnel.

General education teachers have their own complaints about lack of parity in collaborative enterprises. Oftentimes they are noticeably absent from lists of resource personnel for helping students with needs, so much so that some special education teachers have noticed the oversight and have asked why no one questioned them about what *they* had learned from the classroom teachers (Pugach & Johnson, 1989). They felt that not having been trained as specialists suggested that they were less able than the "experts" to consult with and assist. Meanwhile, as classroom teachers they are not going to wait with open arms for the specialists to come and save them. School life will proceed even in the absence of a consulting teacher or co-teacher. School bells will ring, classroom doors will open, and the school day will go on. All of this could foster a message of diminished parity among general education, special education, and related services and support personnel. Teachers who feel like second-class colleagues, not accepted or appreciated as a vital part of the staff, may develop defenses that erode their enthusiasm and effectiveness.

Role confusion and inequality may also fuel stress that leads to professional burnout. So continuous, specific recognition and reinforcement of consulting and collaborating teacher contributions toward student success are important for credibility and success of the role and professional morale of school personnel.

Role Expectations.   Sometimes colleagues have unreasonable expectations for partnerships or team involvement. They may be anticipating instant success and miraculous student progress in a very short while. When positive results with students are slow in forthcoming, attitudes may range from guarded skepticism to open disapproval of collaborative efforts. But they may simply be expecting too much too soon. A co-teacher or a special services consultant cannot provide an instant panacea for every student's difficulties. Furthermore, teachers sometimes neglect to monitor and record results carefully, so gradual day-to-day progress is not noticed. This is much like not seeing a child for some months and then thinking, "My, how she has grown." Then, too, consultees might pressure consultants unfairly by expecting them to "fix" the student, and then if this does not happen rather soon, impatiently dismiss consultation and collaboration as a waste of precious time.

As noted earlier, some consulting teachers expect to work only with students, not adults, and prefer it that way. "I was trained to work with kids, and that's what I enjoy," confessed one consulting teacher when assigned to an indirect service role. This preference presents a difficult situation for both consultee and collaborator. A team approach or co-teaching format may be awkward for the staunchly autonomous teacher at first. Unrealistic and unreasonable expectations must be set aside in the early planning stages of school collaboration practices. Co-educators should set reasonable goals for themselves and not try to do too much too soon. Another point to be considered is that sometimes the most difficult part of a collaborative consultation experience is stepping aside once the consultee experiences some success with students.

Collaborating consultants may wonder occasionally that "If I consult effectively, I may be working myself out of a job." However, that is highly unlikely. The more successful the consultation services are, the more teachers and administrators are apt to value them for both their immediate contribution and their long-range positive ripple effects. As one example, students missed in initial referrals often are noted and subsequently helped as a result of the interaction among classroom teachers and consulting teachers. One astute classroom teacher commented after using a checklist that she and the gifted program consulting teacher had drawn up, "I won't be recommending Chuck for special education testing yet, but I am definitely thinking differently about his many strengths now."

Involvement of as many co-educators as possible through needs assessments, interviews, professional development activities, and both formal and informal communications, will do much to alleviate inappropriate expectations for consulting and partnership roles. If collaborators can engage in successful teamwork with the more receptive and cooperative colleagues in their schools, it will generate confidence in the approach.

Framework

A framework for school consultation, collaboration, and co-teaching calls for structures that provide adequate blocks of time, management of schedules, suitable facilities in which to meet, and organization of details so that the interactive processes are carried out as conveniently and nonintrusively as possible. These conditions are deceptively simple to describe but much more difficult to put into operation.

Structure.   It is one thing to design a hypothetical method of consultation, but quite another to plan multiple methods for application in different situations, and then even more challenging to select and put into motion the right method for each situation. This is easier, of course, if preceded by thoughtful role clarification, genuine role parity, and appropriate role expectations.

Those who collaborate will want to generate a number of methods for consultation and collaboration in a variety of grade levels, subject areas, special needs categories, and school, community, and family contexts. The consultation structure should fit the context of the system. Traditional models and newer models for a variety of school contexts have been developed and put into practice. But school personnel should collaborate to design their own collaborative consultation and co-teaching systems to custom fit their school needs. Taking a survey of teachers to ask how they would use collaborative activities would be a good way to begin. Studying and observing co-teaching and collaborative and consultative structures in other school systems also can be helpful.

Resources.   Time is the ultimate nonrenewable resource. One of the most overwhelming and frustrating obstacles to collaborative activity is lack of time for it. The time needed for interfacing with colleagues and the scheduling of time blocks that fit into schedules of everyone involved are major deterrents to successful interactions. Sometimes willing teachers use their own planning time for consultation, but that is not an ideal way to instill positive attitudes toward a collaborative approach. The typical school day is simply not designed for incorporating collaboration time into the schedule without much careful planning. Even if a schedule for meeting and following up could be arranged, it may be next to impossible to find significant blocks of compatible time for all potential participants. Working out such a plan is often like working a complex puzzle; it is one of the most formidable tasks of those who want to collaborate, particularly those who have direct teaching responsibilities at specific times. Thus it is up to administrators to acknowledge the need for this quality time and to assume strong leadership in enabling it to happen. When administrators lend their authority to this endeavor, school personnel are more likely to find ways of getting together and to use that time productively. Unfortunately, when consulting teachers initiate consultation and collaboration, it is very likely that these activities come out of their own time—that is, before school, after school, during lunch hours, perhaps even on weekends. Even so, this *temporary* accommodation should be replaced as soon as possible with a more formal structure for allocation of time during the school day. This is not only for their well-being, but to emphasize that consultation and collaboration are not simply add-on services to be carried out by a zealous, dedicated, almost superhuman few.

As time is made available for working together, facilities must be accessible in which to conduct the consultation. These areas should be pleasant, quiet, convenient, and relatively private for free exchange of confidences. Such places are often at a premium in a bustling school community.

Management.   As everyone knows, school districts struggle to find money for ever-increasing educational needs. So there is a risk of letting fiscal issues, rather than factors that focus specifically on student needs, dictate the service delivery method. One such factor is the teacher caseload issue and it must be addressed carefully. Large caseloads may seem to save money in the short run, but not in the long run if student performance declines or if there is much attrition from the teaching profession. If a collaborating teacher's caseload is too great, direct service will be inadequate, possibilities for indirect services will be diminished, acceptance of the approach falters, and the program risks rejection.

Recommended caseload numbers vary depending on school context, travel time required, grade levels, exceptionalities and special needs served, and structure(s) of the interaction method. The numbers must be kept manageable to fulfill the intent and promise of consultation and collaboration. Part of the solution lies in documenting carefully all team activities *and* also making note of what should have happened but did not because of time constraints. Consultants must negotiate with their administrators for reasonable caseload assignments and blocks of time to communicate.

Although time is at a premium for busy educators, recent trends in computer technology and other electronic media are improving their situations. Teachers who work in partnerships with colleagues must be very organized and efficient. in recent years tedious, time-consuming tasks such as developing IEPs, preparing reports, collecting and recording academic and behavioral data, and communicating with families and support staff, have been made easier by technological advances. Software templates, e-mail, electronic calendars, and a variety of organizational tools give teachers more time. Tools and vehicles such as these also have allowed teachers to be more connected in networks that enhance collegiality and teamwork.

Technology has revolutionized the processes of collaboration and consultation among educational colleagues. School personnel who collaborate must communicate often and must coordinate plans and practices. With help from modern means of technology, communication can take place asynchronously rather than waiting for congruent schedules and compatible locations. Information can be retrieved on just about any topic teachers or students would want or need, and data can be analyzed and stored efficiently. Furthermore, technology can improve achievement and self-esteem of many students with disabilities and serve as a powerful motivator for students who have experienced failure and frustration in school.

Evaluation and Support

The fourth of the key elements in school consultation, collaboration, and co-teaching involves evaluation and support. Co-educators must document the effectiveness of consultation and collaboration in order to ensure continued support for this kind of educational service and avoid the tendency to overlook small, consistent gains. School personnel are understandably skeptical of indirect services if they do not prove their mettle. Co-educators may be involved initially because they are told to, or because they have been talked into giving it a try, or even because they are intrigued with the possibilities or just want to be collegial. But their interest will wane if the processes become a hassle and a burden, especially if positive results are not forthcoming and convincing.

Assessment.   Assessment is essential for providing evaluative data to measure outcomes of collaborative school consultation and co-teaching. School personnel will be more accepting if success is demonstrated with carefully collected, valid data. Unfortunately, evaluations of collaboration and consultation processes have been minimal and often not well planned and conducted. A few procedures such as rating scales of judgments that represent a variety of skills and activities, and survey estimates of engaged time for the required activities, have been used. Administrators, advisory council members, and policymakers should study carefully the procedures that have been tried and use their skills to design helpful and practical assessment techniques that fit their school contexts. In keeping with the philosophy of collaboration, personnel from diverse roles should design the evaluation tools and procedures cooperatively.

Not only should processes and content be evaluated, but the context of the school setting should be as well. For example, a consultant may have excellent communication skills and a wealth of content with which to consult and collaborate, but if the existing school context provides no time and space for interaction, positive results will be slim to none. Consultants will want to evaluate every stage of the collaborative processes to keep focusing on the right goals. (Evaluation will be addressed in more detail in Chapter 6.)

Assessment and evaluation should include a variety of data-collection methods to provide the kinds of information needed by target groups. Consultation and collaboration practices must not be judged inadequate for the wrong reasons or erroneous assumptions. If time has not been allocated for the interactions, if school personnel have not had preparation and encouragement, and if administrator support is lacking, those elements should be targeted for improvement before the collaborative process itself is faulted.

Acceptance.   Participation in collaborative programs must be a *willing* decision and ensure parity for all who are involved in order for the programs to be accepted. Administrator acceptance and encouragement will help in this regard to a great extent. By using techniques such as publicizing the successes and promoting the benefits of consultations and teamwork that have taken place, schools may get the collaboration bandwagon rolling with even the most reluctant persons on board. Most important, however, is involving people right from the start in needs assessments, planning efforts, evaluations, professional development activities, follow-up activities, and more and more personal contacts. This helps to instill ownership and even arouse a little curiosity, not to mention a left-out feeling if not yet on board. Techniques and incentives for promoting acceptance of consultation, collaboration, and teamwork through professional development and advocacy efforts will be discussed in Chapter 12.

Commitment.   Consultation calls for redirection and change in old ways of doing things. Collaboration requires energy and practice. Co-teaching necessitates sharing ownership and taking risks. These realities make involvement by school personnel more difficult and maintenance of their commitment more challenging. In the minds of many educators, consultation has been associated with exclusionary special education programs and assistance in mainstreamed classes. So if teachers miss the opportunity for collaborative consultation service and come to resent having more responsibility for teaching special education students, they may blame collaborative school consultation and collaborative consultants for the situation.

Special education teachers and support personnel need a well-designed plan and a spirited collegial vision that will intrigue and enthuse them about joining in partnerships. Most of all, they need enthusiastic administrator support and sincere encouragement. (This issue will be discussed in more depth in Chapter 12.) Those who would consult, collaborate, and co-teach must recognize and build on every opportunity for dedicated participation by all.

COMPETENCIES OF EFFECTIVE COLLABORATORS, CONSULTANTS, AND TEAM PARTICIPANTS

Consultation, collaboration, and co-teaching competencies emanate from a foundation of understanding school contexts, demonstrating process skills, and delivering helpful content and resources. Guided by principles of caring and sharing, co-educators work together voluntarily and with parity as a team. Collaborative school consultants prepare themselves through teacher education programs and professional development activities for working together. When they collaborate and co-teach, they model the interactive skills their students will need for the future in their own lives.

Collaborative consultants support students, families, their schools, and the community while advocating for schools and students at every opportunity. What role could be better suited to the aspirations of would-be teachers as described in the opening lines of this chapter?

Competencies for teaching and collaborating will be addressed in each chapter as they emanate from the topics and are amplified in Applications and To Do activities. In Chapter 12, the characteristics will be summarized and a competencies checklist will be provided as a tool for assessment. Some readers may want to look ahead at the checklist (see Figure 12.8 on page 426). Others may wish to wait. Still others might find it interesting and beneficial to work as a group in creating their own checklists now or later for collaborative, consultative, and co-teaching skills.

BENEFITS FROM COLLABORATIVE
SCHOOL CONSULTATION

School environments that promote collaborative consultation tend to involve all school personnel in the teaching and learning processes. Information is shared and knowledge levels about student characteristics and needs, and strategies for meeting those needs, are broadened. Importantly, many of the strategies are helpful with other students who have similar but less severe needs. A number of specific benefits of school consultation and collaboration can be anticipated.

First, there is much-needed support and assistance for students in the inclusive classroom. Consulting special education teachers help classroom teachers develop repertoires of materials and instructional strategies. Many find this more efficient than racing from one student to another in a resource room as all work on individual assignments. As one learning disabilities teacher succinctly put it, "In my resource room, by the time I get to the last student, I find that the first student is stuck and has made no progress. So I frantically run through the whole cycle again. Tennis shoes are a must for my job!" Consulting teachers also find ways to help classroom teachers become confident and successful with special needs students. At times they can assume an instructional role in the classroom, which frees the classroom teacher to study student progress, set up arrangements for special projects, or work intensively with a small group of students. When general classroom and special education teachers collaborate, each has ownership and involvement in serving special needs.

Collaborative efforts to serve students in heterogeneous settings help minimize stigmatizing effects of labels such as "delayed," "having disabilities," "exceptional," or even "gifted." They also can reduce referrals to remedial programs. In a study of special education in an inclusionary middle school, Knowles (1997) found that collaboration and teamwork decreased special education referrals and grade-level retention of students. Fewer referrals for special education services means reduced expenditures for costly and time-consuming psychological assessments and special education interventions. Educators can focus more time and energy on teaching and facilitating, and less on testing and measuring. In addition, a ripple effect extends services to students by encouraging modifications and alternatives for their special needs.

A successful consultation process becomes a supportive tool that teachers increasingly value and use. As inclusive school systems become more prevalent, collaborative consultation will become even more critical for school program success. Consultation services contribute to the total school program as a bridge between the parallel systems of special education and general education (Greenburg, 1987) and are an effective way of alleviating confusion over goals and relationships of general and special education (Will, 1984).

Administrators can benefit from eased pressure and planning loads when classroom teachers are efficient in working with a wide range of student needs. Principals find it stimulating to visit and observe in classrooms as team participants, collaborating on ways of helping every student succeed in the school and reinforcing teacher successes with all of their students. This is for many administrators a welcome change from the typical classroom visitations they make for purposes of teacher evaluation.

Another important and frequently overlooked benefit is the maintenance of continuity in learning programs as students progress through their K–12 school experiences. This, too, is a savings in time, energy, and resources of the educational staff and often the parents as well. Transition periods in the student's school life will be discussed in Chapter 11.

A collaborative consultation approach is a natural system for nurturing harmonious staff interactions. Teachers who have become isolated or autonomous in their teaching styles and instructional outlook often discover that working with other adults for common goals is quite stimulating. Sharing ideas can add to creativity, open-endedness, and flexibility in developing educational programs for students with special needs. In addition, more emphasis and coordination can be given to cross-school and long-range planning, with an increased use of outside resources for student needs.

Collaborative consultants are catalysts for professional development. They can identify areas in which faculty need awareness and information sessions, and coordinate workshops to help all school personnel learn specific educational techniques (McKenzie, Egner, Knight, Perelman, Schneider, & Garvin, 1970). Just as removal of the catalyst stops a chemical process, so can the absence of collaborative consulting teachers curtail individualization of curriculum and differentiation of strategies for special needs (Bietau, 1994).

Parents or caregivers of the exceptional student often become extremely frustrated with the labeling, fragmented curriculum, and isolation from peers endured by their children. So they respond enthusiastically when they learn that several educators are functioning as a team for the student. Their attitudes toward school improve and they are more likely to become more involved in planning and carrying through with the interventions (Idol, 1988), more eager to share their ideas, and more helpful in monitoring their child's learning. They are particularly supportive when consulting services allow students in special education programs to remain in their neighborhood schools and to receive more assistance from interagency sources for their child's special needs.

APPLICATION 1.3
COLLABORATION THROUGHOUT THE GLOBAL COMMUNITY

The word *collaboration* is showing up more and more in newscasts, speeches, documentaries, sports reviews, entertainment and media discussions, political panels, printed material, organizational reports, web logs, casual conversations, science breakthroughs, community meetings, and many other arenas of our daily lives. Listen and watch for uses of the word. Tally on a piece of paper each time you see or hear the word and note in what context it appeared. If making a tally is not convenient, then just make a mental note, "There it is. I did hear or see *collaborate* mentioned today." Then consolidate your findings with those of others who are doing it and discuss when, where, and how the word was used.

ETHICS FOR WORKING TOGETHER
AS CO-EDUCATORS

A collaborative ethic is a set of values or principles that supports collegial styles of interaction among coequal individuals engaging voluntarily in making decisions or solving problems (Friend & Cook, 1990; Phillips & McCullough, 1990; Welch, Sheridan, Fuhriman,

Hart, Connell, & Stoddart, 1992). Specific ethics for collaboration and consultation describe a system of values and principles by which beliefs and actions about working together can be judged right or wrong, good or bad, just or unjust, in order to guide practices and inspire excellence.

Educators might ask why there is need for studying ethical principles and practices when their lofty professional aims and aspirations are already built on principled attitudes and behaviors. A better way to address the issue would be to determine, as models for the leaders of tomorrow, how educators can by their own actions and shared beliefs, convey to students the critical need for ethics in *every* field of endeavor. They can begin by modeling ethical principles in every facet of their roles, including interrelationships and teamwork with professional colleagues. These skills will be keys to success in virtually any work role that students may have in the future.

Each chapter of this book will conclude with a look at ethical considerations pertaining to the chapter's content. Conclusions can be drawn from each chapter about the ways in which consultants, collaborators, and co-teachers should conduct their responsibilities ethically within an ethical climate, and all will be summarized in Chapter 12.

Collaborators should work to create environments in which an ethic of care (Noddings, 1992) dominates professional interactions conducted for the purpose of educating children and youth (Pugach & Johnson, 1995). They must strive also to maintain personal integrity, even under pressure from others in their group, by standing firm as a model and monitoring potential violations of ethical principles by others.

Ethical collaborators respect the worth and potential of every individual. They acknowledge that every child is a minority of one with unique backgrounds, situations, abilities, and needs. They strive to serve special needs and abilities with diligence and perseverance, not because it is legislated but because it is the right thing to do. They acknowledge without rancor that some educators may not be keen on collaborating or co-teaching, but they continue to encourage participation by colleagues when it is of likely benefit for students. Special needs of students are the focus of most collaborative interactions. In addressing those special needs, it is important to keep in mind that consultants have complex roles with responsibilities that include the protection of privacy and caretaking of confidential material.

TIPS FOR WORKING TOGETHER IN SCHOOLS

1. Value and find ways to demonstrate beyond token lip service the worth of consultation, collaboration, and teamwork as tools for planning and coordinating instruction.
2. Do not wait to be approached for opportunities to consult, collaborate, and co-teach.
3. Try not to press for personally favored solutions to school needs, co-educator needs, or student needs. Strive instead for collaborative efforts to solve problems together, even if it means giving up some of your own agenda.
4. Refrain from assuming that colleagues are waiting around to be "saved."
5. Do not share problems or concerns with classroom teachers unless they can have significant input or you have a suggestion for them that might help.
6. Ask for help when you are facing a problem, because it has a humanizing, rapport-building effect.

7. Interact with every co-educator in the building(s) regularly.

8. Learn all you can about methods of consulting, collaborating, co-teaching, and engaging in other kinds of collegial teamwork, determining what worked and what didn't work that would be applicable to your environment.

9. Leave the door open, both figuratively and literally, for future partnerships and collaborations.

10. Encourage each member of a collaborative group to share knowledge and perceptions about an issue, in order to establish a solid framework in which to discuss the issue.

CHAPTER REVIEW

1. Educators of the twenty-first century can no longer be expected to work effectively in isolated environments and autonomous roles. Every child is "a minority of one" with special needs and abilities. A wide array of services and school personnel, working in collaboration, is needed to prepare all students for their future careers, continuing education, and responsibilities of citizenship.

2. Collaborative consultation and team activities such as co-teaching in school contexts describes interaction in which school personnel, families, and community agencies collaborate as a team within the school context to identify learning and behavioral needs, and to plan, implement, and evaluate educational programs that serve those needs. The collaborative school consultant is a facilitator of effective communication, cooperation, and coordination who works with co-educators in a team effort to serve the special learning and behavioral needs of students.

3. Collaborative consultation is a way of working together to identify the special needs of students; plan as a team for goal setting, curriculum, and assessment that will meet those needs in an inclusive setting; and interact with other school personnel, communities, and families for the welfare of students, schools, and communities.

4. Key elements in school consultation and collaboration are preparation for the consultative and collaborative roles at preservice, graduate, and experienced-teacher levels; role delineation with role clarity, parity, and appropriate expectations; a framework of structure, resources, and management; and evaluation and support through assessment, commitment, and acceptance. A consultant, consultee (or mediator), and client (or target) in one school-related situation may function in either of the other two roles under different circumstances. Several questions reflect the practical concerns of consultants and consulting teachers: What do I do? How do I begin? What is my schedule for a day/week/year? How will I know I am succeeding? How can I prepare for this kind of role?

5. Many benefits accrue from successful collaborative consultation and co-teaching. These include much-needed support and assistance for students with disabilities within in the inclusive classroom. Collaboration and teamwork can decrease special education referrals and grade-level retention of students, meaning reduced costs. Ripple effects bring about modifications and alternatives for students' special needs. Collaborative consultants are catalysts for professional development and can help ease burdens of building administrators. Parents respond enthusiastically when they learn that several educators are functioning as a team for the student. Competencies needed to bring about these benefits include context skills of understanding the role, working in parity and collegiality with others, and adhering to ethical principles; process skills of communication, organization, and management; and content skills for co-teaching and co-facilitating, addressing special needs of students in collaboration with resource and support personnel, and continuing to grow professionally.

6. Educators must convey to students the critical need for ethics in every field of endeavor. In their very visible teaching roles they can model ethical principles for students. In their interactions with professional colleagues they can model personal integrity and doing the right things in ways that demonstrate the collaborative ethics their students will need to be successful in virtually every work role of their future.

TO DO AND THINK ABOUT

1. Using material in this chapter, a dictionary, interviews, recollections from teaching experiences, discussion with colleagues or classmates, and any other pertinent references, develop a paragraph or two about collaborative consultation and co-teaching activities among co-educators to reflect your thoughts at this time.

2. Interview three school professionals (elementary, middle school, and high school levels if possible) and two parents to find out their views of consultation services, collaborative activities, and co-teaching in schools. If they ask, "What do you mean by collaboration, and consultation, and co-teaching?" you can approach this in one of two ways—giving them descriptions, perhaps based on those you developed in #1 above, or encouraging them to define the concepts in their own way. Compare the interview results, and draw inferences from your findings. Note any indication of willingness to collaborate or a glimmer of budding interest in consultation, and consider how these positive signs might be followed up productively.

3. Develop a chart for identifying obstacles that may appear in executing the four key elements of collaboration and consultation, namely, preparation, role delineation, framework, and evaluation, and add a section for proposing ways of sidestepping or overcoming those obstacles.

4. Before looking at the competencies checklist provided in Chapter 12, make a list of competencies you think are important for collaborative school consultants who will be working with other educators in groups or in pairs as co-teachers. If possible, compare your list with those done by others and exchange ideas.

5. In groups, discuss the topic of collaborative ethics by generating key words—for example, principles, values, fairness, communicating, caring. Record the words on chart paper or chalkboard so all can see them. Next, with these pooled words as catalysts, formulate a description of a collaborative ethical climate for educators that would work for your school context. Then talk about why ethical principles are so important in school-based education. Finally, generate ideas for ways in which ethical behaviors can be encouraged and modeled by co-educators in educational environments.

ADDITIONAL READINGS AND RESOURCES

Journal for Educational and Psychological Consultation. All issues have theory-based and research-based articles on the use of collaboration and consultation in teaching, psychology, counseling, and other education-based professions.

Thomas, C. C., Correa, V. I., & Morsink, C. V. (2001). *Interactive teaming: Enhancing programs for students with special needs* (3rd ed.). Upper Saddle River, NJ: Prentice Hall.
Unit I on context and foundations for interactive teaming.

Welch, M. (1998.) The IDEA of collaboration in special education: An introspective examination of para-digms and promise. *Journal of Educational and Psychological Consultation, 9*(2), 119–142.

Williams, J. M., & Martin, S. M. (2001). Implementing the Individuals with Disabilities Education Act of 1997: The consultant's role. *Journal of Educational and Psychological Consultation, 12*(1), 59–81.

Yocum, D. J., & Cossairt, A. (1996). Consultation courses offered in special education teacher training programs: A national survey. *Journal of Educational and Psychological Consultation, 7*(3), 251–258.

CHAPTER THREE

CONTEXT:
History and
Models

Foundations and Frameworks for Consultation, Collaboration, and Teamwork

Consultation, collaboration, and teamwork probably began around cave fires ages ago, as humans discovered it was good to talk things over. It is likely that as they learned to explore wider territories, construct things, and then trade those things, they found it helpful to communicate by smoke signal and drumbeat. They formed connections of networks and began to consult and collaborate with those they trusted. Through social interaction they learned useful things from others and enjoyed expressing their own views as well. When they planned hunting and food-gathering forays and eventually began to plant and harvest, they developed methods for teamwork that gave them even more success as hunters, gatherers, and growers.

So it has been that throughout the ages people improved their quality of life by working together. Now, as our global world "shrinks," interpersonal skills are even more essential for progress and well-being in our increasingly complex, interconnected world. Individuals will continue to have their own professional perspectives and personal preferences, but those who interact and work together successfully will fare best.

Relating to others, communicating, and respecting the viewpoints of others should begin at an early age. Toddlers at home, in their neighborhoods, and perhaps in day care centers, are expected to outgrow egocentrism and learn how to interact with others. Preschool children are encouraged to work cooperatively with others. Schools become their next learning fields for interrelating. Educators who cooperate, negotiate, and model collaboration and productive teamwork are teaching students how to succeed in the world they will inherit and lead.

FOCUSING QUESTIONS

1. What school improvement and reform issues have influenced the growth of inclusive schools and collaborative teaching environments?

2. What legislation propels schools toward collaborative school consultation, instructional teams, co-teaching, and partnerships with families?

72 From Chapter 3 of *Collaboration, Consultation, and Teamwork for Students with Special Needs*, 6/e. Peggy Dettmer. Linda P. Thurston. Ann Knackendoffel. Norma J. Dyck. Copyright © 2009 by Pearson Merrill. All rights reserved.

3. What, in brief, are the historical, theoretical, and research bases of collaborative school consultation?

4. What are the common structural components in collaborative school consultation methods?

5. What models of consultation, collaboration, and teamwork have evolved in education?

6. How might educators tailor methods for consultation, collaboration, and co-teaching to make them well suited to their school contexts?

KEY TERMS

Americans with Disabilities Act (ADA)
approach
collaborative consultation models
Conjoint Behavioral Consultation model (CBC)
consultee-centered consultation models
early intervention
free and appropriate public education (FAPE)
IDEA 1997, IDEA 2004
inclusion

Instructional Consultation model (IC)
intersubjectivity
least restrictive environment (LRE)
mainstreaming
method
mode
model
No Child *Held* Behind (NC*H*B)
No Child Left Behind (NCLB)
perspective

prototype
Public Laws 89-313, 94-142, 99-457, and 101-476
regular education initiative (REI)
Resource/Consulting Teacher Program model (R/CT)
Schoolwide Enrichment Model (SEM)
semantics
system
Teacher Assistance Teams model (TAT)
triadic model

SCENARIO 3

The setting is a school administration office where the superintendent, the high school principal, and the special education director are having an early-morning conference.

Special Education Director: I've assigned five people on our special education staff to begin serving as consulting teachers in the schools we targeted at our last meeting.

Principal: I understand the high school is to be one of those schools.

Special Education Director: Yes, several classroom teachers will be involved. I've visited briefly with the English teacher who is getting a new student with learning disabilities and I'll work with one of the consulting teachers to collaborate and perhaps try some co-teaching.

Principal: I'm all for trying a new approach, but at this point I'm not sure my staff understands very much about how this method of service is going to affect them.

Superintendent: Are you saying we need to spend a little more time at the drawing board and get the kinks out of our plan before tossing it out to the teachers?

Principal: Yes, and I think the parents also will want to know what will be happening. They'll want us to tell them specifically how this will benefit their child.

Special Education Director: I've been compiling a file of theoretical background, research studies, program descriptions, even some cartoons and fun sayings, that focus on consultation and collaboration approaches and hopefully will lighten up some of the gray areas of their concerns. I'll get copies of the best of it to you and the principals of the other designated schools. Perhaps we should plan in-service sessions for teachers and some awareness sessions for parents, too, before we proceed, especially if we anticipate trying some co-teaching.

Superintendent: That sounds good. Draft an outline and we'll discuss it at next week's meeting. I'll get the word out to the other principals to be here.

MOVEMENTS FOR SCHOOL IMPROVEMENT

A little history from the past several decades will serve as background for the changing climate that led to the current educational environment. In the 1960s advocates representing special needs pressed for the right of those with mental retardation to have opportunities as similar as possible to those in mainstream society. In addition, the public's attention to needs of preschoolers from disadvantaged environments gained momentum.

In 1965, passage of the Elementary and Secondary Education Act (ESEA) authorized funding and made specific provisions for students with disabilities (Talley & Schrag, 1999). Reauthorizations of that legislation in 1988 and 1994 mandated parent involvement and coordination in early childhood programs such as Head Start, encouraging school and community-linked services through the Community Schools Partnership Act. Consultation and collaboration became essential factors in coordinating the array of services provided for students with special needs.

During the 1970s, 1980s, 1990s, and early 2000s, educators witnessed an explosion of reports, proposals, and legislative mandates calling for educational reform. Issues in the 1970s focused on accountability, lengthening of time in school, and increased investments in education. Demands for cost containment and growing concerns over labeling of students fueled interest in a merger of general education and special education. The primary impetus for the merger was the mainstreaming movement with its concept of least restrictive environment (LRE). This was catalyzed in 1975 by passage of Public Law 94-142 (that is, put forth by the 94th Congress as their 142nd piece of legislation). After that legislation was passed, educators could no longer arbitrarily place individuals with disabilities in a special school or self-contained classroom. A continuum of service options was to be available and the type of service or placement was to be as close to the normal environment as possible, with general education teachers responsible for the success of those students. In order to meet this new responsibility, general education teachers were to receive help from special education personnel. This was an important provision.

During the second wave of reform in the 1980s, the individual school became the unit of decision making. This movement promoted the development of collegial, participatory environments among students and staff, with particular emphasis on personalizing school environments and designing curriculum for deeper understanding (Michaels, 1988). One component of this second wave was school restructuring. Many states initiated some form of school restructuring; however, few schools were truly restructured. Where restructuring efforts occurred, they tended to be idiosyncratic in that they were carried out by a small group of teachers, creating only marginal changes (Timar, 1989).

A position paper issued by Madeline Will (1986), former director of the U.S. Office of Special Education and Rehabilitative Services, stated that too many children were being inappropriately identified and placed in learning disabilities programs. In that paper, Will called for *collaboration* between special education personnel and general education personnel to provide special services within the general classroom. This generated the regular education initiative (REI), referred to by some educators as the general education initiative (GEI), that caused major changes in the way education is delivered. All students, with the exception of those with severe disabilities, were from that time to be served primarily in a regular education setting. The rationale for the REI was that:

- The changes would serve many students not currently eligible for special education services.
- The stigma of placement in special education programs that were separate from age peers would be eliminated.
- Early intervention and prevention would be provided before more serious learning deficiencies could occur.
- Cooperative school-parent relationships would be enhanced (Will, 1986).

In 1986, P.L. 94-142 was amended by P.L. 99-457, which mandated free and appropriate public education (FAPE) for preschool children ages 3–5 with disabilities. An Individualized Family Service Plan (IFSP) was required for each child served, thus extending the concept of the IEP to provide support for child *and* family (Smith, 1998).

Early intervention programs for infants and toddlers with disabilities proliferated following the 1986 legislation. Parents and other caregivers outside the school now had an even more integral part in the education of these children. Because most disabilities of children in early intervention programs are severe, an array of services is essential.

Families are to have an integral part in the therapy through home-based programs. Families are described in a broad sense, not necessarily as a father-and-mother unit. Family includes parents, grandparents, older siblings, aunts and uncles, and others who function in the caregiver role. The IFSP is developed by a multidisciplinary team with family members as active participants. Children are served according to family needs, allowing for a wide range of services with parent training as one of those services. Family choices are considered in all decisions.

In 1990, early in the third wave of reform, Public Law 94-142 was amended with the passage of Public Law 101-476, the Individuals with Disabilities Education Act (IDEA). That legislation's primary elements were:

- All references to children as handicapped were changed to children with disabilities.
- New categories of autism and traumatic brain injury (TBI) were added, to be served with increased collaboration among all special education teachers, classroom teachers, and related services personnel.
- More emphasis was placed on requirements to provide transition services for students 16 years of age and older.

Two distinct groups emerged to advocate for REI—the high-incidence group (many cases) that included learning disabilities, behavioral disorders, and mild/moderate mental retardation, and the low-incidence group (fewer cases) that included students with severe intellectual disabilities. Both groups shared three goals:

1. To merge special and general education into one inclusive system
2. To increase dramatically the number of children with disabilities in mainstream classrooms
3. To strengthen academic achievement of students with mild and moderate disabilities, as well as that of underachievers without disabilities.

To attain these goals, total restructuring would be needed in schools. "Increasingly, special education reform is symbolized by the term 'inclusive schools,'" (Fuchs and Fuchs, 1994, p. 299).

Also passed in 1990 was the Americans with Disabilities Act (ADA). This law prohibited discrimination against people of all ages who have disabilities in matters of transportation, public access, local government, and telecommunications. It required schools to make all reasonable accommodations for access by students and it extended provisions concerning fairness in employment to employers who do not receive federal funds (Smith, 1998).

The *America 2000* report presented in 1991 by President George H. W. Bush and Secretary of Education Lamar Alexander, and the 1994 federal school reform package known as Goals 2000 that was signed into law by President Bill Clinton, identified goals to be met in the nation's schools by the year 2000. The latter report emphasized that home and school partnerships are essential for student success. After these reports were publicized, public pressure to improve schools escalated.

In 1997, after much study and discussion nationwide, reauthorization and amendments for IDEA were approved by Congress and signed into law by President Clinton. This legislation, known as IDEA 1997, contained the following:

- Provisions for improved parent-professional partnerships
- Requirement for states to provide mediation for parents and schools in resolving differences
- Requirement that states would have training for paraeducators to prepare for their roles
- Requirement for general education teachers to participate on IEP teams when students are or will be placed in a general education classroom
- Increased cost sharing among agencies with reduced financial burdens for special education locally
- Accountability of education for students with disabilities by way of participation in state and districtwide assessment programs
- Assurance that children with behavioral disorders who exhibit dangerous behaviors are not to be deprived of educational services, but educators could more easily remove them from their current educational placement if needed
- Tighter disclosure requirements, with families having greater access to their children's records and more information available in IEPs

A focus of IDEA 1997 was collaboration among general educators and special educators, parents, related services personnel, and other service providers; this inclusion meant that general educators in particular must be actively engaged in selecting program modifications and supports, alternative-grading procedures, and assistive technology devices (Williams & Martin, 2001). Transition services and interagency linkages were noted as being vital areas of assistance from collaborating consultants.

In general, the special education community was pleased with components of IDEA 1997. A few concerns remained, not the least of which was the *increase*, rather than a much hoped-for decrease, in the paperwork that so erodes the time and morale of special educators.

Inclusive Schools

The concept of inclusion that swept the nation in recent years did not suddenly emerge out of a vacuum. It emanated from the long line of special education movements and mandates briefly described above and summarized in Figure 3.1.

Inclusive schools *include* students with special needs in the total school experience, rather than exclude them by placement in special schools or classrooms. In full inclusion, support services come to the student in the general education setting. In partial inclusion students may be served in another instructional setting when appropriate for their individual needs, but receive most of their instruction in the general education setting.

From its rather quiet beginning, the inclusive schools movement snowballed into a popular position whereby special education and regular education were expected to merge into a unified school system. The merger was intended to modify many aspects of the rigidly compartmentalized, often stigmatizing, and very expensive special education structure. Furthermore, proponents of inclusive schools made the case that *all* students are unique individuals with special needs requiring differentiated individual attention; therefore, practices used effectively for exceptional students should be made available to all students (McLeskey, Henry, & Hodges, 1998).

In O'Neil (1994–1995), Sapon-Shevin made an appealing case that educators should not have to defend inclusion—rather, they should insist that others should have to defend *exclusion* if they are going to support that position. A collaborative climate with teachers working together for all students in inclusive settings is a realistic way to settle the debate. Collaborative consultation can be advocated for students with disabilities as providing better service, more time, greater levels of teacher attention, and more opportunities for socializing with age peers in natural settings.

The legislation did not define inclusion. But several useful definitions are available in the literature, including these:

- *Inclusion:* Educating each child to the maximum extent appropriate in the school and classroom he or she would otherwise attend (Rogers, 1993). The current focus for inclusion is on location of instruction and grouping of students, it is arbitrary across states and across districts within a state, and ideally it involves a regular education teacher and a special education teacher co-teaching in one classroom (Beakley, 1997).

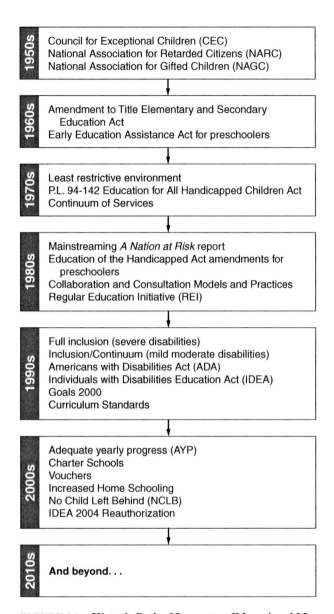

FIGURE 3.1   Historic Path of Important Educational Movements

- *Full (or Total) Inclusion:* Instructional practices and technological supports are available to accommodate all students in the schools and classrooms they would otherwise attend if not disabled (Rogers, 1993).
- *Inclusive Schools:* Schools where all members accept their fair share of responsibility for all children, including those with disabilities. Aids and resources are

utilized where needed regardless of official classifications of disability (Fuchs & Fuchs, 1994).

The National Center on Educational Restructuring and Inclusion (NCERI) conducted a study in 1994 to determine the status of the inclusion movement. The center found that inclusive programs were increasingly being implemented in many states across the country. At that time they identified six factors that are necessary for successful inclusion in schools: visionary leadership, collaboration, refocused use of assessment, supports for family and students, funding, and effective family involvement.

Collaboration is essential to inclusion because successful inclusion presumes that "no one teacher can or ought to be expected to have all the expertise required to meet the educational needs of all students in the classroom" (Lipsky, 1994, p. 5). All educators share responsibility for student achievement and behavior. There must be total commitment from principal to school custodian (Federico, Herrold, & Venn, 1999). Every inclusive school looks different, but all inclusive schools are characterized by a sense of community, high standards, collaboration and cooperation, changing roles and an array of services, partnership with families, flexible learning environments, strategies based on research, new forms of accountability, and ongoing professional development (Federico et al., 1999; Working Forum on Inclusive Schools, 1994).

A Continuing Dialogue about Inclusion.   Responses to inclusion have been complex; they are shaped by multiple variables, and these variables change over time (Salend & Duhaney, 1999). So while supportive educators may applaud the spirit of inclusion and the benefits of inclusive settings, others do not regard inclusion as everybody's panacea. Narrow definitions, myopic practices, and most of all, failure to prepare school personnel in collaborative and co-teaching strategies can short-circuit the well-meant intentions. Critics point to situations in which teachers receive little to no assistance and sometimes are not even informed about the nature of their students' disabilities. Some contend that special education teachers have difficulties managing educational programs of students scheduled among several classrooms.

In some schools several children with severe disabilities are assigned to the same classroom. This does not approximate a typical classroom situation because perhaps only 1 child in 100 will have severe disabilities. This situation can create an extremely frustrating environment for the classroom teacher (Rogers, 1993). Parents of students with disabilities sometimes make the case that their children have fewer services and, in particular, do not receive the direct services they may require. Problems can develop in inclusive settings for children with disabilities if they are "dumped wholesale" into classrooms where their teachers have no time or training for collaboration and teamwork. Sometimes special educators lament loss of control over the learning environment and fear loss of specialized services for students with disabilities (Salend & Duhaney, 1999), as do their parents. To add to the concerns, a backlash among some parents of children who do not have disabilities indicates that they feel their children's education is being compromised by the myriad demands on teachers in inclusive environments.

VanTassel-Baska (1998) notes that studies are limited for education of gifted and talented students within inclusive settings, but those that do exist reveal some troubling trends. Research shows that students with high ability and remarkable talents too often do not receive instruction intensive enough for their learning needs in inclusive classrooms. This concern will be addressed further in Chapter 7.

In a qualitative study of inclusive elementary school programs, Wood (1998) found that in the initial stages of inclusion, teachers maintained discrete role boundaries through an informal but clear division of labor. However, as the school year progressed, role perceptions became less rigid as the teaming process became more cooperative. More recent emphasis on collaborative climates, professional development activities, heightened interest and involvement by parents and communities, and intensive advocacy efforts toward inclusion by both general and special educators, have boosted the acceptance of inclusion throughout the land.

Reauthorization of the Individuals with Disabilities Education Act

Two significant pieces of legislation were due for reauthorization in the first decade of the new century. In 2004, the U.S. Congress reauthorized IDEA 1997 with passage of IDEA 2004. Areas targeted for improvement or change involved:

- High expectations for students with disabilities, to increase abilities for employment and independent living
- Professional development and training of all preservice and school personnel who work with children having disabilities, including skills and knowledge and use of scientifically based (research-based) instructional processes to the maximum extent possible
- Compatibility with No Child Left Behind performance goals for adequate yearly progress
- IEPs that include research-based methodology
- Elimination of short-term objectives and benchmarks except for students taking alternate assessments
- IEPs that provide clear, measurable annual goals, including academic goals and functional goals (routine activities of daily living having evaluation procedures that meet standards for all of the other evaluation procedures)
- Required parental consent for initial evaluation and before implementing services presented in the IEP
- Specification of the roles of school personnel to attend IEP conferences, including parents, not fewer than one regular education teacher, not fewer than one special education teacher, an individual who can interpret instructional implications of evaluations, and a representative of the school district who has supervisory responsibilities and is knowledgeable about the general education curriculum and outside agency resources
- Free and appropriate public education required for all, even those suspended or expelled
- Measurable goals with evaluation procedures that meet standards for all of the other evaluation procedures

Authorization of No Child Left Behind Legislation

The No Child Left Behind Act (NCLB) passed by the U.S. Congress in 2001 and signed by President George W. Bush on January 8, 2002, mandated requirements and added specificity to elements of the 1965 Elementary and Secondary Education Act. Purposes of this legislation were summarized under accountability, assessment, and high standards. Goals of the legislation were as lofty and most likely as undoable as President Clinton's Goals 2000 that mandated, among other things, having "All Children Enter School Ready to Learn."

NCLB unleashed a flurry of high-stakes testing in specific curricular areas (reading and math as first subjects to be tested), inclusion of children with disabilities in the testing scheme, intensive preparations for the tests, high-profile reports of schools that made or failed to make adequate yearly progress (AYP), higher standards for teacher certification, and more accountability of schools for student achievement. This legislation activated considerable discussion, much of it quite critical, in the professional literature, among school personnel, families, and in the Congress. Many educators stress that education is not conducive to high-stakes testing. Children do not learn the same amount at the same rate, as pointed out in Chapter 2. Success of schools cannot be measured by tests. Furthermore, test results should be used to guide instruction, not to signify school failure.

One of the harshest criticisms of NCLB has been that the emphasis on testing has narrowed the school curriculum considerably. Another is that the focus on students below proficiency has shifted attention and resources from very able learners who need challenge and advancement; consequently, they are being *held* behind (NC*H*B). Still another concern is that standardized tests and assessment of adequate yearly progress in cognitive areas do not assess student growth in the emotional, physical, self-expressive, and social areas that also are vital for student development (Dettmer, 2006). Children need development in fine arts, physical education, practical arts, problem solving, and working together collaboratively. All of these problems are compounded by failure of the federal government to adequately fund the legislation.

A number of revisions were proposed for a reauthorization of NCLB slated to happen during September 2007, but the process faltered under considerable controversy and debate during a politically volatile period. Changes considered for the reauthorization include, in a broad sense, making it more flexible and broad-based to serve its original purposes. Examples would be a wider selection of tests that provide more authentic assessment, supplemental education services for schools that are falling behind, limiting of students to be tested for whom English is a second or even a third language, and better data-processing systems to ascertain progress and diagnose needs.

Proponents of NCLB say the partnerships that are emerging have been encouraging and the resultant experienced-based information has been constructive. Most acknowledge that NCLB has caused a narrowing of the curriculum and some teaching to the test, but some schools are working to develop more flexible tests. They further believe that the responses to such concerns are providing new energy to work toward the accountability and high standards that were mandated.

Expanded goals for NCLB could include improving high school graduation rates, providing better tests to measure accountability, having stronger emphasis on preparing students for work and college, including assessments that reflect critical thinking and problem solving, and retaining excellent teachers by means of career ladders and mentors.

A BRIEF HISTORY OF COLLABORATIVE
SCHOOL CONSULTATION

The advent of special education in public schools probably dates back to the mid-nineteenth century, when state after state (Rhode Island in 1840, then Massachusetts in 1952, and followed in time by all others) passed compulsory school attendance laws mandating formal education for every school-age child regardless of disability, giftedness, or other special need. And now, in the twenty-first century, as school doors open each morning and school bells ring, students congregate and classes begin, students bring their special needs to school to be addressed. Up to one-third of all school-age children can be described as experiencing difficulties in school by reason of special needs. If the significant learning needs of gifted students were included, this figure would be increased substantially.

These realities, along with various social issues of the times, have spurred interest in school consultation, collaboration, and other forms of teamwork such as co-teaching, mentoring, cooperative learning, and peer tutoring. The result has been an escalating number of conferences, publications, research studies, pilot programs, federal and state grants, training projects, as well as development of several teacher preparation courses and programs, for understanding and applying collaborative practices in schools.

Collaborative School Consultation before 1970

School consultation probably originated in the mental health and management fields (Reynolds & Birch, 1988). Caplan (1970) had developed consultation programs to train staff members for working with troubled adolescents in Israel at the close of World War II. Building upon this Caplanian mental health consultation concept (Caplan, Caplan, & Erchul, 1995), mental health services escalated and moved into school settings, where consultation services of school psychologists produced promising results. The role of consultation in school psychology was broadened to encourage collaborative relationships (Gallessich, 1974; Pryzwansky, 1974). Such relationships were nurtured to help teachers, administrators, and parents deal with future problems as well as immediate concerns.

Examples of consulting in the areas of speech and language therapy, and in hearing-impaired and visually impaired programs, date from the late 1950s. Emphasis on teacher consultation for learning disabled and behavior-disordered students surfaces in the literature as early as the mid-1960s. At that time consultants for the most part were not special educators, but clinical psychologists and psychiatric social workers.

Also, by the mid-1960s the term *school consultation* was listed in *Psychological Abstracts* (Friend, 1988). School counselors began to promote the concept of proactive service, so that by the early 1970s consultation was being recommended as an integral part of contemporary counseling service. This interest in collaborative relationships on the part of counselors and psychologists reflected a desire to influence the individuals, groups, and systems that most profoundly affect students (Brown, Wyne, Blackburn, & Powell, 1979).

The behavioral movement had been gaining momentum in the late 1960s and it fueled interest in alternative models for intervention and the efficient use of time and other resources. This interest sparked development of a text by Tharp and Wetzel (1969) in which they presented a triadic consultation model using behavioral principles in school settings. The triadic model is the basic pattern upon which many subsequent models and methods for consultation have been constructed.

Passage of the Elementary and Secondary Education Act (ESEA) in 1965 authorized funding and made specific provisions for students with disabilities (Talley & Schrag, 1999). Reauthorizations in 1988 and 1994 mandated parent involvement and coordination in programs such as Head Start, encouraging school and community-linked services through the Community Schools Partnership Act. Consultation and collaboration became essential factors in coordinating the array of services provided for students with special needs.

By 1970 the special education literature contained references to a method of training consulting teachers to serve students in special education at the elementary level (McKenzie et al., 1970). The first direct explication of a consulting teacher service delivery model for students with mild disabilities was by McKenzie, Egner, Knight, Perelman, Schneider, and Garvin in 1970. This group described a program at the University of Vermont for preparation of consulting teachers and a plan for implementing a consulting teacher model in the state (Lilly & Givens-Ogle, 1981).

Collaborative School Consultation from 1970 to 2000

As noted earlier, the decade of the 1970s was a very busy time in the field of special education. Intensive special education advocacy, federal policy making for exceptional students, and technological advancements influenced special education practices for students who were at that time described as being handicapped (Nazzaro, 1977). The Education for All Handicapped Children's Act (EHA) was passed in 1975 and signed by President Gerald Ford, reauthorized in 1990 as the Individuals with Disabilities Education Act (IDEA), amended as IDEA 1997, and reauthorized in 2004. These legislative actions contained national guidelines on service delivery of education for students with disabilities (Talley & Schrag, 1999). One of the many guidelines was prescription of multidisciplinary and multi-dimensional services to be coordinated for maximizing student learning and development. By the mid-1970s consultation was being regarded as a significant factor in serving students with special needs. Special education became a major catalyst for promoting consultation and collaboration in schools (Friend, 1988).

Consultation became one of the most significant educational trends by the mid-1980s for serving students with special needs. To analyze the trend, West and Brown (1987) sent a questionnaire to directors of special education in the fifty states. Thirty-five state directors responded. Twenty-six of the respondents stated that service delivery models in their states included consultation as an expected role of the special educator. The 26 states reported a total of ten different professional titles for consultation as a job responsibility of special educators. About three-fourths of the respondents acknowledged the need for service delivery models that include consultation. However, only seven indicated that specific requirements for competency in consultation were included in their policies.

As interest in school consultation escalated during the 1980s, the National Task Force on Collaborative School Consultation, sponsored by the Teacher Education Division (TED) of the Council for Exceptional Children (CEC), sent a publication to state departments of education with recommendations for teacher consultation services in a special education services continuum (Heron & Kimball, 1988). Several guidelines were presented for development of consultative assistance options; definition of a consulting teacher role and recommended pupil-teacher ratio; and requirements for preservice, inservice, and certification preparation programs. The report included a list of education professionals skilled in school consultation and a list of publications featuring school consultation.

By 1990 a new journal focusing on school consultation, the *Journal of Educational and Psychological Consultation* (JEPC), appeared. A preconvention workshop sponsored by the Teacher Education Division of the Council for Exceptional Children on school consultation and collaboration programs and practices was a featured event at the 1990 annual CEC conference in Toronto. Early leaders in school consultation reconceptualized models to fit more appropriately with inclusive schools and expanded roles of school personnel. Caplan's mental health consultation model evolved into mental health collaboration as a better choice of practice for school-based professionals (Caplan, Caplan, & Erchul, 1995). Bergan (1995) similarly described an evolution from the school psychologist's behavioral consultation focus on assessment, labeling, and placement activities to an expanded role of consultative and collaborative problem solving for students' needs. The framework for behavioral consultation was revised to become a case-centered, problem-solving approach that could be teacher-based, parent-based, or conjoint-based (parent-teacher) consultation in which the consultee's involvement is critical to success of positive client outcomes (Kratochwill & Pittman, 2002).

In the field of education for gifted students, discussion of collaborative consultation practices was minimal but gradually increased and promised to be one of the most viable fields for its extensive use (Dettmer, 1989). For more than two decades Dettmer and Lane (1989) and Idol-Maestas and Celentano (1986) stressed the need for collaborative consultation practices to assist with learning needs of gifted and talented students who spend most of their school day in regular classrooms. Dyck and Dettmer (1989) promoted methods for facilitating learning programs of twice exceptional, gifted learning-disabled students within a consulting teacher plan.

Collaborative School Consultation since 2000

The general public in the new millennium is aware that teaching is not just the responsibility of professional educators within the school's walls. Community members and resource personnel beyond school campuses are needed as collaborators and team members who can help plan and direct rich, authentic learning experiences for students.

Also gaining prominence is an awareness of the need for collaboration among general and special education teachers that will give students opportunities for learning and practicing skills related to standards set forth by governing bodies of each area. The practice of teaming across classrooms is being utilized by many dedicated teachers as an approach that can bring students closer to achieving the standards (Kluth & Straut, 2001).

The next several decades of this millennium are critical for professional educators as they learn to work together and to *enjoy* doing it. It will be very important for them to model such behaviors because their students also will be expected to work collaboratively as adults in their careers and community roles. Strong partnerships between home and school educators will be an increasingly essential part of helping students become capable, ethical leaders for the future.

THEORETICAL AND RESEARCH BASES OF COLLABORATIVE SCHOOL CONSULTATION

Is school consultation theory-based as a practice or an atheoretical practice related to a problem-solving knowledge base? Differing points of view exist.

School consultation is theory-based if identified across more than one literature source focusing on the relationship between consultant and consultee (West & Idol, 1987). On the other hand, if identified by problem-solving methods, then it is knowledge-based in the area of problem solving. At this point it would be good to bear in mind the adage that "there is nothing so practical as a good theory."

West and Idol identified ten prominent models of consultation, of which six are founded on a clearly distinguishable theory or theories: mental health, behavioral, process, advocacy, and two types of organizational consultation. They designated a seventh as a collaborative consultation model having the essential elements for building theory because it features a set of generic principles for building collaborative relationships between consultants and consultees.

During the 1980s when interest in collaboration and consultation escalated, many analyses and discussions of school consultation took place. Heron and Kimball (1988) identified an emerging research base that includes:

- Theory and models (West & Idol, 1987)
- Methodology (Gresham & Kendell, 1987)
- Training and practice (Friend, 1984; Idol & West, 1987)
- Professional preferences for consultation service (Babcock & Pryzwansky, 1983; Medway & Forman, 1980)
- Guidelines (Salend & Salend, 1984)
- Competencies for consultations (West & Cannon, 1988)

Fuchs, Fuchs, Dulan, Roberts, and Fernstrom (1992) share views stated by Pryzwansky (1986) that many studies on consultation are poorly conceptualized and executed. Consultation researchers must assess the integrity of consultation plans, since many plans are not implemented by consultees as designed (Witt & Elliott, 1985). Conducting the research effectively requires careful planning, attention to detail, interpersonal skills, flexibility, positive relationships with school personnel, and research skills (Fuchs et al., 1992). But West and Idol (1987) have pointed out that efforts to conduct research in the complex, multidimensional field of school consultation are impeded by lack of psychometrically reliable and valid instrumentation and controls.

Without question there should be more research to ascertain effects of collaborative consultation and to understand more about the variables related to those effects. Research can be improved by use of control or comparison groups, inclusion of more than one consultant and more than one dependent measure, including follow-up data, and making every effort to control experimenter bias (Bramlett & Murphy, 1998; Fuchs et al., 1992).

According to Slesser, Fine, and Tracy (1990), much of the research on school consultation heretofore has examined behaviors specific to particular models. They propose that further research is needed to examine specific behaviors and attitudes of more successful consultants compared with those who are less successful, because it is likely that many school consultants initiate their own integration of different models. Customization of models will be a recommendation given in this book.

One promising area for exploration is intersubjectivity. Since the 1980s and the rediscovery and analysis of Vygotsky's (1978) work, this aspect of social learning has captured the attention of educational psychologists. His intersubjective attitude of negotiation and joint construction of meaning is a commitment to building shared meaning by finding common ground and exchanging interpretations (Woolfolk, 2001). Colleagues with an intersubjective attitude assert their own positions while respecting those of others and working together to co-construct useful perspectives. Recall the discussion of adult differences and variety of styles in teamwork presented in Chapter 2.

Another area of collaborative and consultative processes that must be considered is disengagement. Winding down or ending a collaborative consultation relationship is likely to be an emotionally sensitive and stressful process. It is a joint decision in which participants feel comfortable applying things that have been learned during the collaboration to new situations. Communication skills are of utmost importance and proper timing is crucial. There is no textbook approach to this (Dougherty, Tack, Fullam, & Hammer, 1996); therefore, it is essential for those involved to prepare themselves for the feelings that come when professional and personal relationships must come to an end.

STRUCTURAL ELEMENTS OF COLLABORATIVE SCHOOL CONSULTATION

Overlapping philosophies of consultation have evolved from a blending of consultation knowledge and practices in several fields. This overlap creates a tangle of philosophy and terminology that could be problematic for educators. So it is helpful to sort out the myriad consultation terms, theories, research findings, and practices, and recast them into useful structures.

When communicating about educational issues, educators will want to avoid using "educationese" (convoluted and redundant phrases), "jargon" (in-house expressions that approximate educational slang), and "alphabet soup" (acronyms that appear to laypeople as a form of code). Communication must be presented in clear language and this requires careful attention to semantics, as discussed in Chapter 1. If the simple word *chair* cited in that chapter is problematic, consider words such as *progress* and its meaning in regard to NCLB, or *misbehavior* as discussed by parents, or *reinforcers* when co-teachers plan teaching strategies, or *homework* as defined by teachers, parents, and some high-profile educational experts. So when some would say, "Never mind, it's just semantics that are causing the problem," educators must keep in mind that it is quite possible semantics *are* the problem, and often a very serious one, in understanding and resolving issues.

Collaborative school consultation is a blend of six elements—system, perspective, approach, prototype, mode, and model. These six can be synthesized into a particular

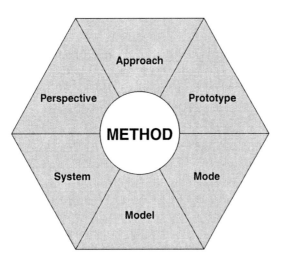

FIGURE 3.2   Structure for Collaborative School Consultation

method having a goodness of fit for a specific educational situation. (See Figure 3.2.) The six elements can be framed as:

1. *System*—entity made up of many parts that serve a common purpose
2. *Perspective*—a particular viewpoint or outlook
3. *Approach*—initial step toward a purpose
4. *Prototype*—pattern
5. *Mode*—form or manner of doing
6. *Model*—example or replica

For brevity and clarity the elements are designated by the uppercase form of their first letter—for example, system is marked with *S*. When two elements begin with identical letters, some other prominent letter in the word is used. Thus the six categories are *S* (system), *P* (perspective), *A* (approach), *R* (p**r**ototype), *E* (mod**e**), and *M* (model).

Systems

A *system* (S) is a unit composed of many diverse parts for a common purpose. The most natural system within which to conduct school consultation and collaboration is, obviously, the school context. However, educators are involved beyond the academic or cognitive aspects of student development, to address physical, emotional, social, and life-orientation aspects. Educators include not only teachers, but parents, related services and support personnel, other caregivers, and the community in general.

Systems (S) in which educators function to serve special needs of students include home and family, community, medical and dental professions, mental health, social work, counseling, extracurricular functions, and advocacy and support groups. Other systems with which consultants and collaborators might be involved from time to time in addressing very specialized needs are therapy, industry, technology, mass communications, cultural enrichment, and special interest areas such as talent development.

Perspectives

A *perspective* (P) is an aspect or object of thought from a particular viewpoint or outlook. Consultation perspectives that have evolved in education and related fields include purchase, doctor-patient, and process.

A *purchase* perspective is one in which a consumer shops for a needed or wanted item. The consumer, in this case the consultee, "shops for" services that will help the consultee serve the client's need. For example, the teacher of a developmentally delayed student might ask personnel at the instructional media center for a list of low-vocabulary, high-interest reading material with which to help the student have immediate success in reading. The purchase perspective makes several assumptions (Neel, 1981): (1) that the consultee describes the need precisely; (2) the consultant has the right "store" and stock for that need; (3) the consultant also has enough "inventory" (strategies and resources) to fill the request; and (4) the consultee can assume the costs of time, energy, or modification of classroom procedures.

As a consumer the consultee is free to accept or reject the strategy or resource, use it enthusiastically, put off trying it, or ignore it as a "bad buy." Even if the strategy is effective for that case, the consultee may need to go again to the consultant for similar needs of other clients. Little change in consultee skills for future situations is likely as a result of such consumer-type interaction. Thus the overall costs are rather high and the benefits are limited to specific situations.

The *doctor-patient* perspective casts the collaborating consultant in the role of diagnostician and prescriptor. The consultee knows there is a problem, but is not in a position to correct it. Consultees are responsible for revealing helpful information to the consultant. Again, this perspective makes several assumptions: (1) The consultee describes the problem to the consultant accurately and completely; (2) the consultant can explain the diagnosis clearly and convince the consultee of its worth; (3) the diagnosis is not premature; and (4) the prescribed remedy is not *iatrogenic* (a term from the medical profession meaning that the professionals' treatments turn out to be more debilitating than the illness they were designed to treat). An iatrogenic effect from educational services would create more problems for students, educators, or the school context than the initial condition did. For example, taking high-ability students from their general classrooms to meet with gifted program facilitators could result in resentment and antagonism from their peers and perhaps even from their classroom teachers, so that if pressed to choose, many students would reject academic enrichment in order to remain in good graces with their friends. Or having a restless, misbehaving toddler stay inside during playtime will make the child even more restless during the next quiet time.

A classroom teacher might use a doctor-patient perspective by calling on a special education teacher and describing the student's learning or behavior problem. The collaborative consultant's role would be to observe, review existing data, perhaps talk to other specialists, and then make diagnostic and prescriptive decisions. As in the medical field, there is generally little follow-up activity on the consultant's part with the doctor-patient perspective, and the consultee does not always follow through with conscientious attention to the consultant's recommendations.

In a *process* perspective, the consultant helps the client perceive, understand, and act on the problem (Neel, 1981; Schein, 1969). Consultative service does not replace the consultee's direct service to the client. In contrast to the purchase and doctor-patient perspectives, the consultant neither diagnoses nor prescribes. As Neel (1981) puts it, the consultee becomes the consultant's client for that particular problem.

Schein (1978) sorts process consultation into two types—a catalyst type in which the consultant does not know a solution but is skilled toward helping the consultee figure one out, and the facilitator type in which the consultant contributes ideas toward the solution. In both catalyst and facilitator types of process consultation the consultant helps the consultee clarify the problem, develop solutions, and implement the plan. Skills and resources used to solve the immediate problem may be used later for other problems.

All of these perspectives—purchase, doctor-patient, and the two types of process— have strengths; therefore, each is likely to be employed at one time or another in schools. One factor influencing the adoption of a particular perspective is the nature of the problem. For example, in a noncrisis situation the consultee may value the process approach. In crisis situations the consultee may need a quick solution, even if temporary, for the problem. In such cases the purchase or doctor-patient perspectives would be preferred. Situations that immediately affect the physical and psychological well-being of students and school personnel require immediate attention and cannot wait for process consultation.

When process consultation is employed regularly, many of the skills and resources that are developed for solving a particular problem can be used again and again in situations involving similar problems. This makes process consultation both time-efficient and cost-effective for schools.

Approaches

An *approach* (A) is a *formal* or *informal* preliminary step toward a purpose.

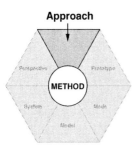

Formal collaborative consultations occur in preplanned meetings such as staffings, conferences for developing IEPs, arranged interactions between school personnel and support personnel, and organized staff development activities. They also take place in scheduled conferences with families, related services personnel, and community resource personnel.

In contrast, informal consultations often occur "on the run." These interactions have been called "vertical consultations" because people tend to engage in them while standing on playgrounds, in parking lots, at ball games, even in grocery stores. They are dubbed "one-legged consultations" when they happen in hallways with a leg propped against the wall (Hall & Hord, 1987; McDonald, 1989). Conversations also take place frequently in the teacher workroom. This aspect will be addressed more fully in Chapter 12 as a type of informal staff development. It is very important to note and record these informal interactions as consultations because they *do* require expenditures of time and energy on the part of both consultant(s) and consultee(s). Highlighting them as consultations will help establish the concept of school consultation and promote efforts to construct a suitable framework that includes allocation of quality time for interaction. Informal consultations should be encouraged because they can initiate more structured consultation and collaboration. Sometimes they become catalysts for meaningful inservice and staff development activities as well. In other cases they may initiate team effort that would have been overlooked or neglected in the daily hustle and bustle of school life.

Prototypes

A *prototype* (R) is a pattern. Consultation prototypes include mental health consultation, behavioral consultation, process consultation, and advocacy consultation. Only the first two will be featured here.

The *mental health* prototype has a long history (Conoley & Conoley, 1988). As noted earlier, the concept originated in the 1960s with the work of psychiatrist Gerald Caplan, who conceived of consultation as a relationship between two professional people in which responsibility for the client rests on the consultee (Hansen, Himes, & Meier, 1990).

Caplan (1970) proposed that consultee difficulties in dealing with a client's problems usually are caused by any one, or all, of four interfering themes:

1. Lack of knowledge about the problem and its conditions
2. Lack of skill to address the problem in appropriate ways
3. Lack of self-confidence in dealing with the problem
4. Lack of professional objectivity when approaching the problem

The consultant not only helps resolve the problem at hand, but enhances the consultee's ability to handle similar situations in the future. When the mental health prototype is used for consultation and the issue of theme interference is introduced, consultee change may very well precede client change. Therefore, assessment of success should focus on consultee attitudes and behaviors more than on client changes (Conoley & Conoley, 1988). School-based mental health consultation is characterized by consultant attention to teacher feelings and the meaning the teacher attaches to the student's behavior (Slesser, Fine, & Tracy, 1990).

The *behavioral consultation* prototype also purports to improve the performance of both consultee and client. It focuses on clear, explicit problem-solving procedures (Slesser, Fine, & Tracy, 1990). It is based on social learning theory, with skills and knowledge contributing more to consultee success than unconscious themes like objectivity or self-confidence (Bergan, 1977). Behavioral consultation probably is more familiar to educators, and therefore more easily introduced into the school context than mental health consultation. Indeed, it is the prototype on which the majority of collaborative consultation models are based. The consultant is required to define the problem, isolate environmental variables that support that problem, and plan interventions to reduce the problem. Bergan (1995) notes that his four-stage model of a consultative problem-solving process was grounded on successful identification of the problem as the first stage. Problem analysis, implementation, and evaluation followed this stage.

Conoley and Conoley (1988) regard behavioral consultation as the easiest prototype to evaluate because problem delineation and specific goal setting occur within the process. Evaluation results can be used to modify plans and to promote consultation services among other potential consultees. But behavioral consultation can fail to bring results when it focuses on problematic social behavior such as aggression or being off-task, if that behavior really emanates from poor or inadequate academic skills (Cipani, 1985).

Modes

A *mode* (E) is a particular style or manner of doing something. Modes for school consultation are direct consultation for the delivery of service to clients, or indirect consultation for delivery of service to consultees.

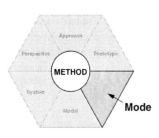

Mode

In a direct mode the consultant works directly with a special-needs student. For example, a learning disabilities consulting teacher or a speech pathologist specialist might use a particular technique with the student while a parent or classroom teacher consultee observes and assists with the technique. Direct service typically is provided to students subsequent to a referral (Bergan, 1977). The consultant may conduct observations and discuss the learning or behavior with the student (Bergan, 1977; Heron & Harris, 1987). The consultant becomes an advocate and the student has an opportunity to participate in decisions made pertinent to that need. Another example of direct service is teaching coping skills to students to use at home or at school (Graubard, Rosenberg, & Miller, 1971; Heron & Harris, 1987).

The *indirect* service delivery mode calls for "backstage" involvement among consultants and consultees to serve client needs. The consultant and consultee interact and problem-solve together. Then the consultee provides related direct service to the client. So school consultation is indirect service to students resulting from the direct service to teachers or parents.

Models

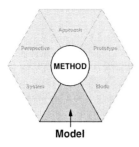

Model

Models are many things—patterns, examples for imitation, representations in miniature, descriptions, analogies, or displays. But a model is not the real thing, just an approximation of it. A model functions as an example through which to study, replicate, approximate, or manipulate intricate things. Models are useful for examining things or ideas when they are too big to construct (a model of the solar system) or too small to copy (a DNA molecule). They help explain and illustrate things that cannot be replicated because they are too costly (a supersonic jet plane), too complex (the

United Nations system), or too time-intensive (travel to outer space). Such qualities make the model a useful structure on which to pattern the complex human processes of collaboration, consultation, and co-teaching in order to implement services that will help students who have exceptional learning needs.

A few of the many well-known models that have been adopted or adapted for collaboration and consultation in schools over the past twenty-five years are:

- Triadic model
- Resource/Consulting Teacher Program model
- Instructional Consultation model
- Conjoint Behavioral Consultation model
- Consultee-centered consultation model
- Teacher Assistance Teams model
- Responsive Systems Consultation model
- Collaborative consultation and its variant models

The *triadic* model, developed by Tharp and Wetzel (1969) and Tharp (1975), is the classic one from which many school consultation and collaboration models have evolved. It includes three roles—consultant, consultee (or mediator), and client (or target). In this most basic of the existing models, services are not offered directly, but through an intermediary (Tharp, 1975). The service flows from the consultant through the mediator to the target. The consultant role is typically, although not always, performed by an educational specialist such as a learning disabilities teacher or a school psychologist. The consultee is usually, but not always, the classroom teacher. The client or target is most often, but not always, the student with the exceptional learning need. An educational need may be a disability or an advanced ability requiring special services for the student. The triadic model requires that both consultant and consultee take ownership of the problem and share accountability for the success or failure of the program that is developed (Idol, Paolucci-Whitcomb, & Nevin, 1995). (See Figure 3.3.)

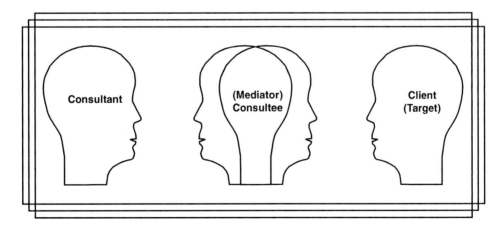

FIGURE 3.3   Example of a Basic Triadic Consultation

When studying the models, it is important to recall the discussion in Chapter 1 about roles. Roles are interchangeable among individuals, depending on the school context and the educational need. For example, on occasion a learning disabilities consulting teacher might be a consultee who seeks information and expertise from a general classroom teacher consultant. At another time a student might be the consultant for a resource room teacher as consultee, and parents as the clients who are targets for interventions intended to help their child. Tharp gives the following example:

> Ms. Jones the second-grade teacher may serve as mediator between Brown, the psychologist, and John, the problem child. At the same time, she may be the target of her principal's training program and the consultant to her aide-mediator in the service of Susie's reading problem. The triadic model, then, describes relative position in the chain of social influence. (Tharp, 1975, p. 128)

Tharp identifies several strengths of the triadic model, including the clarity it provides in delineating social roles and responsibilities, and the availability of evaluation data from two sources—mediator behavior and target behavior. However, it may not be the most effective model for every school context and content area given the process skills and resources that are available. Here is a summary highlighting the triadic model's strong points and possible concerns:

■ *Strong Points:* Appropriate in crisis situations; a good way to get started with the consultee; quick and direct; informal and simple; keeps problem in perspective; has objectivity on consultant's part; provides student anonymity if needed; is time efficient; can lead into more intensive collaborative consultation; may be all that is needed.

■ *Possible Concerns:* Has little or no carryover to other situations; probably will be needed again for same or similar situations; only one other point of view available; consultant will need expert skills; essential data may be unavailable; consultant may be held accountable for lack of progress; there is little or no follow-up.

The *Resource/Consulting Teacher Program* (R/CT) model was implemented at the University of Illinois and replicated in both rural and large urban areas (Idol, Paolucci-Whitcomb, & Nevin, 1986). It is based on the triadic model, with numerous opportunities for interaction among teachers, students, and parents. The resource/consulting teacher offers direct service to students through tutorials or small-group instruction and indirect service to students through consultation with classroom teachers for a portion of the school day. Students who are not staffed into special education programs can be served along with exceptional students mainstreamed into general classrooms. Parents are sometimes included in the consultation. (See Figure 3.4.)

In the R/CT model, emphasis is placed on training students in the curricula used within each mainstreamed student's general classroom (Idol-Maestas, 1983). Close cooperation and collaboration between the R/CT and the classroom teacher are required so that teacher expectations and reinforcement are the same for both resource room and regular class setting (Idol-Maestas, 1981). This accentuates the importance of sharing perspectives and preferences as discussed in Chapter 2.

■ *Strong Points:* Provides direct and indirect service; stipulates specific and relatively generous percentages of time for interaction when determining caseloads; includes

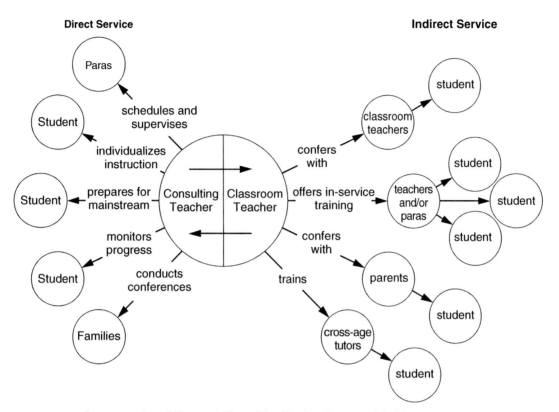

FIGURE 3.4 Interpretation of Resource/Consulting Teacher Program Model

parent involvement; is an "in-house" approach to problems; allows opportunity for student involvement; is compatible with interrelated methods; encourages ownership by many roles in problem solving; more closely approximates classroom setting; spreads responsibility around; provides opportunity for regular contact between consultant and consultee.

■ *Possible Concerns:* Energy-draining; caseloads can be high for the consulting teacher; indirect services are not weighted as heavily as direct services; provides delayed or no reinforcement for the consultant; requires strong administrator support and cooperation.

The *Instructional Consultation* (IC) model merges skill in collaborative consultation with expertise in specific areas of content. The model responds to several premises that have been offered by educational experts. First, teacher behavior does make a crucial difference to children's achievement (Rosenfield, 1995). Second, many tasks assigned to students are not well matched to their instructional levels. Bloom (1976) asserted that alterable variables, as opposed to such variables as IQ, are more important in planning instruction. Children should be regarded as having learning disabilities only if they fail to learn *after* having appropriate instruction (Rosenfield, 1995). Furthermore, when students are referred for special services, their classroom teachers should have ongoing assistance in developing and managing their learning programs.

The IC process begins with entry-level discussion between consultant and teacher about roles, expectations, and commitment. Consultants are case managers who have relinquished the expert role and configured their professional relationships to be collaborative and egalitarian. Steps proceed through problem identification and analysis, classroom observation, procedures such as curriculum-based assessment, implementation of interventions, ongoing evaluation, and termination of the consultation relationship. At termination, a written record of agreed-on findings is submitted to involved parties.

Rosenfield lays out challenges of providing continuing education to practitioners of this model. Online supervision and coaching are two supporting practices. Each team member is required to develop and apply consulting skills in order to create effective multidisciplinary teams. Another challenge is introduced by the variations in participants' pre-service teacher preparation for applying consultation (Gravois, Knotek, & Babinski, 2002). Co-educators have to arrive at understandings and "be on the same page." This reinforces points about perspectives and preferences presented in Chapter 2. In addition, the goals and processes of this model are aligned with Vygotsky's social construction principles (Knotek, Rosenfield, Gravois, & Babinski, 2003). The interpersonal process of the consultation, problem-solving skills, language, and support personnel helps the consultee acquire new insight into the problem.

■ *Strong Points:* Follows the existing stage of consultation; removes attitudes that internal deficits within the child or the family create the learning and behavioral problems; focuses on the student-teacher-task interactions (Rosenfield, 1995); and helps transform schools into learning communities.

■ *Possible Concerns:* Does not relieve teachers of the responsibility for student learning; requires excellent communication skills; calls for teachers to have data-collection time and skill; needs consultant knowledge of high-quality instruction; is more problematic at the secondary level where a student has an array of teachers; must include a strategy for exiting from the consultation.

The *Conjoint Behavioral Consultation* (CBC) model offers home-school collaboration and shared problem solving (Wilkinson, 2005a). Behavioral problems in the classroom are intrusive and distracting to learning. Unfortunately, many classroom teachers have had little or no training in behavior management techniques. This relatively new model is an indirect, structured model of consultation service delivery for parents, teachers, and school personnel to join in and share responsibility for addressing academic, social, or behavioral needs (Wilkinson, 2005a). Home and school collaborators share problem solving as they work to pinpoint the problem or problems, develop a plan, and conjointly evaluate the success of the plan. A method of data collection for behaviors is conjointly developed.

■ *Strong Points:* Research on the model is ongoing; school educators and home educators respond well to the conjoint involvement of families, teachers, and school psychologists.

■ *Possible Concerns:* Some of the research is single-case study and a more robust design would help draw conclusions about attribution of improved behavior (Wilkinson, 2005a).

The *consultee-centered consultation* model is based on Caplan's work and is a non-prescriptive model that involves interaction between consultant and consultee, with the first task being to identify existing conceptualizations (Sandoval, 2003). Active listening and an attitude of onedownsmanship are important tools for the consultant. Next steps call for relationship building while maintaining rapport, problem identification, and generating a new theory. Some cognitive dissonance is expected as the participants ask questions and reframe facts. The goal is not to bring the consultee to an understanding that has been determined in advance by the consultant, but to construct together a concept that fits the situation and permits action (Sandoval, 2003). This model leaves the responsibility to accept or reject suggestions up to the consultee. Consultee-centered consultation is common in Swedish schools and is often used in preschools and childcare institutions (Hylander, 2003).

■ *Strong Points:* The learner (consultee) is actively participating and not passively receiving information; long-term and ripple-effect benefits in other situations can be expected; both consultant and consultee learn (Ingraham, 2003).

■ *Possible Concerns:* Needs more research on discourse of consultants; requires that consultants are calm and not shocked by a situation as presented for consultation; calls for self-disclosure by consultee (Ingraham, 2003); consultee must expect change and so may need to tolerate risks.

The *Teacher Assistance Teams* (TAT) model was developed in the 1970s as a way for classroom teachers to self-refer for assistance from a team of two or three skilled teachers in their building who have been elected as a problem-solving team (Pugach & Johnson, 1995). The team typically meets in problem-solving sessions for about thirty minutes. The approach also was intended as a means of reducing referrals to special education. It is regarded as a very nondirective approach to problem solving in which classroom teachers are regarded as professionals capable of using the problem-solving process effectively. The model also has been employed by special education pairs and others who have similar roles. As an in-house assistance plan it could be helpful for novice teachers who might otherwise be reluctant to ask for help due to apprehension that they might be regarded as less than competent.

■ *Strong Points:* Involves several teachers as experts; treats the consultee as a capable professional and not incompetent because of requesting assistance; reduces the number of inappropriate referrals (Pugach & Johnson, 1995).

■ *Possible Concerns:* Needs structure in the meetings even though it is a nondirective approach; requires teacher commitment to the recommended changes.

The *Responsive Systems Consultation* (RSC) model will resonate with co-educators who believe that learning and behavioral concerns result from the contexts and interactions experienced by the student. As some would put it, the problem is in the unsuitability of the environment for the student, not a misfit of the student in the environment. RSC takes a behavioral approach with collaborative consultation characteristics (Denton, Hasbrouck, & Sekaquaptewa, 2003). Parents and teachers work together in interview settings to achieve common goals.

Most *collaborative consultation* models are derived from Tharp and Wetzel (1969) and Tharp (1975) and include three components—(C) consultant, M (mediator), and (T) target (Idol et al., 1995). Collaborative consultation is a problem-centered approach requiring all parties in the consultation to participate in development of exemplary programs (Idol et al., 1995). The consultant and consultee are equal partners with diverse expertise in identifying problems, planning intervention strategies, and implementing recommendations that carry mutual responsibility (Idol et al., 1986; Raymond, McIntosh, & Moore, 1986).

The communication is not hierarchical or one-way. Rather, there is a sense of parity that blends the skills and knowledge of both consultant and consultee, with disagreements viewed as opportunities for constructive extraction of the most useful information (Idol et al., 1995). In addition, both consultant and consultee work directly with the student. In research to investigate teacher responses to consultative services, Schulte, Osborne, and Kauffman (1993) found that most teachers who were surveyed viewed collaborative consultation as an acceptable alternative to resource rooms. However, scheduling and congruence of teacher time slots can impose limits on success.

Idol, Nevin, and Paolucci-Whitcomb (1995) list six generic principles that participants need for success:

1. Situational leadership for guidance
2. Cooperative goal structures for conflict resolution
3. Appropriate interview skills
4. Active listening skills
5. Oral and written communication without "educationese" or jargon
6. Positive nonverbal language

Pryzwansky (1974) emphasized the need for mutual consent on the part of both consultant and consultee, mutual commitment to the objectives, and shared responsibility for implementation and evaluation of the plan. To reiterate, the collaborative school consultation process must be voluntary and nonsupervisory, and carried out with a demeanor of onedownsmanship. The consultant, mediator, and target have reciprocally reinforcing effects on one another and this encourages more collaborative consultation at a later date (Idol-Maestas, 1983). Each collaborator, as part of the team, contributes a clearly defined portion of the effort so that all come together to create a complete plan or solution.

Variations of collaborative consultation can be structured for particular contexts. For example, one teacher in a small rural school with as many as six different lesson preparations who is coaching a different sport each season finds a combination of the collaborative and triadic models very time efficient. It can be conducted informally to utilize both consultant and consultee knowledge efficiently. John-Steiner, Weber, and Minnis (1998) make the case for a theory of collaboration that promotes multiple definitions and multiple models of collaborative practice.

More Variations on Triadic and Collaborative School Consultation Models.   Many experts assert that the very best model is a combination of the best features from many models to create one that is tailor-made for a designated school context. Additional variations of collaborative consultation that lend themselves to further adaptation for local contexts are outlined in the section that follows.

Class-Within-a-Class (CWC). This is an innovative delivery model that reduces dependence on pull-out programs by serving learning disabled students full-time in general classes. Special education teachers go into the classrooms during instruction time to collaborate and consult with the teacher and provide additional support to students with exceptional learning needs.

Schoolwide Enrichment Model (SEM). This well-researched model (Renzulli & Reis, 1985) provides three types of challenging learning experiences for gifted and talented students in the regular classroom. It involves close collaboration between general education teachers and gifted program facilitators and includes intensive staff development to prepare all participants for their roles. Teachers and facilitators are co-educators in providing gifted and talented students with curriculum options and alternatives such as flexible pacing, enrichment, personalized instruction, and challenging group experiences.

Type 1 offers exploratory activities such as field trips, interest centers, demonstrations, and resource speakers for all students. Type 2 includes methods and materials designed to promote development of critical and creative thinking skills and problem-solving skills, again for all students. As many as 15 percent to 20 percent of students in the regular classroom can be declared eligible for enrichment and served by Type 1 and Type 2 learning experiences in general classrooms (VanTassel-Baska & Brown, 2007). Type 3 often takes place in the resource room or off-campus. It typically is provided for highly able students who become independent investigators and researchers and develop products that are critiqued by authentic audiences of professionals who have expertise in the student's area of investigation.

Resource Consultation Model. The concept was developed originally by Curtis, Curtis, and Graden (1988) and adapted for education of gifted students. The consultation is a problem-solving process shared by all school personnel in which the primary goal is to use limited and expensive resources more effectively and efficiently to better serve students (Kirschenbaum, Armstrong, & Landrum, 1999). It can occur at one of three levels—collaboration on a less formal and less structured basis; assistance from gifted education personnel (an option that turns out to be chosen 85 percent of the time); or team intervention if several school personnel will be affected, such as in a consultation matter involving radical acceleration.

■ *Summary of Strong Points for Collaborative Models:* In general, they fit current school reform goals; inspire professional growth for all through shared expertise; provide many points of view; focus on situations encompassing the whole school context; involve general *and* special education staff and often resource and support personnel as well; generate many ideas; maximize opportunities for constructive use of adult differences; allow administrators to assume a facilitative role; facilitate liaisons with community agents; are pleasing to families because many school personnel are working with their child.

■ *Summary of Possible Concerns:* Little or no training of educators in collaborative consultation and co-teaching; shortage of time and compatibility of schedules for interacting; working with adults not the preference of some educators; require solid, not token, administrator support; confidentiality harder to ensure with many people involved; could diffuse responsibility so much that no one feels ultimately responsible; can take time to see results.

Co-teaching as a team is one of the most powerful forms of consultation combined with collaboration, appearing on the educational scene in the 1960s and having a resurgence of interest among educators in the 1990s (Pugach & Johnson, 1995). Co-teaching and its variations will be the focal topic of Chapter 7.

DEVELOPMENT AND APPLICATION OF PLANS FOR COLLABORATIVE SCHOOL CONSULTATION

When planning for collaborative school consultation, it is helpful to use an informal, journalistic-style template that directs the discussion, such as:

- Why is this type of service best?
- What do we expect to occur?
- Who will be involved?
- When will it take place and for how long?
- Where will it be happening?
- How will we put the plan into operation and assess results?

Then, returning to the six components in Figure 3.3 for constructing a method, planners can decide which elements and to what extent they will be structured to help frame the plan:

1. System (school systems, other social systems)
2. Perspective (purchase, doctor-patient, process)
3. Approach (formal, informal)
4. Prototype (mental health, behavioral)
5. Mode (direct, indirect)
6. Model (triadic, Resource/Consulting Teacher Program, Instructional Consultation, Conjoint Behavioral Consultation, consultee-centered consultation, Teacher Assistance Teams, and other collaborative consultation variations).

Referring again to Figure 3.2, the Method area in the center draws from each of the six components to synthesize all into a method with goodness of fit for the particular school situation. Several practice situations that follow will provide opportunities to plan and implement school consultation, collaboration, and/or teamwork. To work through the situations, it is helpful to consider the why, who, what, when, where, and how, and choose among options for system, perspective, approach, prototype, mode, and model. It is not necessary to dwell on interaction and coordination processes at this time.

When thinking about a situation and one of the structures that could be useful, it is stimulating to address complex circumstances in the way that the eminent thinker Albert Einstein did, that is, as a thought problem to be explored in the mind and not in a laboratory or a classroom. The idea is to manipulate variables and concepts mentally, "seeing" them from all angles and withholding judgment until all conceivable avenues have been explored in one's mind. Thought problems are opportunities for intently reflecting on real problems and possibilities before presenting them for discussion and critique by others. This abstract way of pondering problems rather than manipulating elements in the real world, is a practice Einstein employed quite successfully. Indeed, much of the time this kind of thinking does occur informally when co-educators are contemplating multifaceted processes such as collaborative consultation and co-teaching.

APPLICATION 3.1
FORMULATING AN APPROPRIATE METHOD
FOR SPECIFIC SITUATIONS

SAMPLE SITUATIONS

Before reflecting on one or more of the following sample situations, consider these combinations that have been used at one time or another for different circumstances:

■ One person or group may decide that the best way to address a situation is with the *triadic* model and a *purchase* perspective, using *indirect* service from the consultant to the client, in an *informal, mental health* prototype of interaction within the *school system.*

■ Another may address a client's need by choosing the *Conjoint Behavioral Consultation* model, with a *process* perspective, in a *formal* and *direct* way, using the *behavioral* prototype in the *social service* system.

■ Yet another individual or group may approach a particular problem through a variation of a *collaborative consultation* model, with a *process* perspective, using *direct* service to the client from both consultant and consultee, in a *formal* way that approximates a *behavioral* prototype, in a *community work setting* as the system.

Also, when thinking about possibilities, it is helpful to think about what might be major obstacles in carrying out the proposed method and also to consider what could emerge as major benefits and positive ripple effects beyond the immediate situation.

Situation 1: Ten-year-old Clarisse is new to the school and is placed in the TMR program. Her teacher quickly learns that she prefers to observe rather than participate, and will not join in group activities. In her previous school, according to her parents, Clarisse had been allowed to lie on the floor most of the day so she would not have tantrums about participation. Her new teacher and paraprofessional want Clarisse to demonstrate her capabilities, but do not want her to get off to a bad start in the new school and do not want parents to feel negative toward her new teachers. The teacher knows this is a crucial time for Clarisse and wonders what to do.

Situation 2: The speech pathologist has been asked by the gifted program facilitator to consult with her regarding a highly gifted child who has minor speech problems, but is being pressured by parents and kindergarten teacher to "stop the baby talk." The child is becoming very nervous and at times withdraws from conversation and play. How can the speech pathologist structure collaborative consultation to help?

Situation 3: A school psychologist is conferring with a teacher about a high school student she has just evaluated. The student is often a behavior problem, and the psychologist is discussing methods for setting up behavior limits with appropriate contingencies and rewards. The teacher makes numerous references to the principal as a person who likes for teachers to be self-sufficient and not "make waves." How should the school psychologist handle this?

Situation 4: A fifth-grade student with learning disabilities (LD) is not having success in social studies. The student has a serious reading problem, but is a good listener and stays on task. The LD resource teacher suspects that the classroom teacher is not willing to modify materials and expectations for the child. The teacher has not discussed this situation with the LD teacher, but the student has in a roundabout way. Parent-teacher conferences are scheduled for the following week. What should happen here, and who will make it happen?

Situation 5: Parents of a student with learning disabilities have asked the special education consulting teacher to approach the student's classroom teacher about what they think is excessive and too-difficult homework. The parents say it is disrupting their home life and frustrating the student. How can this situation be addressed?

Situation 6: A high school learning disabilities consultant is visiting with a principal at the principal's request. The principal expresses concern about the quality of teaching demonstrated by two faculty members and asks the consultant to observe them and then provide feedback. How should the consultant handle this situation?

Situation 7: A pediatrician contacts the director of special education and asks her to meet with a group of local doctors to discuss characteristics and needs of children with disabilities. How should this opportunity be structured for maximum benefit to all?

Situation 8: A middle school student has been failing in several subjects during the semester and has become more and more sullen and withdrawn over the past several weeks. Two of her teachers have arrived independently at the strong possibility that she is being abused by a male relative who is living with her family in the home. What actions need to be taken here?

Situation 9: Schoolwide achievement tests will be administered soon. According to IDEA regulations, special education students are to be included in these assessments or documentation must be made as to reasons for excluding them from the tests. The consulting teacher is conferring with a teacher who has several students with exceptional learning needs in her inclusive classroom about their ability to take these tests. The pressure of responding to demands of NCLB loom in the minds of both teachers. Where should these co-educators go with their concerns?

Situation 10: A fifth-grade boy with a quiet and sensitive nature who prefers to work and play with girls and shuns athletics, is not accepted by other boys in his class. He is being harassed and bullied by several of them on the playground, in restrooms, and on the way home from school. He has not talked about his plight to teachers, but two of his classmates have described some of the events to their classroom teacher. What should the teacher do about the boy, the alleged bullies, and the informers?

Situation 11: An energetic new teacher is full of ideas that often are initiated with little planning or step-by-step instruction for students. She allows the students to be self-directed and to move from one activity to another as their interests impel them. A slow-learning student is floundering in this unstructured setting. The special education director has been alerted to the situation by the school principal, who had been approached by the student's mother with her concerns. There is no other classroom at the student's grade level in this school to which the student might be transferred, and now that several weeks of school have gone by, it would be too late to consider such a step anyway. What might be done?

Situation 12: A teenage student went hunting over the weekend. He had lost his hunting knife with which he dressed out game, so he borrowed one from a friend. Now he drives to school on Monday with the knife in his backpack, intending to return it to his friend in the parking lot. But they do not connect and he is distracted by an altercation that is happening, so he forgets about the knife. But somebody learns about it later in the day and reports his backpack item. He is called to the principal's office. His special education teacher for learning disabilities and attention deficit disorder with hyperactivity (ADHD), his single mother, and law officers are summoned. Then his coach becomes involved because this student is a star athlete whose eligibility to play is crucial to the team's success. How should this situation best be addressed?

Situation 13: A preschool child with behavior disorders hits other children for no apparent cause in the inclusive day care center. The teacher has tried behavior management strategies and time-out periods. But the child impulsively strikes out whenever another child enters her physical "space." How should the Early Childhood Special Education (ECSE) teacher approach the grandparent caregiver and who else could be involved to help?

ETHICAL CONSIDERATIONS FOR DEVELOPING FOUNDATIONS AND FRAMEWORKS

Methods for collaborative consultation in schools are as varied as the school personnel who will use them and the school climates in which they will be used. Models may be drawn on for building the framework(s), but ultimately the development process will be a collaborative endeavor that is itself an example of the method to be developed for students.

If collaborative efforts markedly reduce the time and instruction needed for direct services to students with special needs, there will be a risk of diminishing returns (Friend & Cook, 1992). This is mentioned occasionally by parents as a reason for opposing interactive processes such as inclusive classrooms, and collaboration and co-teaching practices. This issue must be examined with objectivity (is it a valid point?), then discussed candidly with parents and resolved.

Cooperation is a facilitative endeavor, but not in the same way as collaboration. Cooperation often involves giving up something—changing one's perspectives to a degree or matters of one's preferences to a certain extent. Sometimes cooperation is a necessary engagement. Negotiation and arbitration impose similar demands and are complex social behaviors. But collaboration combines all three. It requires work, and more work, for relatively autonomous individuals to arrive at the same goal along different pathways.

Occasionally it is in the best interest of all concerned, and the student in particular, for co-educators to decide they must disengage from a collaborative endeavor or a shared teaching process. Having previously discussed a transition plan or an exit procedure can obviate feelings of inadequacy and failure among all concerned. The situation should be handled objectively according to the prior agreement and not taken as personal rejection.

TIPS FOR STRUCTURING FOUNDATIONS OF COLLABORATIVE ENDEAVORS

1. Be knowledgeable about the history and outcomes of school improvement and reform movements.
2. Keep up-to-date on educational issues and concerns.
3. Be informed about educational legislation and litigation.
4. Be on the alert for new methods or revisions of existing methods through which consultation and collaboration can occur in your school context.
5. Read current research on school consultation and collaboration, and highlight references to these processes in other professional material you read.
6. Visit programs where models different from those in your school(s) are being used.
7. Find sessions at professional conferences that feature different models and methods, and attend them to broaden your knowledge about educational systems.
8. Create specific ways that teachers can get your help and make those ways known.
9. Clarify expectations by having dialogue with people in all roles in the school context. Expectations will vary from person to person, and the first question must be, How important are these differences?
10. Be flexible and adaptable. Change takes time, and it must be preceded by awareness of the need to change.

CHAPTER REVIEW

1. Every decade from the 1960s on has had important movements and legislation that address the welfare of students with special needs. These efforts have sparked educational accountability, restructuring, mainstreaming in a least restrictive environment (LRE), assurance of free and appropriate public education (FAPE), the regular education initiative (REI), inclusion, and increasing interest in collaborative consultation among co-educators.

2. The reauthorization of the Individuals with Disabilities Act in 2004 and pending reauthorization of the No Child Left Behind Act contain mandates for ensuring student achievement and directives for managing environments so students can succeed. IDEA stipulates high expectations for students with exceptional learning needs as well as professional development and training of all preservice and school personnel who work with the students, replacement of IEP objectives and benchmarks with measurable annual goals, compatibility with NCLB performance goals, and parental consent for evaluation and services. NCLB focuses on accountability of schools and teachers for student learning, assessment of learning with high-stakes testing, and high standards for student learning and teacher credentialing.

3. School consultation evolved from practices in the mental health and medical services fields. Differing points of view are held about the existence of a theoretical base of school consultation. Some researchers consider school consultation theory-based if the relationship between consultant and consultee can be identified across more than one literature source. Research in school consultation and collaboration has been conducted to assess situational variables, outcome variables, and organizational change. There is need for more reliable and valid instrumentation, more specific definition of variables, and more careful control of variables during the research.

4. Structural elements to develop effective methods of school consultation can be categorized as: Systems (institutions and contexts); Perspectives (purchase, doctor-patient, problem-solving); Approaches (formal, informal); Prototypes (mental health, behavioral); Modes (direct, indirect); and a variety of Models.

5. Several collaborative consultation models are the triadic model (the basic model for most collaborative consultation models), Resource/Consulting Teacher Program model, the Instructional Consultation model, the Conjoint Behavioral Consultation model, the consultee-centered consultation model, the Teacher Assistance Teams model, the Responsive Systems Consultation model, and numerous other variations of the collaborative consultation model.

6. Educators should introduce into their school context one or more structures combining opportunities for consultation, collaboration, and co-teaching that will be well suited to the local schools, co-educators, families, and most of all taking into account students' needs and what will serve them best.

TO DO AND THINK ABOUT

1. Pinpoint several changes that have occurred in special education during the past several decades, and suggest implications they have for school consultation methods. For example, if you decide on inclusion, it could be analyzed as follows:

Select an article or book on inclusion. Before reading it, put your "knows" in Column 1 on the left and your "wants" in Column 2 in the middle. After your reading, complete Column 3 on the right. Return to your paper periodically as you study more about students with special needs, adding more information to the respective columns.

COLUMN 1	COLUMN 2	COLUMN 3
What I KNEW about Inclusion	What MORE I Want to Know about Inclusion	What I HAVE learned about Inclusion NOW

2. Locate articles focusing on consultation, collaboration, and teamwork. Summarize the highlights, and prepare a "fact sheet" or information bulletin for other school personnel such as building administrator or school board member.

3. Have the complete articles from which you shared information in #2 available for any who might ask to read the entire work.

4. Brainstorm with a group to list current issues and major problems in education. After generating as many ideas as possible, mark those that seem most amenable to solutions afforded by consultation, collaboration, and teamwork. You might want to asterisk those that in the past have "belonged" to special education, and discuss what part general education plays in dealing with those issues now.

5. Visit schools where consultation and collaboration play an integral role in serving students' special needs. Observe the consultation systems, perspectives, approaches, prototypes, modes, and models that appear to be in use in those schools. Then summarize the results into brief, innovative descriptions of the methods that seem to have evolved from the synthesis of these components. If you feel inspired to do so, sketch a graphic to illustrate your description.

6. Just as in most fields of human endeavor, stereotypes are "out there" regarding consultation and collaboration. Here are a few of the more pejorative phrases about collaboration and consultation. Propose some ways these negative perceptions could be dismantled with some collaborative consulting among teaching colleagues.

> "A consultant drives over from the central office and borrows your watch to tell you what time it is."
>
> "Collaboration is just the latest buzzword."
>
> "The consultant is someone from two counties away wearing a suit and carrying a briefcase."
>
> "A consultant is a big-bucks speaker who just pulls in, pops off, and pulls out."
>
> "Collaboration is where we convene a meeting and then we take minutes to waste hours."
>
> "Expert? Oh, yes, X marks the spot of the little spurt under pressure."

ADDITIONAL READINGS AND RESOURCES

Bassett, D. S., Jackson, L., Ferrell, K. A., Luckner, J., Hagerty, P. J., Bunsen, T. D., & MacIsaac, D. (1996). Multiple perspectives on inclusive education: Reflections of a university faculty. *Teacher Education and Special Education, 19*(4), 355–386.

Denton, C. A., Hasbrouck, J. E., & Sekaquaptewa, S. (2003). The consulting teacher: A descriptive case study in Responsive Systems Consultation. *Journal of Educational and Psychological Consultation, 14*(1), 41–73.

A case study analysis illustrating the consulting teacher's role in implementing the Responsive Systems Consultation (RSC), a behavioral approach that features relationships within contexts. The consultation case involves two consulting teachers and a novice second-grade teacher addressing behavioral and academic problems of a student.

Erchul, W. P., & Martens, B. K. (1997). *School consultation: Conceptual and empirical bases of practice.* New York: Plenum.

For more information about the models described in this chapter, consult the following sources.

Idol-Maestes, L., & Ritter, S. (1985). A follow-up study of resource/consulting teachers: Factors that facilitate and inhibit teacher consultation. *Teacher Education and Special Education, 8,* 121–131.

Illsley, S. D., & Sladeczek, I. E. (2001). Conjoint behavioral consultation: Outcome measures beyond the client level. *Journal of Educational and Psychological Consultation, 12*(4), 397–404.

Descriptions of five children and their families illustrate the effectiveness of Conjoint Behavioral Consultation in reducing conduct problem behaviors.

Pugach, M. C., & Johnson, L. J. (1995). *Collaborative practitioners, collaborative schools.* Denver, CO: Love.

This source describes the Teacher Assistance Teams model.

Renzulli, J. S., & Reis, S. M. *The schoolwide enrichment model: A comprehensive plan for educational excellence.* Mansfield Center, CT: Creative Learning Press.

Rosenfield, S. (1995). Instructional consultation: A model for service delivery in the schools. *Journal of Educational and Psychological Consultation, 6*(4), 297–316.

Scruggs, T. E., & Mastropieri, M. A. (1996). Teacher perceptions of mainstreaming/inclusion, 1958–1995: A research synthesis. *Exceptional Children, 63*(1), 59–74.

Sheridan, S. M., Kratochwill, T. R., & Bergan, J. R. (1996). *Conjoint Behavioral Consultation: A procedural manual.* New York: Plenum.

Smith, J. D. (1998). The history of special education: Essays honoring the bicentennial of the work of Jean Itard. *Remedial and Special Education, 19*(4), entire issue.

Tharp, R. (1975). The triadic model of consultation. In C. Parker (Ed.), *Psychological consultation in the schools: Helping teachers meet special needs.* Reston, VA: Council for Exceptional Children.

Welch, M., Sheridan, S. M., Fuhriman, A., Hart, A. W., Connell, M. L., & Stoddart, T. (1992). Preparing professionals for educational partnerships: An interdisciplinary approach. *Journal of Educational and Psychological Consultation, 3*(1), 1–23.

Wilkinson, L. A. (2005). Bridging the research-to-practice gap in school-based consultation: An example using case studies. *Journal of Education and Psychological Consultation, 16*(3), 175–200.

Wilkinson, L. A. (2005). Supporting the inclusion of a student with Asperger's syndrome: A case study using conjoint behavioral consultation and self-management. *Educational Psychology in Practice, 21,* 307–326.

Williams, J. M., & Martin, S. M. (2001). Implementing the Individuals with Disabilities Education Act of 1997: The consultant's role. *Journal of Educational and Psychological Consultation, 12*(1), 59–81.

In addition, the following references may be helpful for other topics in the chapter.

Journal of Educational and Psychological Consultation, all issues.

The journal, as noted in this chapter, was initiated in 1990 and is published four times a year for the purpose of improving scientific understanding of consultation and offering practical strategies for effective, efficient consultation to individuals and organizations. Central administrators of schools would do well to subscribe to this journal that includes research, theory, and practice across all school role groups from speech pathologists to school psychologists to preservice teachers to parents and much more.

Educational Leadership. (December 1994/January 1995), *52*(4).

Topical issue on the inclusive school.

CHAPTER FOUR

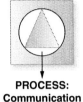

PROCESS:
Communication

Communication Processes in Collaborative School Consultation and Co-Teaching

Communication is one of the greatest achievements of humankind. A vital component of human relationships in general, it is also the foundation of cooperation and collaboration among educators. Communication is not simply delivering a message. Communication involves talking, listening, managing interpersonal conflict, and addressing concerns together. Components of successful communication are understanding, trust, autonomy, and flexibility. Effective communicators withhold judgment and minimize efforts to control the path of communication.

While problems and conflicts are unavoidable elements of life, good communication skills facilitate problem solving and resolution of conflicts. Ineffective communication creates a void that breeds misunderstanding and distrust. Elements of trust, commitment, and effective interaction are critical for conflict-free relationships. Effective communication becomes a foundation for cooperation and collaboration among school personnel, parents, students, and others involved in education.

FOCUSING QUESTIONS

1. What is a primary reason people fail in collaborative efforts?
2. What are key components of the communication process?
3. How does one establish rapport in order to facilitate effective communication?
4. What are major verbal and nonverbal skills for communicating effectively?
5. What are the primary roadblocks to communication?
6. How can a school consultant be appropriately assertive and cope with resistance, negativity, and anger to manage conflict?

From Chapter 4 of *Consultation, and Teamwork for Students with Special Needs*, 6/e. Peggy Dettmer. Linda P. Thurston. Ann Knackendoffel. Norma J. Dyck. Copyright © 2009 by Pearson Merrill. All rights reserved.

KEY TERMS

anger	conflict management	resistance
assertiveness	empathy, empathic	Responsive Listening
body language	negativity	Checklist
communication	nonverbal communication	roadblocks to
computer-mediated	paraphrasing	communication
communication (CMC)	rapport	verbal communication

SCENARIO 4

The setting is the hallway of a junior high school in midafternoon, where the general math instructor, a first-year teacher, is venting to a colleague.

Math Teacher: What a day! On top of the fire drill this morning and those forms that we got in our boxes to be filled out by Friday, I had a disastrous encounter with a parent. Guess I flunked Parent Communication 101.

Colleague: Oh, one of those, huh?

Math Teacher: Jay's mother walked into my room right before fourth-hour, and accused me of not doing my job. It was awful!

Colleague: (frowns, shakes head)

Math Teacher: Thank goodness there weren't any kids around. But the music teacher was there telling me about next week's program. This parent really let me have it. I was stunned, not only by the accusation, but by the way she delivered it. My whole body went on "red alert." My heart was pounding, and that chili dog I had for lunch got caught in my digestive system. Then my palms got sweaty. I could hardly squeak out a sound because my mouth was so dry. I wanted to yell back at her, but I couldn't!

Colleague: Probably just as well. Quick emotional reactions don't seem to work very well when communication breaks down. I found out the hard way that it doesn't help to respond at all during that first barrage of words. Sounds like you did the right thing.

Math Teacher: Well, it really was hard. So you've had things like this happen to you?

Colleague: Um-humm. I see we don't have time for me to tell you about it, because here come our troops for their next hour of knowledge. But I can tell you all about it later if you want. Come to my room after school and we'll compare notes—maybe even plan some strategies for the future just in case. And, by the way, welcome to the club!

COMMUNICATION FOR EFFECTIVE SCHOOL RELATIONSHIPS

Teachers manage many kinds of relationships in their work with children who have special needs. Some relationships grow throughout the year or over several years, others are established and stable, while still others are new, tentative, and tenuous. No matter what the type of relationship, and no matter whether it is with families, colleagues, paraeducators, or other human service providers, communication is the key to successful relationships. Furthermore, communication in the twenty-first century has become paradoxically more simple and more complex due to the effects of modern technology.

In the chapter "Enter Technology, Exit Talking" of her 2006 book, Sonya Hamlin says that "even hello has changed" as a result of modern technology (p. 3). Her discussion lists examples of how technology has changed the ways we communicate:

- We e-mail the person in the office next door.
- We have a list of 15 phone numbers to reach our family.
- We pull up in our driveway and use our cell phone to see if anyone is home to help carry in the groceries.
- We get up in the morning and go online before getting our coffee.
- We don't stay in touch with friends because we don't have their e-mail addresses.

Computers, cell phones, the Internet, and even television have changed communication in the last decade. However, while all these media may be part of our repertoire when it comes to collaborating with school, home, and community partners, face-to-face interactions are still the standard and most effective type of communication for most collaboration. People typically communicate in one form or another for about 70 percent of their waking moments. Unfortunately, lack of effective communication skills is a major reason for work-related failure.

A supportive, communicative relationship among special education teachers, general classroom teachers, and parents is critical to the success of children with exceptional learning needs in inclusive classrooms. Trends in education emphasize the necessity for greatly strengthened communication among all who are involved with a student's educational program. Special educators who are to serve as consultants and team members for helping students with special needs succeed, must model and promote exemplary communication and interaction skills.

Consulting is not a one-person exercise. A consultant will pay a high price for a "Rambo" style of interaction ("My idea can beat up your idea," or "I'm right and that's just the way it is."). Communication that minimizes conflict and enables teachers to maintain self-esteem may be the most important and most "delicate" process in consulting (Gersten, Darch, Davis, & George, 1991.) Unfortunately, development of communication skills is not typically included in teacher education programs. Because the development and use of "people skills" is the most difficult aspect of collaboration for many educators, more and more educators are stressing the need for specific training in collaboration and communication skills to serve special needs students.

Challenges of Communication

Communication requires four elements:

1. A message
2. A sender of the message
3. A receiver of the message
4. The medium

Semantics play a fundamental role in both sending and receiving messages. As stressed earlier, a person who says, "Oh, it's no big deal—just an issue of semantics" is missing a major point. The semantics frequently *are* the issue and should never be taken for granted. The vital role of semantics in consultation, collaboration, and teamwork cannot be ignored.

Body language also plays a key role in communication. Studies of kinesics, or communication through body language, show that the impact of a message is about 7 percent verbal, 38 percent vocal, and 55 percent facial. The eyebrows are particularly meaningful in conveying messages.

Placing, or removing, a physical barrier would be another aspect of communication. We communicate nonverbally much of the time and in many more ways than we tend to realize. Nonverbal modes of communication include use of space, movements, posture, eye contact, attention to the clock, positions of feet and legs when sitting, use of furniture, facial expressions, gestures, mannerisms, volume of voice, rate of voice, and level of energy (Gazda, Asbury, Balzer, Childers, Phelps, & Walters, 1999).

In order to communicate effectively, the message sender must convey the purpose of the message in a facilitative style with clarity to the receiver. As the noted theologian John Powell put it, "I can't tell you what you *said,* but only what I *heard.*" Miscommunication breeds misunderstanding. A gap in meaning between what the message sender gives and what the message receiver gets can at best be described as distortion, or as communication trash in extreme cases. A person may send the message, "You look nice today," and have it understood by the receiver as, "Gee, then I usually don't look very good." A classroom teacher wanting to reinforce efforts of the learning disabilities teacher might say "Gerry seems to get much better grades on tests in the resource room," but the resource teacher may hear, "You're helping too much and Gerry can't cope outside your protection." (See Figure 4.1, which graphically illustrates a potential range of distorted communication.)

Vague semantics, distorted messages, and psychological filters disrupt the message as it passes (or doesn't pass) between the sender and the receiver. Examples of filters are differing values, ambiguous language, stereotypes and assumptions, levels of self-esteem, and personal experiences. Preconceived ideas constantly filter the messages we receive, prevent

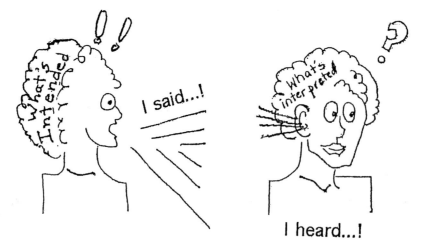

FIGURE 4.1   Miscommunication

us from hearing what others are saying, and provide only what people want to hear (Buscaglia, 1986). This can be demonstrated with the well-known game of "Gossip." Players stand in a long line or a circle, while one of them silently reads or quietly receives a message. Then that person whispers the message to the next one, and that message continues to be delivered to each one in turn. After passing through the filters of many people and stated aloud by the very last one, the message in most cases is drastically different from the original message. The game results are usually humorous. Real-life results are not always so funny.

APPLICATION 4.1
SENDING, RECEIVING, AND SHARING MESSAGES

In groups of three, with one person designated as Interviewer, another as Interviewee, and the third one Responder, conduct three-minute interviews to learn more about each other. After each interview change roles, so that each person has a turn to serve in all three capacities. Each Responder may make brief notes to use during a one-minute Share Time to introduce his or her Interviewee to the whole group. Use questions of this nature, or others given by the convener: What are your special talents? Apprehensions? Pet peeves? Successes you have had? Long-range goals? Things you want to learn more about?

Ethnic and Gender Differences in Communication

Language is the window through which the reality of others' experiences is revealed. Gender and ethnicity are other factors that may cloud that window and lead to systematic misjudgments in interpreting communication. Misunderstanding may not be due simply to miscommunication. Other factors such as the sex or cultural background of the sender or the receiver may be responsible. Examples of gender differences in conversational style affecting both sender and receiver of the message are discussed by sociolinguist Deborah Tannen and others (Tannen, 1991, 1994; Banks & Banks, 2007). Tannen's research describes differences in communication styles between females (both girls and women) and males (both boys and men):

- Amount of time listening versus talking
- Interrupting
- Physical alignment during conversation
- Use of indirectness and silence
- Topical cohesion

For example, men and boys' conversations tend to be diffuse, while those of women and girls are more tightly focused with minimal topics. Educational consultants should be aware that such types of communication style differences might lead them to be misunderstood or cause them to misunderstand their consultees.

The caveat for gender also applies to cross-cultural interactions. Most consultants are aware that different languages or different dialects may have different words for the same object. Some languages have no words for terms we use in education. For example, there is no word in Spanish for assertiveness or self-advocacy.

Verbal and nonverbal communication must be attuned to ethnic, racial, linguistic, and cultural differences. Because language and culture are so inextricably bound together, communicating with potential collaborative partners who are from different cultural and linguistic backgrounds is a very complex process (Lynch & Hanson, 1998). Chisholm (1994) has these suggestions for educators as they develop cross-cultural communication competencies:

- Develop awareness of your own cultural perspective and realize that your cultural perspective is not a universal norm.
- Develop mechanisms to cope with the stress of dealing with the unfamiliar.
- Understand that cultural context and personal experience have meaning. For example, the word *wedding* will convey a different meaning to persons from different cultural contexts, because the gender and familial role expectations, ceremonial traditions, and shared values vary across these cultures.
- Realize that logical reasoning and discourse styles are culture-specific.
- Learn about cultural aspects of nonverbal communication. For example, eye contact in a classroom may signal disrespect and inattention in one culture but may mean respect in another culture. There are cultural differences in use of space, touch, appearance, voice tone, and body language. Unwary educational consultants in such cases could lose much esteem for engaging in consultations in the same manner as they might do elsewhere.

As will be discussed specifically in Chapter 9 and elsewhere throughout the book, consultants will continue to be challenged by the cultural diversity of collaborators. Increasing diversity among colleagues, families, and communities requires that educational consultants recognize and continuously consider the impact of culture on communication in their work.

Computer-Mediated Communication

It is estimated that more than 147 million people across the country use e-mail daily. All told, people dash off millions of e-mails a day for work and pleasure, and most do not stop to consider how those hurried messages are being received or interpreted. Even in school settings, educators are sending e-mail instead of writing letters, phoning, or meeting face-to-face. In the case of school-based collaboration with colleagues, community organizations, and families, e-mail can greatly facilitate or hinder ongoing collaborative efforts. Because Internet communication, like other forms of written communication, lacks "tone of voice" and other nonverbal elements, this type of communication may make it more difficult for educators to get a message across clearly and result in miscommunication. Extra time and work are required to repair damage caused by an unread e-mail, a misinterpreted message, or an unclear communication related to an e-mail or classroom Web site.

Computer-mediated communication (CMC) is the process of human communication via computers. CMC includes task-oriented and personal communication and involves communication via both personal and mainframe computers. It includes both asynchronous communication via e-mail or electronic bulletin boards, and synchronous communication such as chat rooms or instant messaging (IM). Finally, CMC refers to all types of communication such as the World Wide Web, e-mail, message boards, and blogs (web logs or online journals).

CMC is an excellent tool for collaboration. It has the potential to provide a range of opportunities for interaction, information, and community among people of all ages, cultures, and socioeconomic classes. It also holds the potential for individuals to interact as peers and to overcome the physical constraints of communication (Gold, 1997). With the appropriate technology, collaboration among those in a virtual community is not hindered by language, culture, or disability.

However, just as with social etiquette rules that are designed to help people "think before they act," network etiquette ("netiquette") is designed to make communication easier and unlikely to cause harm by a stray or misguided comment or action via the Internet. Strawbridge (2006), in *Netiquette: Internet Etiquette in the Age of the Blog*, suggests a total of 157 netiquette rules that include rules for e-mail, mail lists, blogs, online services, and Web sites. Several of these suggestions are especially relevant to educators and others in team-building and collaborative work. Recommendations from Strawbridge, other experts, online communicators, and consulting teachers' experiences stress ten major points:

1. When sending an e-mail to a group, use "BCC" (blind copy) rather than listing all those addressed in the "To" line, because when a group e-mail is received and all addresses are in the "To" line, they are visible to all recipients. Often people do not like to have their e-mail address given to people they don't know or don't wish to have receive it; doing so could be considered a breach of privacy. Also be very careful about "Forward to" and "Reply to All" and other "group-send" buttons. There are horror stories about sending messages inadvertently to the wrong recipients!

2. E-mail greetings are not as formal as those for written letters. Start with the recipient's name or "Hello." If it is someone you don't know well, using a first name may come across as overly familiar. When sending an e-mail to a group of people, use such greetings as "Colleagues," "After-School Grant Proposal Team," or "Dear Families."

3. Each line should contain no more than 65 characters, allowing software to wrap sentences to the next line without making short lines and long lines in the same message. Use short, well-written sentences, with a space between paragraphs.

4. Use standard English and avoid abbreviations or popular contractions of text messaging. Most people can figure out that "pls hlp" means please help, but recipients whose language is not primarily English will have trouble with some of these expressions. E-mail is meant to be helpful and efficient, not puzzling and time-consuming. Written communication presents enough challenges without receivers having to interpret text shorthand!

5. Keep the writing style professional. Avoid "emoticons" and hone your writing and vocabulary skills rather than using such things as smiley faces. Use a readable font and remember that colors and special formatting can make your message difficult for the recipient to read. Sending hard-to-read messages is not a good practice for teachers of those with special (visual or learning) needs! Do not write in all capital letters or in all small letters.

6. Use a signature block for your professional e-mail that is about 4 lines long with 70 or fewer characters per line and includes information to help the recipient contact you.

7. Although e-mails should be short and to the point, an appropriate level of small talk lightens the mood and shows that you are accessible. But tailor it to the individual and remember that brevity is best. Mark Twain is said to have told a recipient, "If I'd had more time, I would have made this message shorter." Shorter may be harder, but it is more effective.

8. Reread for grammar and spelling, and for parts that could be confusing or embarrassing to anyone, even the sender. Never say in an e-mail what you wouldn't say in a crowded room, suggests Strawbridge (2006).

9. Whenever possible, don't deal with conflict, bad behavior, or negative comments in an e-mail. If you need to convey bad news, a face-to-face meeting allows both parties the full range of nonverbal cues given out by the other person.

10. Don't send attachments unless they are absolutely necessary. Many people are wary of attachments because of viruses; plain text e-mails without attachments do not carry viruses. When you do feel the need to send an attachment, use formatting that can be read regardless of the software readers might have on their computers. It is frustrating to receive an important attachment that cannot be opened in a timely fashion.

Computer-mediated communication is a great tool but in general it is not well used. Many organizations, businesses, and more and more schools are adopting and implementing etiquette rules for use of the Internet by their employees so there will be more efficiency and better protection from liability. Netiquette is an important consideration when educators use e-mail or other types of electronic communication. The overall purpose is to provide more effective communication.

Nonverbal Communication

The successful collaborative consultant models facilitative nonverbal communication, or body language, during interactions and attends carefully to the body language of others. Nonverbal communication can be organized into six categories: Eye contact; gestures; paralanguage (volume, rate, pitch, and pronunciation of the verbal communication); posture; overall facial expression; and as a new category to be added to the traditional five already named, clothing and setting for the interaction (White, 2000).

Eyes and the brows above them are expressive instruments for conveying thoughts as well as feelings. Gestures send signals, and facial expressions disclose thoughts and feelings. When gestures and facial expressions do not match verbal content, mixed signals result. For example, teachers send mixed signals when they smile as they outline class rules and procedures, but display stern faces when introducing a learning activity. A consulting teacher might err similarly when interacting with parents or co-teachers. Voice tone, pitch, volume, and speed can affect the receiver of a message in positive or negative ways.

Slouching posture or turning away will imply lack of interest or rejection. Clothing worn by educators should be comfortable, of course, but also should be chosen to suit the environment. A consulting teacher was told by her colleagues at one school that she "dressed to supervise, not to work," so she learned to "dress down" for that setting, with sneakers and no jewelry. For her afternoon schedule in a school with a more dressy style, she changed to heeled shoes, a blazer, and a scarf or necklace. Not expecting to notice much difference, she was amazed to find more acceptance for her role at both schools.

SKILLS FOR COMMUNICATING

In order to be effective communicators, senders and receivers of messages need skills that include rapport building, responsive listening, assertiveness, tools for dealing with resistance, and conflict-management techniques. With well-developed communication skills, consultants and consultees will be able to engage more effectively in collaborative problem solving.

Five major sets of skills are integral to successful communication:

1. Rapport-building skills
2. Responsive listening
3. Assertion skills
4. Conflict management skills
5. Collaborative problem-solving skills

Rapport building is the first step in establishing a collaborative relationship. Responsive listening skills enable a person to understand what another is saying and to convey that the problems and feelings have been understood. When listening methods are used appropriately by a consultant, the consultee plays an active role in problem solving without becoming dependent on the consultant.

Assertion skills include verbal and nonverbal behaviors that enable collaborators to maintain respect, satisfy their professional needs, and defend their rights without dominating, manipulating, or controlling others. Conflict management skills help individuals deal with the emotional turbulence that typically accompanies conflict. Conflict management skills also have a multiplier effect of fostering closer relationships when a conflict is resolved. Collaborative problem-solving skills help resolve the conflicting needs so that all parties are satisfied. Problems then "stay solved," and relationships are developed and preserved. Problem solving is discussed in Chapter 5.

Rapport-Building Skills

Collaboration with other professionals that is in the best interests of students with special needs often means simply sitting down and making some joint decisions. At other times, however, it must be preceded by considerable rapport building. Successful consultation necessitates good rapport between the participants in the consulting relationship. It is important to keep in mind that both the consultant and the consultee should provide ideas toward solving the problem. Respect must be a two-way condition for generating and accepting ideas. Rapport building is vital for building an appropriate consultation climate.

When we take time to build positive relationships with others that are based on mutual respect and trust, others are more likely to:

- Want to work with us
- Care about our reactions to them

- Try to meet our expectations
- Accept our feedback and coaching
- Imitate our behavior

We are more likely to:

- Listen to and try to understand their unique situations
- Accept them as they are and not judge them for what they are not
- Respond appropriately to their concerns and criticisms
- Advocate for, and support and encourage them in their efforts on behalf of, students with special needs

What behaviors are central to the process of building a trusting, supportive relationship? When asked this question, many teachers mention trust, respect, feeling that it is okay not to have all the answers, feeling free to ask questions, and feeling all right about disagreeing with the other person. People want to feel that the other person is *really* listening. Trust is developed when one addresses the concerns of others and looks for opportunities to demonstrate responsiveness to others' needs.

Respecting differences in others is an important aspect of building and maintaining rapport. Although teachers and other school personnel are generally adept at recognizing and respecting individual differences in children, they may find this more difficult to accomplish with adults. Accepting differences in adults may be particularly difficult when the adults have different values, skills, and attitudes. Effective consultants accept people as they really are rather than wishing they were different. Rapport building is not such a formidable process when the consultant respects individual differences and holds high expectations for others.

Responsive Listening Skills

Plutarch said, "Know how to listen and you will profit even from those who talk badly." Shakespeare referred to the "disease" of *not* listening. Listening is the foundation of communication. A person listens to establish rapport with another person. People listen when others are upset or angry, or when they do not know what to say or fear speaking out will result in trouble. People listen so others will listen to them. Listening is a process of perpetual motion that focuses on the other person as speaker and responds to that other person's ideas, rather than concentrating on one's own thoughts and feelings. Thus, effective listening is *responsive listening* because it is responding, both verbally and nonverbally, to the words and actions of the speaker.

Successful consultants listen responsively and empathically to build trust and promote understanding. Responsive listening improves relationships, and minimizes resistance and negativity. Although most people are convinced of the importance of listening in building collegial relationships and preventing and solving problems, few are as adept at this skill as they would like or need to be. There are several reasons for this. First, most people have not been taught to listen effectively. They have been taught to talk—especially if they are teachers, administrators, or psychologists. Educators are good at talking and regard it as an essential part of their roles. But effective talkers must be careful not to let the lines of communication get tangled up in a tendency to talk too much or too often.

According to Thomas Gordon, one of the early promoters of effective communication, listening helps keep the "locus of responsibility" with the one who owns the problem (Gordon, 2000). Therefore, if one's role as a consultant is to promote problem-solving without fostering dependence on the part of the consultee, listening will keep the focus of the problem-solving where it belongs. Listening also is important in showing empathy and acceptance, two vital ingredients in a relationship that fosters growth and psychological health (Gordon, 2000).

Responsive, effective listening makes it possible to gather information essential to one's role in the education of children with special needs. It helps others feel better, often by reducing tension and anxiety, increasing feelings of personal well-being, and encouraging greater hope and optimism. This kind of listening encourages others to express themselves freely and fully. It enhances your value to others, and often contributes significantly to positive change in others' self-understanding and problem-solving abilities.

If listening is so important, why is it so hard? Listening is difficult because it is hard to keep an open mind about the speaker. People may be hesitant to listen because they think listening implies agreeing. Openness certainly is important in effective communication. However, listening is much more than just hearing. Consultants must demonstrate tolerance toward differences and appreciation of richly diverse ideas and values while they are engaged in consulting relationships. A consultant's own values about child rearing, education, or the treatment of children with special needs become personal filters that make it difficult to really listen to those whose values are very different. For example, it may be hard to listen to a consultee parent who thinks it is appropriate for a very gifted daughter to drop out of school at the age of sixteen to help on the family farm because "She'll be getting married before too long and farm work will prepare her to be a wife better than schoolwork ever can." It takes discipline to listen to comments such as this when your mind is reacting negatively and wants to put together some very pointed arguments. A good thing to remember in such cases is that "when we add our two cents' worth in the middle of listening, that's just about what the communication is worth!" (Murphy, 1987).

Listening is indeed hard work. If the listener is tired or anxious or bursting with excitement and energy, it is particularly hard to listen carefully. Feelings of the listener also act as filters to impede listening. Other roadblocks to responsive listening are making assumptions about the message (mind-reading), thinking about our own response (rehearsing), and reacting defensively.

Improving listening skills can help establish collaborative relationships with colleagues, even those with whom it is a challenge to communicate. When consultants and consultees improve their listening skills, they have a head start on solving problems, sidestepping resistance, and preventing conflicts.

There are three major components of responsive listening:

1. Nonverbal listening (discerning others' needs and observing their nonverbal gestures)
2. Encouraging the sending of messages (encouraging others to express themselves fully)
3. Showing understanding of the message (reviewing what they conveyed), or paraphrasing

Nonverbal Listening Skills. Responsive listeners use appropriate body language to send out the message that they are listening effectively. Nonverbal listening behavior of a good listener is described by Tony Hillerman in his 1990 best-seller *Coyote Waits:* "Jacobs was silent for awhile, thinking about it, her face full of sympathy. She was a talented listener. When you talked to this woman, she attended. She had all her antennae out. The world was shut out. Nothing mattered but the words she was hearing" (Hillerman, 1990, pp. 148–149).

Nonverbal listening may be less than effective for those people who do several things at once, such as watch a television show and write a letter, or talk to a colleague and grade papers, or prepare supper while listening to a child's synopsis of the day. This is because nonverbal components of listening should demonstrate to the speaker that the receiver is respecting the speaker enough to concentrate on the message and is following the speaker's thoughts to find the *real* message. Careful listening conveys attitudes of flexibility, empathy, and caring, even if the speaker is using words and expressions that cloud the message. A person who is attentive leans forward slightly, engages in a comfortable level of eye contact, nods, and gives low-key responses such as "oh," and "uh-huh," and "umm-humm." The responsive listener's facial expression matches the message. If that message is serious, the expression reflects seriousness. If the message is delivered with a smile, the listener shows empathy by smiling.

The hardest part of nonverbal listening is keeping it nonverbal. It helps the listener to think about a tennis game and remember that during the listening part of the "game," the ball is in the speaker's court. The speaker has the privilege of saying anything, no matter how seemingly silly or irrelevant. The listener just keeps sending the ball back by nodding, or saying "I see" or other basically nonverbal behaviors, until he or she "hears" the sender's message. This entails using nonverbal behaviors and "listening" to the nonverbal as well as the verbal messages of the sender. The listener recognizes and minimizes personal filters, perceives and interprets the filters of the sender, and encourages continued communication until able to understand the message from the sender's perspective. Responsive listeners avoid anticipating what the speaker will say and *never* complete a speaker's sentence.

After listeners have listened until they really hear the message, understand the speaker's position, and recognize the feelings behind the message, it is their turn to speak. But they must be judicious about what they do say. Several well-known, humorous "recipes" apply to this need.

- Recipe for speaking—stand up, speak up, then shut up.
- Recipe for giving a good speech—add shortening.
- It takes six letters of the alphabet to spell the word *listen.* Rearrange the letters to spell another word that is a necessary part of responsive listening.[1]
- In the middle of listening, the *t* doesn't make a sound.

Verbal Listening Skills.   Although the first rule of the good listener is to keep one's mouth shut, there are several types of verbal responses that show that the listener is following the thoughts and feelings expressed by the speaker. Verbal responses are added to nonverbal listening responses to communicate that the listener understands what the other is saying from that speaker's specific point of view. Specific verbal aspects of listening also keep the speaker talking. There are several reasons for this which are specific to the consulting process:

- The consultant will be less inclined to assume ownership of the problem.
- Speakers will clarify their own thoughts as they keep talking.

[1]Did you get *silent?*

- More information will become available to help understand the speaker's point of view.
- Speakers begin to solve their own problems as they talk them through.
- The consultant continues to refine responsive listening skills.

Three verbal listening skills that promote talking by the speaker are inviting, encouraging, and questioning cautiously. Inviting means providing an opportunity for others to talk, by signaling to them that you are interested in listening if they are interested in speaking. Examples are "You seem to have something on your mind," or "I'd like to hear about your problem," or "What's going on for you now?"

Verbal responses of encouragement are added to nodding and mirroring of facial responses. "I see," "uh-hum," and "oh" are examples of verbal behaviors that encourage continued talking. These listener responses suggest: "Continue. I understand. I'm listening." (Gordon, 1977).

Cautious questioning is the final mechanism for promoting continued talking. Most educators are competent questioners, so the caution here is to use minimal questioning. During the listening part of communication, the message is controlled by the speaker. It is always the speaker's serve. Intensive and frequent questioning gives control of the communication to the listener. This is antithetical to the consulting process, which should be about collaboration rather than power and control. Questions should be used to clarify what the speaker has said, so that the message can be understood by the listener—for example, "Is this what you mean?" or "Please explain what you mean by 'attitude problem.'"

Paraphrasing Skills. Responsive listening means demonstrating that the listener understands the essence of the message. After listening by using nonverbal and minimal verbal responses, a consultant who is really listening probably will begin to understand the message of the speaker. To show that the message was heard, or to assess whether what was "heard" was the same message the sender intended and was not altered by distortion, the listener should paraphrase the message. This requires the listener to think carefully about the message and reflect it back to the speaker without changing the content or intent of the message.

There is no simple formula for reflecting or paraphrasing, but two good strategies are to be as accurate as possible and as brief as possible. A paraphrase may begin in one of several ways: "It sounds as if . . ." or "Is what you mean . . . ?" or "So, it seems to me you want [think] [feel] . . ." or "Let me see if I understand. You're saying. . ." Paraphrasing allows listeners to check their understanding of the message. It is easy to mishear or misinterpret the message, especially if the words are ambiguous. Correct interpretation of the message will result in a nod from the speaker, who may feel that at last someone has really listened. Or the speaker may correct the message by saying, "No, that's not what I meant. It's this way. . ." The listener may paraphrase the content of the message. For example, "It seems to me that you're saying . . ." would reflect the content of the message back to the speaker. "You appear to be very frustrated about . . . " reflects the emotional part of the message. It is important to use the speaker's words as much as possible in the paraphrase words and to remain concise in responses. By paraphrasing appropriately, a listener demonstrates comprehension of the message or receipt of new information. This aspect of hearing and listening is essential in communication, and in assertion, problem solving, and conflict management as well.

Just by recognizing a consultee's anger, or sadness, or frustration, a consultant can begin to build a trusting relationship with a consultee. The listener doesn't necessarily have to agree with the content or emotion that is heard. It may appear absurd or illogical. Nevertheless, the consultant's responsibility is not to change another's momentary tendency; rather, it is to develop a supportive working relationship via effective communication, paving the way to successful cooperation and problem-solving while avoiding conflict and resistance.

Parents often comment that they have approached a teacher with a problem, realizing that they didn't want a specific answer, but just a kindly ear—a sounding board, or a friendly shoulder. Responsive listening is important in establishing collaborative relationships and maintaining them. It is also a necessary precursor to problem solving in which both parties strive to listen and get a mutual understanding of the problem before a problem is addressed.

So when is responsive listening to be used? The answer is—*all* the time. Use it when establishing a relationship, when starting to problem-solve, when emotions are high, when one's conversation doesn't seem to be getting anywhere, and when the speaker seems confused, uncertain, or doesn't know what else to do.

This complex process may not be necessary if two people have already developed a good working relationship and only a word or two is needed for mutual understanding. It also may not be appropriate if one of the two is not willing to talk. Sometimes "communication postponement" is best when you are too tired or too emotionally upset to be a responsive listener. When a consultant cannot listen because of any of these reasons, it is not wise to pretend to be listening, while actually thinking about something else or nothing at all. Instead, a reluctant listener should explain that he or she does not have the energy to talk about the problem now, but wishes to at a later time, for example: "I need a chance to think about this. May I talk to you later?" or "Look, I'm too upset to work on this very productively right now. Let's talk about it first thing tomorrow." Figure 4.2 summarizes responsive listening skills that help avoid blocked communication.

Assertiveness

By the time the consultant has listened effectively and the collaborative relationship has been developed or enhanced, many consultants are more than ready to start talking. Once the sender's message is understood and emotional levels are reduced, it is the listener's turn to be the sender. Now the consultant gets to talk. However, it is not always easy to communicate one's thoughts, feelings, and opinions without infringing on the rights, feelings, or opinions of others. This is the time for assertiveness.

Assertiveness skills allow consultants to achieve their goals without damaging the relationship or another's self-esteem. The basic aspects of assertive communication are:

- Use an "I" message instead of a "you" message.
- Say "and" instead of "but."
- State the behavior objectively.
- Name your own feelings.
- Say what you want to happen.
- Express concern for others (empathy).
- Use assertive body language.

FIGURE 4.2   Responsive Listening Checklist

	Yes	No
A. *Appropriate Nonverbals*		
1. Good eye contact	_____	_____
2. Facial expression mirrored	_____	_____
3. Body orientation toward other person	_____	_____
B. *Appropriate Verbals*		
1. Door openers	_____	_____
2. Good level of encouraging phrases	_____	_____
3. Cautious questions	_____	_____
C. *Appropriate Responding Behaviors*		
1. Reflected content (paraphrasing)	_____	_____
2. Reflected feelings	_____	_____
3. Brief clarifying questions	_____	_____
4. Summarizations	_____	_____
D. *Avoidance of Roadblocks*		
1. No advice giving	_____	_____
2. No inappropriate questions	_____	_____
3. Minimal volunteered solutions	_____	_____
4. No judging	_____	_____

Open and honest consultants say what they want to happen and what their feelings are. That does not mean they always get what they want. Saying what you want and how you feel will clarify the picture and ensure that the other(s) won't have to guess what you want or think. Even if others disagree with the ideas and opinions, they can never disagree with the feelings and wishes. Those are very personal and are expressed in a personal manner by starting the interaction with "I," rather than presenting feelings and opinions as truth or expert answer.

In stating an idea or position assertively, consultants should describe the problem in terms of its impact on the consultant, rather than in terms of what was done or said by the other person. "I feel let down" works better than "You broke your part of the agreement". If a consultant makes a "you" statement about the consultee which the consultee thinks is wrong, the consultant will only get an angry reaction and the consultant's concerns will be ignored.

Concern for Others during the Interaction.   Expressing concern for others can take many forms. This skill demonstrates that although people have thoughts and feelings which differ from those of others, they can still respect the feelings and ideas of others. "I realize it is a tremendous challenge to manage thirty-five children in the same classroom." This statement shows the consultant understands the management problems of the teacher. As the consultant goes on to state preferences in working with the teacher, the teacher is more likely to listen and work cooperatively. The consultee will see that the consultant is aware of the problems that must be dealt with daily. "It seems to me that . . . ," "I understand . . . ," "I realize . . . ," and "It looks like . . . " are phrases consultants can use to express concern for the other person in the collaborative relationship. If the consultant cannot complete these sentences with the appropriate information, the next step is to go back to the listening part of the communication.

How to Be Concerned and Assertive. Assertive people own their personal feelings and opinions. Being aware of this helps them state their wants and feelings. "You" sentences sound accusing, even when that is not intended, which can lead to defensiveness in others. For example, saying to a parent, "You should provide a place and quiet time for Hannah to do her homework," is more accusatory than saying, "I am frustrated when Hannah isn't getting her homework done, and I would like to work with you to think of some ways to help her get it done." Using "and" rather than "but" is particularly important in expressing thoughts without diminishing a relationship. This is a particularly difficult assertion skill. To the listener the word *but* erases the preceding phrase and prevents the intended message from coming through.

It is important to state behavior specifically. By describing behavior objectively, a consultant or consultee sounds less judgmental. It is easy to let blaming and judgmental words creep into language. Without meaning to, the speaker throws up a barrier that blocks the communication and the relationship.

APPLICATION 4.2
COMMUNICATING POSITIVELY

Compare the first statement with the second one:

1. "I would like to have a schedule of rehearsals for the holiday pageant. It is frustrating when I drive out to work with Maxine and Juanita and they are practicing for the musical and can't come to the resource room."

2. "When you don't let me know ahead of time that the girls won't be allowed to come and work with me, I have to waste my time driving and can't get anything accomplished."

In reflecting on these statements, which one is less judgmental and accusatory? Can these two contrasting statements create differing listener attitudes toward the speakers? For many listeners the judgmental words and phrases in the second sentence ("you don't let me know," "won't be allowed," "waste my time") sound blaming. They introduce a whole array of red flags.

Assertive communication includes demonstrating supportive body language. A firm voice, straight posture, eye contact, and body orientation toward the receiver of the message will have a desirable effect. Assertive body language affirms that the sender owns his

FIGURE 4.3   Assertiveness Checklist

	Usually	Sometimes	Never
1. Conveys "I" instead of "you" message	_____	_____	_____
2. Says "and" rather than "but"	_____	_____	_____
3. States behavior objectively	_____	_____	_____
4. Says what he or she wants to have happen	_____	_____	_____
5. States feelings	_____	_____	_____
6. Expresses concern	_____	_____	_____
7. Speaks firmly, clearly	_____	_____	_____
8. Has assertive posture	_____	_____	_____
9. Avoids aggressive language	_____	_____	_____

or her own feelings and opinions but also respects the other person's feelings and opinions. This is a difficult balance to achieve. Body language and verbal language must match or the messages will be confusing. Skills for being assertive are listed in Figure 4.3.

What we say and how we say it have tremendous impact on the reactions and acceptance of others. When consultants and consultees communicate in ways that accurately reflect their feelings, focus on objective descriptions of behavior and situations, and think in a concrete manner about what they want to happen, assertive communication will build strong, respectful relationships. Assertive communication is the basis for solving problems and resolving conflicts.

The Art of Apologizing.   Sometimes, despite good communication skills and careful relationship building and problem solving, consultants make errors and mistakes. Good consultants never blame someone else for communication breakdowns; they accept responsibility for their own communication. This is demonstrated when a consultant says, "Let me explain in a different way" instead of "Can't you understand?" Good consultants also use the art of apologizing.

One of the biggest misconceptions in the area of consultation and collaboration is that apologizing puts consultants and teachers at a disadvantage when working with colleagues and parents. It is simply not true that strong, knowledgeable people never say they're sorry. In fact, apologizing is a powerful strategy because it demonstrates honesty and confidence. Apologizing offers a chance to mend fences in professional relationships. Some suggestions from psychologist Barry Lubetkin (1996) about how to apologize include allowing the person you've wronged to vent her or his feelings first, apologize as soon as possible, don't say "I'm sorry, but. . . .," and say it once and let that be enough. Most importantly, apologies are empty if you keep repeating the behavior or the mistake.

Roadblocks to Communication

Roadblocks are barriers to successful interaction, halting the development of effective collaborative relationships. They may be verbal behaviors or nonverbal behaviors that send out messages such as, "I'm not listening," or "It doesn't matter what you think," or "Your ideas and feelings are silly and unimportant." Responsible school consultants most assuredly do not intend to send blocking messages. But by being busy, not concentrating, using poor listening skills, or allowing themselves to be directed by filters such as emotions and judgment, well-meaning consultants inadvertently send blocking messages.

Barriers to communication among educators and families may sometimes take the form of specific conditions such as learning disabilities of the adults involved. When education consultants work with parents, paraeducators or other adults who may have a learning disability themselves, some suggestions for improving communication are:

- Break large tasks or bodies of information into smaller ones
- Give information in a very structured manner
- Offer "organizational tools" such as notes, colored files or flyers for color coding, paper for taking notes or printed notes
- Be very careful about being critical
- Offer plenty of positive feedback, when warranted
- Encourage them to tape meetings or instructions
- Communicate frequently and offer information in smaller segments
- Frequently test the accuracy of communication by asking them to repeat or rephrase what was said

Nonverbal Roadblocks.   Nonverbal roadblocks include facing away when the speaker talks, displaying inappropriate facial expressions such as smiling when the sender is saying something serious, distracting with body movements such as repetitively tapping a pencil, and grading papers or writing reports while "listening." Interrupting a speaker to attend to something or someone else—the phone, a sound outside the window, or a knock at the door—also halts communication and contributes in a subtle way toward undermining the spirit of collaboration.

Verbal Roadblocks.   Gordon (1977) lists 12 verbal barriers to communication. These have been called the "Dirty Dozen," and they can be grouped into three types of verbal roadblocks that prevent meaningful interaction (Bolton, 1986):

1. Judging
2. Sending solutions
3. Avoiding others' concerns

The first category, judging, includes criticizing, name-calling, and diagnosing or analyzing why a person is behaving a particular way. False or non-specific praise and evaluative words or phrases, send a message of judgment toward the speaker. "You're not thinking clearly," "You'll do a wonderful job of using curriculum-based assessment!" and "You don't really believe that—you're just tired today" are examples of judging. (Notice that each of these statements begins with the word *you*.) Avoiding judgment about parents or others helps teachers avoid deficit-based thinking which hurts everyone it touches (Lovett, 1996). Nonjudgmental communication conveys equity in the relationship, a critical factor in teamwork.

Educators are particularly adept with the next category of verbal roadblocks—sending solutions. These include directing or ordering, warning, moralizing or preaching, advising, and using logical arguments or lecturing. A few of these can become a careless consultant's entire verbal repertoire. "Not knowing the question," Bolton says (1986, p. 37), "it was easy for him to give the answer." "Stop complaining," and "Don't talk like that," and "If you don't send Jim to the resource room on time . . . " are examples of directing or warning. Moralizing sends a message of "I'm a better educator than you are." Such communication usually starts with "You should . . . " or "You ought to. . . . " When consultees have problems, the last thing they need is to be told what they *should* do. Using "should" makes a consultant sound rigid and pedantic. Avoid giving the impression that you are more concerned with rules or shoulds than with the relationship with the consultee.

Advising, lecturing, and logical argument are all too often part of the educator's tools of the trade. Teachers tend to use roadblock types of communication techniques frequently with students. The habits they develop cause them to overlook the reality that use of such tactics with adults can drive a wedge into an already precarious relationship. Consultants must avoid such tactics as assuming the posture of the "sage-on-the-stage," imparting wisdom in the manner of a learned professor to undergraduate students, lecturing, moralizing, and advising. Unfortunately, these methods imply superiority, which is detrimental to the collaborative process.

Avoiding others' concerns is a third category of verbal roadblocks. This category implies "no big deal" to the message-receiver. Avoidance messages include reassuring or sympathizing, such as "You'll feel better tomorrow" or "Everyone goes through this stage," or interrogating to get more than the necessary information, thereby delaying the problem solving. Other avoidance messages include intensive questioning in the manner of The Grand Inquisition, and humoring or distracting, "Let's get off this and talk about something else." Avoiding the concerns that others express sends the message that their concerns are not important.

Other powerful roadblocks to communication are too much sending, not enough receiving; excessive kindness (Fisher, 1993); reluctance to express negative information (Rinke, 1997); and inadequate feedback, that is, the sender does not find out if the message has been received, acknowledged or understood (Fisher, 1993). When consultants use roadblocks, they are making themselves, their feelings, and their opinions the focus of the interaction, rather than allowing the focus to be the issues, concerns, or problems of the consultee. When they set up roadblocks, listeners do not listen responsively or encourage others to communicate clearly, openly, and effectively. Because it is so easy to inadvertently use a communication block through speaking, it is wise to remember the adage, "We are blessed with two ears and one mouth, a constant reminder that we should listen twice as much as we talk." Indeed, the more one talks, the more likely a person is to make errors, and the less opportunity that person will have to learn something.

Terms, Labels, and Phrases as Roadblocks.   Inappropriate use of terms and labels can erect roadblocks to communication. Educators should adhere to the following points when speaking or writing about people with disabilities:

■ Do not focus on the disability, but instead on issues affecting quality of life for them, such as housing, affordable health care, and employment opportunity.

- Do not portray successful people with disabilities as superhuman, for all persons with disabilities cannot achieve this level of success.
- Use people-first language, such as "a student with autism," rather than "an autistic student."
- Emphasize abilities and not limitations, such as "uses a wheelchair," rather than "wheelchair-bound."
- Terms such as *physically challenged* are considered condescending, and saying "victim of" is regarded as sensationalizing.
- Do not imply disease by saying "patient" or "case" when discussing disabilities.

Acceptable, contemporary terminology facilitates active listening and improves verbal communication.

MANAGING RESISTANCE, NEGATIVITY, ANGER, AND CONFLICT

Communication is the key to collaboration and problem solving. Without back and forth discussions, there can be no agreement. Problem solving often breaks down because communications break down first, because people aren't paying attention or because they misunderstand the other side, or because emotions were not dealt with as a separate and primary issue.

In problem solving it is critical to separate the person from the problem. Collaborative consultants will find themselves often needing to deal with emotions, as well as any errors in perceptions or communication, as separate issues which must be resolved on their own. Emotions may take the form of resistance, anger, negativity, or outright conflict. If emotions are not recognized and dealt with skillfully, they may become barriers to effective communication when they are experienced by the consultant or consultee. Sometimes, regardless of how diplomatic people are in dealing with the emotions of others, they run into barriers of resistance in their attempts to communicate.

It is estimated that as much as 80 percent of problem solving with others is getting through the resistance. Resistance is a trait of human nature that surfaces when people are asked to change. Researchers have found that people resist change for a number of reasons. They may:

- Have a vested interest in the status quo
- Have low tolerance for change
- Feel strongly that the change would be undesirable
- Be unclear about what the change would entail or bring about
- Fear the unknown

A wise person once suggested, "How can we ask others to change when it is so hard to change ourselves?" Resistance often has nothing to do with an individual personally, or even with the new idea. The resistance is simply a reaction to change of any kind. Change implies imperfection with the way things are being done, and this makes people defensive. However, it is good to remember the adage from another wise person, "Change is the only thing that is permanent."

Many people get defensive or resistant or just stop listening when others disagree with them. This often happens because they feel they are being attacked personally. Parents who are asked what time a sleepy student goes to bed at night may feel defensive because they feel you are attacking or questioning their parenting, even though you may just want to rule out lack of sleep for some of the behaviors the child is exhibiting in the classroom.

Why Collaborative Partners Resist

It is human nature to be uncomfortable when another person disagrees. It is also human nature to get upset when someone resists efforts to make changes, implement plans, or modify systems to be more responsive to children with special needs. The need for change can generate powerful emotions. Most people are uncomfortable when experiencing the strong emotions of others. When someone yells or argues, the first impulse is to become defensive, argue the other point of view, and defend one's own ideas. Although a school consultant may intend to remain cool and calm and collected in the interactions that involve exceptional children, occasionally another individual says something that pushes a "hot button" and the consultant becomes upset, or angry, or defensive.

Special education consulting teachers who have been asked to describe examples of resistance they have experienced toward their roles provide these examples:

- Consultees (classroom teachers) won't share how they feel.
- They act excited about an idea, but never get around to doing it.
- They won't discuss it with you, but they do so liberally with others behind your back.
- They may try, but give up too soon.
- They take out their frustrations on the students.
- They are too quick to say that a strategy won't work in their situation.
- They dredge up a past example where something similar didn't work.
- They keep asking for more and more details or information before trying an idea.
- They change the subject, or suddenly have to be somewhere else.
- They state that there is not enough time to implement the strategy.
- They intellectualize with a myriad of reasons it won't work.
- They are simply silent.
- They just prefer the status quo.

When resistance spawns counter-resistance and anger, an upward spiral of emotion is created that can make consulting unpleasant and painful. Bolton (1986) describes resistance as a push, push-back phenomenon. When a person meets resistance with more resistance, defensiveness, logical argument, or any other potential roadblock, resistance increases and dialogue can develop into open warfare. Then the dialogue may become personal or hurtful. Nobody listens at that point, and a potentially healthy relationship is damaged and very difficult to salvage.

How to Deal with Resistance and Negativity

An important strategy for dealing with resistance and defensiveness is to handle one's own defensiveness, stop pushing so that the other person will not be able to push-back, delay reactions, keep quiet, and *listen.* This takes practice, patience, tolerance, and commitment.

It is important to deal with emotions such as resistance, defensiveness, or anger before proceeding to problem solving. People are not inclined to listen until they have been listened to. They will not be convinced of another's sincerity and openness, or become capable of thinking logically, when the filter of emotions is clouding their thinking.

Negative people and negative emotions sap the energy of educational consultants. Reactions to negativity, to conflict, and to resistance can block communication and ruin potentially productive relationships. It is important to remember that negative people are not going to change. The person who has to change is the consultant.

The first point is to refrain from taking negativity personally. Such individuals just may be having a bad time at that point in their lives. A positive approach would be to deal with negativity as a challenge from which much can learned about working with people. When there is a breakthrough in the communication and problem solving, such folks can become one's staunchest allies and supporters.

Accommodating negative or resistant school colleagues or family members of students at their best times and on their turf can be a first step toward this alliance. Communicate in writing in order to diffuse emotional reactions and convey the message one wishes to send. Following up later and remaining patient will model a spirit of acceptance that is spiced with invincibility yet grounded in purpose.

For application of practical techniques, William Ury of the Program on Negotiation at Harvard Law School, stresses that one of the keys to working with difficult people is controlling one's own behavior (Ury, 1991). The natural reaction to resistance, challenges, and negativity is to strike back, give in, or break off the communication. A negative reaction to resistance leads to a vicious cycle of action and reaction and leads to communication and relationship breakdowns. Instead of reacting, seek to regain a mental balance and stay focused. So his suggestion is, don't react.

Ury (1991) provides two strategies for curbing one's own natural reactions to resistance and negativity. The first is to "go to the balcony". This means distancing oneself from the action-reaction cycle. Step back and take a deep breath and try to see the situation objectively. Imagine yourself climbing to the balcony overlooking the stage where the action-reaction drama has been taking place. Here, you can calmly look at the situation, with a detached or third-party perspective. Going to the balcony means removing yourself from your natural impulses and emotions. Remember, when your "hot buttons" get pushed or when you find yourself getting emotional and reacting instead of acting, go to the balcony!

Another strategy Ury (1991) suggests is to keep your eyes on the prize. Dealing with emotional and difficult situations in collaborative efforts usually diverts us from our goals and causes distress, so always keep your mind on the larger picture. In the collaborative consultant's case, the prize is optimal developmental and educational outcomes for students with special needs. If we remember that the communication process is crucial to the relationships among the stakeholders in a student's education, we will remember that diversions are worth dealing with and the eventual outcome is well worth the process.

Roger Fisher, director of the Harvard Negotiation Project and a collaborator with William Ury, co-authored a book with Sharp titled *Getting It Done: How to Lead When You're Not in Charge* (Fisher & Sharp, 1999). The book has been called the definitive book on collaboration, which they term "lateral leadership." Their formula to improve collaboration is: Ask, offer, and do. First, ask good questions, that is, questions that get others collaboratively thinking about a problem and looking for a solution. Open questions encourage others to be full and equal participants in the process. Second, offer your own thoughts, data, ideas, or suggestions. Contribute one piece of the puzzle. Third, model the behavior you would like to see. This method lessens resistance and helps create a climate of mutual support and feedback.

Yankelovich (2001), a social scientist and advisor to large corporations and government factions, believes that there are several "potholes that make the road to dialogue difficult to travel" (p. 130). These potholes are common causes of resistance and defensiveness. Yankelovich targets five potholes and then offers suggestions for avoiding them:

1. *Holding back.* Reasons people hold back are usually that trust has not been built, or they feel latent hostility, or they sense the potential for embarrassment. Try building trust with such strategies as breaking the ice by talking about personal experiences and by doing a small amount of self-disclosure.

2. *Staying in the box and not thinking or acting outside traditional boundaries.* This can be seen as resistance to change or to creative suggestions for solving problems. Focus on common interests, not divisive ones. Respect all suggestions; and bring assumptions out into the open.

3. *Prematurely moving into action.* We tend to act quickly on our problems. This, according to Yankelovich (2001), is one of our culture's great strengths as well as a limitation. Work to achieve mutual understanding before rushing into action.

4. *Listening without hearing.* The three core requirements of collaborative communication are equality, empathic listening, and treating the surfacing assumptions nonjudgmentally.

5. *Showboating.* Although we live in an era that values self-expression, subordinating one's personality to a certain extent is needed to empathize fully with someone else's point of view.

APPLICATION 4.3
MANAGING RESISTANCE

Construct a problem situation involving another person that could happen, or has happened, in your school context and interact with a colleague to try these communication techniques:

Dismiss the negativity with "You may be right," and keep moving forward. Be assertive (e.g., "I am bothered by discussing the negative side of things"). Ask for complaints in writing (because some people don't realize how negative they sound). Ask for clarification, also, by suggesting that the person describe the problem and clarify the desired outcome. This leads people to thinking about positive actions. Don't defend attacks, and invite criticism and advice instead. Ask what's wrong. Look for interests behind resistance, negativity, and anger by asking questions. Tentatively agree by saying "that's one opinion."

Switch roles and try another episode. Then have a debriefing session to critique the interactions.

Consultants must "hear their way to success" in managing resistance. This may take five minutes, or months of careful relationship-building. Colleagues cannot always avoid disagreements that are serious enough to create anger and resistance. A comment or question delivered in the wrong manner at the wrong time may be the "hot button" that triggers the antagonism. Consider remarks such as these:

"If you want students to use good note-taking skills, shouldn't you teach them that?"
"Not allowing learning disabled students to use calculators is cruel."
"Why don't you teach in a way to accommodate different learning styles?"
"You penalize gifted students when you keep the class in lockstep with basal readers."

Such remarks can make harried, overworked classroom teachers defensive and resentful. If an occasion arises in which a teacher or parent becomes angry or resistant, responding in the right way will prevent major breakdowns in the communication that is needed.

Why People Get Angry

Anger is felt when a situation is perceived as unfair or threatening, and the person angered feels helpless to rectify that situation (Margolis, 1986). Differences of opinions, values, and behaviors exacerbate these feelings. Coyle (2000) explains anger as a secondary feeling that follows frustration, unmet expectations, loss of self-respect, or fear. The anger is accompanied by anxiety and powerlessness, changing into feelings or actions of power and fight. Anger is directly proportional to a person's feeling of powerlessness. If you ask angry people to tell you what they want, you give them power, thereby reducing their feeling of powerlessness. And sometimes "people vent their anger at those giving them the most help because they feel comfortable directing it there. In most instances, angered people feel unjustly victimized and blame others for their pain and anguish" (Coyle, 2000, p. 43).

How to Deal with the Anger.   Unresolved conflict leads to anger, which undermines morale and thwarts productivity. It is important for the collaborative consultant to respond appropriately to angry people. A first rule is to address the problem rather than the person, then seek to find a shared goal with the angry person. Defer judgment and together explore options. When an angry person is loud and belligerent, speak more softly and calmly. Listen intently with responsiveness, not reaction.

Margolis (1986) recommends that educators learn about those who are angry and get to know them as people, not problems. When they meet with the angry person, they should succinctly state a general and slightly ambiguous purpose for the meeting and ask if that purpose is satisfactory. The tone must be empathic, with careful phrasing of questions and brief summaries at key points during the problem solving phase. The final summary with agreements and commitments should be written down to provide a record for later referral if necessary. Margolis reminds educators to congratulate all for what they have accomplished during the interaction.

Griffin (1998) has these suggestions for dealing with anger:

- Do nothing. Let the person vent. This will drain off some of the energy. Avoid telling the person to calm down; this only makes matters worse. Avoid telling the person to do anything to feel or behave in a certain way.
- After the first wave of rage is over, play it back, minus the rage. Try to understand the person, even if you are uncomfortable with the strong emotion.

■ Ask: "How would you like to resolve this?" Do what you can to transform an "I versus you" conversation into a "We versus the problem" dialogue.

Why Conflict Occurs in School Contexts

Conflict is an inevitable part of life. It occurs when there are unreconciled differences among people in terms of needs, values, goals, and personalities. If conflicting parties cannot give and take by integrating their views and utilizing their differences constructively, interpersonal conflicts will escalate. School consultants and collaborators are not exempt from the dysfunction that often accompanies conflict. So it is important for them to develop tools for transforming vague and ambiguous sources of conflict into identified problems that can be solved collaboratively. Lippitt (1983) suggests that conflict, as a predictable social phenomenon, should not be repressed, because there are many positive aspects to be valued. Conflict can help clarify issues, increase involvement, and promote growth, as well as strengthen relationships and organizational systems when the issues are resolved. Gordon (1977) contends it is undesirable to avoid conflict when there is genuine disagreement, because resentments build up, feelings get displaced, and unpleasantries such as backbiting, gossiping, and general discontent may result.

Teachers, administrators, and parents face many possible occasions for conflict when they are involved with educating children who have special needs. Some conflicts occur because there is too little information or because misunderstandings have been created from incorrect information. These instances are not difficult to resolve because they require only the communication of facts. Other areas of conflict arise from disagreement over teaching methods, assessment methods, goals, and values. Parent goals and teacher goals for the exceptional student may differ significantly, and support personnel may add even more dimensions to the conflict. For example, if a child is instructed by the reading specialist to read more slowly, urged by the learning disabilities teacher to read more rapidly, required by the classroom teacher to read a greater amount of material, and ordered by the parent to get better grades or *else,* effective communication is tenuous or nonexistent, and conflict is inevitable. Some conflict can even be beneficial if it clears the air of lingering disagreement and doubt so that conflicting parties can move ahead. But if differences cannot be resolved through formal or informal conflict-resolution processes, then relationships will surely disintegrate

Perhaps the most difficult area of conflict relates to values. When people have differing values about children, education, or educator roles within the learning context, effective communication is a challenging goal. As discussed earlier in this chapter, rapport-building, listening, and paraphrasing are significant in building relationships among those whose values conflict. The most important step is to listen courteously until a clear message about the value comes through, demonstrating respect for the value even if it conflicts with yours. Then it is time to assert one's own values, and along with the other person try to reach a common goal or seek a practical issue on which to begin problem solving.

How to Resolve School-Related Conflicts

Some conflicts, particularly those involving values, are difficult to prevent and may seem at the time to be irresolvable. However, if all can agree to common goals or common ground for discussion, conflicts can be resolved.

When emotions or conflict inhibit the communication process, first listen responsively and acknowledge what is being said. The other side appreciates the sense of being heard and understood, and the consultant will gain a vivid picture of their interests and concerns. A useful strategy is to focus on interests rather than positions as a way to circumvent potential conflicts during the communication process.

"Always think win/win" is one of Stephen Covey's (1989) seven habits of highly effective people and is a crucial element of effective relationships and problem solving in educational and community settings. If you can't come to a true win/win agreement, Covey suggests, it is better to go for no deal at all. This allows you to preserve the relationship and the possibility for a win/win pact in the future. Win/win agreements flow from solid relationships and taking time to develop a strong level of trust is essential for mutual collaboration. We must resist the urge to succeed at the expense of the other person. This forms a relationship that is open to success on both sides in the future.

Covey (1989) suggests a four-step process for the win/win approach:

1. Try to see the situation from the other person's perspective.
2. Identify the key issues and concerns involved.
3. Make a list of the results that you would consider a fully acceptable solution.
4. Look for new options to get those results.

Resolving conflicts within an "everybody wins" philosophy requires listening skills described earlier in the chapter to find common ground. In dealing with emotions of the speaker, the listener must concentrate with an open mind and attend to the speaker's feelings as well as the facts or ideas that are part of the message. The listener must strive to hear the whole story without interrupting, even if there are strong feelings of disagreement. Conflict usually means that intense emotions are involved. Only by concentrating on the message with an open mind can all parties begin to deal with the conflict. Emotional filters often function as blinders. If the emotions cannot be overcome, the best tactic is to postpone the communication, using assertive responses to do so.

Listening establishes a common intent and develops a starting attitude. Listening to one who is upset helps that person focus on a problem rather than on an emotion. Listening lets people cool down. Bolton (1986) calls this the spiral of resistance, suggesting that if one listens with empathy and does not interrupt, the speaker's anger or high emotion will dissipate. Without saying a word, the listener makes the speaker feel accepted and respected.

It is hard to argue with someone who does not argue back. It is hard to stay mad or upset with someone who seems to understand and empathize. Each time a person listens, a small victory for the advancement of human dignity has been achieved (Schlinder & Lapid, 1989). Only after emotions are brought into the open and recognized can all parties involved move on to seek a common goal.

The initial intent for resolving a conflict should be to learn. This enables all factions to increase mutual understanding and think creatively together. Most people could agree to such a start because it does not address goals or values. It does not even require agreement that a problem exists. It simply establishes the intent to learn by working together. Establishing intent for dialogue should follow the reduction of emotional responses. Of course, as discussed earlier, it is important to avoid roadblocks at all stages of the process.

Consultants and consulting teachers must put aside preconceived notions about their own expertise and learn from those who often know the student best—family members and classroom teachers. Such consultees respond positively to open-ended questions that let them know they are respected and needed. When consultants open their own minds, they unlock the potential of others.

APPLICATION 4.4

PRACTICE MAKES PERFECT, OR EASIER AT LEAST!

With a partner, practice the following ten uncomfortable or embarrassing situations. Use the Figures in this chapter as checklists to monitor verbal and nonverbal communication, for both sending and receiving.

1. Ask a person who drops by to come back later.
2. Say "no" to someone who is urging you to help with a project.
3. Answer the phone when you have about three things going on (voice tone and rate being particularly pertinent here).
4. Receive a compliment graciously.
5. Deliver a compliment so that it is not a distorted message.
6. Ask a colleague to please (for once!) be on time.
7. Enter a roomful of people who are probably unknown to you.
8. Respond when someone has interrupted you.
9. Break into the conversation when someone has monopolized the discussion to everyone's frustration.
10. Apologize for an oversight or ill-chosen remark you made.

Now, as you feel more confident in these real-life "peak" and "pit" situations, practice using them until they become second nature.

After listening constructively, consultants need to help establish ground rules for resolving the conflict. The ground rules should express support, mutual respect, and a commitment to the process. Again, this requires talking and listening, dialoguing, and keeping an open mind. It is important not to dominate the dialogue at this time, and by the same token not to let the other person dominate the conversation. This part of the communication might be called "agreeing to disagree," with the intent of "agreeing to find a point of agreement." It is important to share the allotted interaction time equitably and in a way that facilitates understanding. Consultants must use precise language without exaggerating points, or, as discussed earlier, flaunting educationese or taking inappropriate shortcuts with jargon and alphabet soup acronyms.

Dealing with conflict productively also requires asserting one's ideas, feelings, or opinions. While listening enables the consultant to understand the speaker's perspectives, wants, and goals, assertion skills allow consultants to present their perspective. This often follows a pattern of listen—assert—listen—assert—listen, and so on, until both parties have spoken and have been heard.

FIGURE 4.4   Checklist for Managing Resistance and Conflict

A. *Responsive Listening*

    1. Had assertive posture   _____

    2. Used appropriate nonverbal listening   _____

    3. Did not become defensive   _____

    4. Used minimal verbals in listening   _____

    5. Reflected content   _____

    6. Reflected feelings   _____

    7. Let others do most of the talking   _____

    8. Used only brief, clarifying questions   _____

B. *Assertiveness*

    9. Did not use roadblocks such as giving advice   _____

   10. Used "I" messages   _____

   11. Stated wants and feelings   _____

C. *Recycled the interaction*

   12. Used positive postponement   _____

   13. Did not problem-solve before emotions were controlled   _____

   14. Summarized   _____

   15. Set time to meet again, if applicable   _____

Although there may be resistance after each assertion, it will gradually dissipate so that *real* communication and collaboration can begin to take place. Only after this process has happened can collaborative goal setting and problem solving occur. Figure 4.4. summarizes useful steps for managing resistance and conflict.

There is a well-known story of a man who had three sons. He stipulated in his will that the oldest son should inherit half his camels, the middle son should get one-third of the camels, and the youngest should be the new owner of one-ninth of his camels. When the old man died, he owned seventeen camels. But the sons could not agree on how to divide the camels in accordance with their father's will. Months and months of bitter conflict went by. Finally the three young men sought the advice of a wise woman in the village. She heard their complaints and observed their bitterness, and felt sorry that brothers were fighting and putting the family into turmoil. So she gave the brothers one of her camels. The estate then was divided easily according to the father's wishes. The eldest took home nine camels, the second put six camels beside his tent, and the youngest took home two camels. The men were happy, the father's last wishes were honored, and the wise woman took her own camel back and led it home.

Conflict management is the process of becoming aware of a conflict, diagnosing its nature, and employing an appropriate problem solving method in such a way that it simultaneously achieves the goals of all involved and enhances relationships among them. If the consulting relationship is treated as a collaborative one in which each person's needs are met (the win/win model), then feelings of self-confidence, competence, self-worth and power increase, enhancing the overall capacity of the system for responding to conflict in the future. The win/win relationship is based on honesty, trust, and mutual respect—qualities stressed earlier as vital to a successful consulting relationship. Win/win allows all involved parties to experience positive outcomes. The model works best when all parties use effective communication skills (Fisher & Ury, 1991).

The opposite of successful conflict management is avoiding conflict, ignoring feelings, and bypassing the goals of others. The relationship becomes adversarial, if it is not already so, because for someone to win, another must lose. When conflicts are approached with responsive listening and dealt with honestly and openly, the underlying problem or need can be resolved.

What to Do When Communication Goes Wrong

Fisher and Sharp (1991) also have suggestions for diagnosing setbacks in the collaboration process. Many collaboration setbacks can be traced to four problems:

1. *Telling others what to think or do.* Telling does not inspire others to learn new behavior or adopt new attitudes. Telling someone what to do implies they have a lower status, and in fact, some see it as an accusation. They might respond, "Are you telling me how to do my job?" Telling your collaborators what to do fails to promote understanding of the problems and the perspectives involved. Team members who have not participated in the thinking about a problem have no ownership in the solution. Empower others by helping them see they can make a difference.

2. *Mistaking the person for the problem.* Collaborators must separate the person from the problem and acknowledge good reasons for the other's behaviors. Often this can be an empathic response such as "I know you've been swamped with all those IEP meetings as well as getting ready for the Special Olympics. We really need your input on this grant proposal."

3. *Blaming others.* There is a universal human tendency to blame others for problems; but this is a dead-end attitude for the consultant. Focus on your own actions; if partners don't react the way you want or expect, start with the assumption that you are doing something wrong.

4. *Having faulty working assumptions.* Some consultants make assumptions when working with teachers, community agencies, or families. Examples of working assumptions that inhibit successful collaboration include ideas like: the problems are someone else's fault; there's not much I can do to change the behavior of others; the situation is impossible, so it's best if I just ignore it; and if it didn't work before, don't try again. Successful consultants work to identify faulty working assumptions and to change them to healthier and more positive assumptions, such as: perhaps I can make a difference; the easiest way to change the behavior of others is to change my own; I can choose to help; and thoughtful persistence pays off.

When engineers stress collaboration, they often use the bumblebee analogy. According to the laws of aerodynamics, bumblebees cannot fly. But as everyone knows, they do. By the same token some might say that groups cannot function productively because of the conflicts, personal agendas, and individual preferences that exist among the members. But they do. Groups of people play symphonies, set up businesses, write laws, and develop IEPs for student needs. An understanding of adult individual differences, styles, and preferences, as discussed in Chapter 2, will encourage participants in consultation and collaboration to listen more respectfully and value differences among colleagues. This knowledge, when combined with responsive listening, avoidance of roadblocks, and assertiveness, will enable consultants to deal with resistance and conflict productively. Conflict management puts these skills to practical use in educational settings of school and home.

Educational consultants maximize their effect on the lives and education of children with special needs by using good communication skills. They should always keep in mind the ancient rule we instill in children for crossing the street: "Stop, Look, and Listen." For the collaborative school consultant it means:

- Stop talking, judging, and giving advice.
- Look at the long-term outcome of good communication (keep eyes on the prize).
- Listen to parents, colleagues and others who work in collaboration for children with special needs.

The stop, look, and listen rule sets up consultants for success—in establishing collaborative relationships, in developing rapport, in dealing with conflict and emotions, and in solving problems.

COMMUNICATING ETHICALLY IN COLLABORATIVE WAYS

Effective communication skills form the basis of respectful, egalitarian relationships within an ethical climate that best serves students with special needs. Verbal and nonverbal skills pave the way to effective problem solving and mutual collaboration.

It is often helpful to write down what one plans to say to a teacher or a parent, and note what the effects of different options might be (Laud, 1998). Novice teachers and more experienced teachers who are still honing their communication skills could keep a log for recording selected interactions, analyzing them, and reflecting on alternative ways to communicate if those interactions were not productive.

Along similar lines, when sending written communication, select words and expressions carefully. When in doubt, it is a good idea to have a colleague read your communication before it is sent on its way. A helpful recipe to keep in mind is to set aside anger or frustration, begin the note on a positive tone, state the problem or concern carefully and objectively in the middle of the communication, and conclude with additional positive words.

Listening instead of arguing, establishing ground rules that are considerate of the values and opinions of others, and working toward common goals and expectations for student success will help bring teams to the problem-finding and problem-solving stages with parity and respect. Consultants who remain calm and listen—always listen—will be "hearing their way to success" and helping to create an ethical and collaborative climate.

TIPS FOR COMMUNICATING EFFECTIVELY

1. Avoid communication roadblocks. Research shows that positively worded statements are one-third easier to understand than negative ones (Rinke, 1997).
2. Listen. This helps dissipate negative emotional responses and often helps the other person articulate the problem, perhaps finding a solution then and there.
3. Use assertion. Say what you feel and what your goals are.
4. Be aware of your hot buttons. Knowing your own responses to certain trigger behaviors and words will help you control natural tendencies to argue, get defensive, or simply turn red and sputter.
5. Attend to nonverbal language (kinesics, or body language) as well as to verbal language when communicating.
6. Don't "dump your bucket" of frustrations onto the other person. Jog, shout, practice karate, but avoid pouring out anger and frustration on others. Instead, fill the buckets of others with "warm fuzzies" of empathy and caring.
7. Develop a protocol within the school context for dealing with difficult issues and for settling grievances.
8. Deal with the present. Keep to the issue of the current problem rather than past problems, failures, or personality conflicts.
9. Use understanding of individual differences among adults to bridge communication gaps and manage conflicts in educational settings.
10. Advocate for training that focuses on communication, problem solving, and conflict management.

CHAPTER REVIEW

1. The primary reason people fail in collaborative efforts is because of communication problems. It is too often assumed that communication skill develops with no special attention to the complexities of social interaction.

2. The sender, message, receiver, and medium are four key components of the communication process. Each component is vital. When a message is missent or misheard, many distortions occur which prevent open, honest communication. This happens because of differences in values, language, attitudes, perceptions, gender, ethnicity, and history of sender and receiver.

3. Rapport building requires respect for differences in others, trust, feeling all right about not having all the answers, and being comfortable even when there is disagreement.

4. Major skills in effective communication are responsive listening, asserting, managing conflict, and collaborative problem solving. Both verbal and nonverbal components are included in these skills.

5. Communication can be hampered by verbal roadblocks and nonverbal roadblocks. Verbal roadblocks include responses that are judging, responses that send solutions, and responses that avoid the concerns of others. Nonverbal roadblocks include body language that conveys lack of empathy and concern.

6. Assertive communication allows speakers to state their own views, feelings, and opinions without impeding the ongoing consulting process. Assertiveness means stating one's wants or feelings by starting sentences with "I," using "and" rather than "but," and showing

concern for the other person. Resistance can be managed by using a combination of assertiveness and responsive listening. Resistance, anger, and negativity are residuals of disagreements and unwanted change. Conflict arises when members of educational teams have different feelings, values, needs, and goals. Conflict resolution should follow a win/win model if collaborative efforts are to be maintained.

TO DO AND THINK ABOUT

1. Discuss the following:

    What type of roadblock does each of these comments set up?

    > What you need is more activity. Why don't you develop a hobby?

    > You are such a good friend. I can count on you.

    > Let's talk about something more positive.

    > I know just how you feel.

    > Why did you let her talk to you that way?

    Which of these lines create resistance and defensiveness?

    > What you should do is . . .

    > Do you want to comment on this?

    > Everyone has problems like that.

    > That's a good thought.

    > You mean you'd actually do that?

    > Let's change the subject.

    > What should I do?

    What assertive statements could be made for each situation?

    > A colleague talks to you about his personal problems and you can't get your work done.

    > The paraeducator comes in late frequently.

    > During a committee meeting one member keeps changing the subject and getting the group off-task.

    > A colleague wants to borrow some material but has failed to return things in the past.

    > During a phone conversation with a wordy parent, you need to get some information quickly and hang up soon.

    > The class next door is so rowdy that your class can't work.

2. Discuss these basic assumptions about communication for consultation and add more to the list.

    > The reactions of others depend on your actions, word choices, body language, and listening skills.

    > People generally want to do a good job.

    > People have a powerful need to "save face."

    > No one can force another person to change.

    > Learning to communicate, be assertive, and facilitate conflict resolution is awkward at first.

3. Make a list of phrases that can be "hot buttons" in the school context. Then practice reacting to each one with a colleague who understands your purpose and will say them to you. Note your body language and the body language of your partner. Then discuss how these phrases might help or hinder the collaborative process.

4. Practice the following situations:

    > Expressing anger in constructive ways

    > Getting the interaction back on-task

    > Stating a contrasting view to a supervisor

    > Recommending a better way of doing something

    > Asking again, and again, for materials you loaned some time ago that you need now

5. Restate the following messages so the language is assertive but nonthreatening to the receiver.

    > "You penalize gifted students when you keep the class lockstepped in the basal texts and the workbooks."

    > "If you want students to use good note-taking skills, you should teach them how to take notes."

    > "Not allowing students to use calculators is terribly outmoded."

    > "It is not fair to insist that students with learning disabilities take tests they cannot read."

ADDITIONAL READINGS AND RESOURCES

Bolton, R. (1986). *People skills: How to assert yourself, listen to others, and resolve conflicts.* New York: Simon & Schuster.

Fisher, R., & Sharp, A. (1999). *Getting it DONE: How to lead when you're not in charge.* New York: HarperCollins.

Fisher, R., Ury, B., & Patton, B. (1991). *Getting to YES: Negotiating agreement without giving in.* Boston: Houghton Mifflin.

Lynch, E. W., & Hanson, M. J. (1998). *Developing cross-cultural competence: A guide for working with children and their families* (2nd ed.). Baltimore: Paul H. Brooks.

Stone, D., Patton, B., & Heen, S. (1999). *Difficult conversations: How to discuss what matters most.* New York: Random House.

CHAPTER FIVE

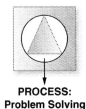

PROCESS:
Problem Solving

Problem-Solving Strategies for Collaborative Consultation and Teamwork

Using a structured process for collaborative school consultation is like preparing food according to a recipe. After the fundamentals of cooking have been mastered, one can adapt those procedures to just about any setting, preference, or creative impulse. In similar fashion, a basic "recipe" for consultation and collaboration can be adapted to any school context, grade level, content area, or special learning need. Just as a recipe should be adaptable for individual preferences, so should a collaborative consultation structure be flexible and adaptable to fit the needs of individual students in their school contexts.

A collaborative style is based on valuing and trusting one another. When educators exercise ingenuity in constructing teaching and learning strategies collaboratively, schools are better contexts in which all can perform at their best. Collaborative school consultation is an ideal scenario for incorporating problem-solving techniques that cultivate flexible, divergent thinking. Teamwork builds esprit de corps.

FOCUSING QUESTIONS

1. What are fundamental components in a problem-solving process?

2. Why is problem identification so important in collaborative consultation?

3. What basic steps should be included in the collaborative school consultation process?

4. What kinds of things should consultants and consultees say and do during their professional interactions?

5. What problem-solving techniques are particularly helpful for collaborative consultation and teamwork?

6. What are interferences and hurdles that must be overcome when problem solving with co-educators?

142 From Chapter 5 of *Collaboration, Consultation, and Teamwork for Students with Special Needs*, 6/e. Peggy Dettmer. Linda P. Thurston. Ann Knackendoffel. Norma J. Dyck. Copyright © 2009 by Pearson Merrill. All rights reserved.

KEY TERMS

brainstorming	jigsaw	problem-solving process
concept mapping (webbing)	lateral thinking	SCAMPER
follow through	metaphorical thinking	Six Thinking Hats
follow up	multiple intelligences	synectics
idea checklist	Plus-Minus-Interesting (PMI)	synergism
Janusian thinking	problem identification	TalkWalk

SCENARIO 5.A

The setting is the office area of an elementary school, where a special education staff member has just checked into the building and meets a fourth-grade teacher.

Classroom Teacher: I understand you're going to be a consulting teacher in our building to work with learning and behavior disorders.

Consulting Teacher: That's right. I hope to meet with all of the staff very soon to find out your needs and how we can work together to address those needs.

Classroom Teacher: Well I, for one, am glad you're here. I have a student who is driving me and my other twenty-four students up the wall.

Consulting Teacher: How so?

Classroom Teacher: Well, since she moved here a few weeks ago she's really upset the classroom system that I've used for years, and used quite successfully, I might add.

Consulting Teacher: Is she having trouble with the material you teach?

Classroom Teacher: No, she's a bright child who finishes everything in good time, and usually does it correctly. But she's extremely active, almost frenetic as she "busy-bodies" around the room.

Consulting Teacher: What specific behaviors concern you?

Classroom Teacher: Well, for one thing she tries to help everyone else when they should be doing their own work. I've worked a lot on developing independent learning skills in my students, and they've made good progress. They don't need to have her tell them what to do.

Consulting Teacher: So her behavior keeps her classmates from being the self-directed learners that they can be?

Classroom Teacher: Right. I have to monitor her activities constantly, which means diverting my attention from all the other students. She bosses her classmates in the learning centers and even on the playground. At this rate she will soon be having serious difficulties with peer relationships.

Consulting Teacher: Which of those behaviors would you like to see changed first?

Classroom Teacher: Well, I need to get her settled into some activities by herself rather than bothering other students.

Consulting Teacher: What have you tried until now to keep her involved with her own work?

Classroom Teacher: I explain to her what I expect, and then try to reinforce appropriate behavior with things she likes to do.

Consulting Teacher: We could make a list of specific changes in behavior you'd like to see, and work out a program to accomplish them. In fact, the technique of webbing might help us explore the possibilities. How about doing one together on this chart paper? Then we will have a record of our ideas. (Consultant and teacher work together to make the web and begin a plan.) . . . There's the bell. Want to meet tomorrow to add any second thoughts to our chart and finalize this plan?

Classroom Teacher: Sounds good. I'd like to get her on track so the class is more settled. Then other children will like her better and she'll be able to learn other things, too. We could meet right here tomorrow, if that's OK with you. It helps a lot to have someone to talk with about this and work out a plan.

THE PROBLEM-SOLVING PROCESS

Educators must exercise perception and judgment in order to ascertain student needs, set reasonable goals, and select the most efficient means addressing those needs and goals. This requires development and implementation of effective problem-solving skills. Problem-solving ability comes more naturally and easily to some than to others. There is no one specific formula or "recipe." Furthermore, problem-solving strategies, particularly as used by groups, can be improved with training and practice.

Pugach and Johnson (1995) suggest that co-educators configure two general categories for problem solving in the context of teacher collaboration: (1) schoolwide problems, and (2) specific student problems. Full inclusion is an example of schoolwide problem solving undertaken in a collaborative way by all school staff. The second category, that of specific student needs, is more commonly dealt with by teachers in a problem-solving mode. Both categories of problems provide an opportunity to broaden the educational options for students with special needs.

In order to address both schoolwide problems and specific student needs, it is helpful to begin with a study of the fundamental problem-solving process. These components are key steps in solving problems effectively and they frame most problem-solving models:

- Data-gathering as guided by the "mess" for which a solution is being sought
- Identification and definition of the problem (*extremely* important)
- Generation of possible actions toward solution
- Critique of proposed actions
- Decision making to select best option(s)
- Implementing the elements of the decision
- Following up to evaluate the outcome(s)

Communicating in Problem-Solving Teams

A problem-solving process that encourages high levels of communication and collaboration will allow educators to share their expertise related to the problem. Learning and behavior problems are not always outcomes of student disabilities. Many students are simply "curriculum-disabled" (Conoley, 1985), requiring a modified or expanded approach to existing curriculum in order to function successfully in school (Pugach & Johnson, 1990). To modify the settings for learning and make accommodations in the educational environment, educators must identify those aspects of students' educational curriculum that are impeding their development.

Delineating the Problem.   The first and most critical step in a problem-solving process is to identify the problem (Bolton, 1986). The most sophisticated teaching methods and the most expensive instructional materials are worthless if student needs are misidentified or overlooked. It can even be argued that inaccurate definition of the problem situation has potential for iatrogenic effects. These effects hurt more than help, just as identifying an illness incorrectly can result in inappropriate treatment and delay or deny use of a better treatment, or perhaps even introduce a harmful one.

Problem identification requires special emphasis if the consultation process is to produce results. Bergan (1995) stresses that when problem identification is successful, the consultation is much more likely to come to a successful conclusion.

Multisourced information about student needs provides a more accurate perspective on learning and behavior problems, along with information about the settings in which they are demonstrated, the severity and frequency of the problems, and the persons who are most affected by those behaviors (Polsgrove & McNeil, 1989). Obtaining information from multiple sources requires effective communication skills by all who can contribute information. See Figure 5.1 to identify sixteen possible data sources.

Communication is such an important aspect of successful school consultation that it was addressed separately in Chapter 4. Expressing thoughts and feelings with clarity and accuracy requires effective listening and appropriate assertiveness. A problem will never be solved if all parties think they are working on different issues. Problems are like artichokes—they come in layers. Only after the outside layers are stripped away can problem solvers get to the heart of the matter. Good listening facilitates movement to the heart of the problem.

Co-educators must examine their own perspectives and preferences to identify any potential aspects that will impede their abilities to problem-solve for the student's needs. The four major interfering themes outlined by Caplan (1970) and introduced in Chapter 3 are revisited here to stress their potential impact on the educator's ability to listen effectively and think divergently on the student's behalf. They are:

1. Lack of understanding about the problem and relevant processes of instruction and learning
2. Lack of skills in posing options for courses of action that could be taken
3. Lack of self-confidence in addressing the situation and dealing with it
4. Lack of professional objectivity when former experiences or beliefs get in the way and have undue influence

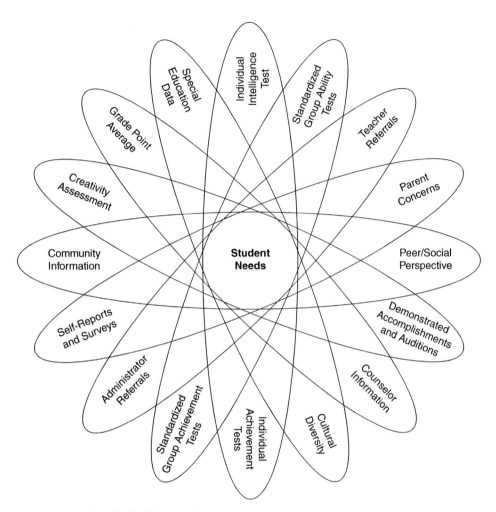

FIGURE 5.1 Case Study Information

Generating Possibilities. Problem solving also involves generating ideas for solutions. Divergent thinking is important to avoid getting stuck in routines and answers. Some consultants find it helpful to encourage the person who "owns" the problem to make the most suggestions. For example, if the problem is making a decision about postsecondary education for a student with learning disabilities, the student and the parents should be encouraged to generate the most options. This is important for several reasons. When people participate in decision making, they feel more ownership of the results than when the decision is forced on them. People are more apt to support decisions they helped create than those imposed on them.

An important second reason for prompting the owner of the problem to give initial suggestions is that consultants should avoid giving advice and being perceived as the expert. Several researchers have shown that a nonexpert approach to educational consulting is especially effective in special education (Idol-Maestes, Lloyd, & Lilly, 1981; Margolis & McGettigan, 1988). The suggestions and opinions of all others need to be listened to with respect and fully understood before additional suggestions are offered.

Problems that come up in school consultation often reveal the need for changes in classroom practices. (Recall that resistance was discussed in Chapter 4.) Advice giving and hierarchical structure may be unintentionally communicated if consultants promote the options generated as being their ideas. Furthermore, if a consultant is regarded as *the* expert, there is pressure on that consultant and false expectations are created. It is hard to win in this kind of situation. The best practice for the collaborating consultant is to communicate equality, flexibility, and a sharing attitude. Three questions assess the equality that is or is not present in a professional consulting relationship:

1. Does the consultant give recognition to the consultee's expertise and opinions?
2. Does the consultant encourage the consultee to generate ideas and make decisions?
3. Do consultees feel free to *not* do as the consultant might recommend?

Eager, competent consultants, who are ready to solve problems and produce quick results, instant cures, and dramatic increases, too often jump in and try to solve problems alone. Consultees may react with resistance or negativism, or perhaps even hostility, by hiding their feelings and withdrawing, blaming others if things do not work out.

It can be difficult for consultants to avoid the "quick fix." But a quick fix is inappropriate (DeBoer, 1986), and it is demeaning to the person who has been struggling with the problem. Others need to feel that the consultant fully understands their unique situation and the source of their frustrations before they are ready to participate in problem solving and listen to the suggestions of colleagues. Consultants must listen before they can expect to be listened to and treated with parity or approached voluntarily by consultees.

All learning situations and all students are unique. In response to a question about classroom management, a wise high school teacher replied, "I don't know all the answers, because I haven't seen all the kids." While students and situations may appear similar in some ways, the combinations of student, teacher, parents, and school and home contexts are unique for each problem. Furthermore, in many cases, people with problems already have their answers. They just need help to clarify issues or an empathic ear to face the emotional aspects of the concern. If people keep talking, they often can solve their own problems. Joint problem identification and idea generating ensures that professional relationships are preserved. Then professional communication is enhanced and professionals maintain a greater feeling of control and self-esteem.

Good collaborative consultants do not "solve" problems—they see that problems get solved. So they facilitate problem solving and "nix the quick fix." As Gordon (1977) asks, Whose problem is it? Who *really* owns the problem? Busy consultants do not need to take on the problems of others, and such action would inhibit consultees from learning and practicing problem-solving skills. Everyone who owns a part of the problem should participate in solving it. That may involve collaboration among several people—teachers, administrators, vocational counselors, social workers, justice system personnel, students, parents, and others. Consultants and consultees should focus on the problem rather than on establishing

FIGURE 5.2 Problem-Solving Process Guide Form

Problem: _____

Expected Outcome: _____

Options	Consequences
1. _____	_____
2. _____	_____
3. _____	_____
4. _____	_____
5. _____	_____
6. _____	_____

Chosen Solution: _____

Responsibilities and Commitments: _____

Follow-Up Date and Time: _____

Source: Linda P. Thurston. Used with permission.

ownership for the problem. All individuals will need to attend carefully to minimizing roadblocks and maximizing assertion and listening skills.

A record sheet for taking notes on the ideas generated can help collaborators communicate effectively and think divergently. Notes taken on problem, options, and consequences are a problem-solving guide and the responsibilities section is a record of expectations and commitments. (See Figure 5.2.) Also, Garmston (1995) recommends providing a rationale to participants in collaboration before initiating the group activity, then inserting a few moments for reflection and journaling after the activity and before the summarizing group discussion.

Implementing Agreed-On Plans. The problem-solving group selects a workable solution all are willing to adopt, at least on a trial or experimental basis. The consultant promotes mutual participation in the decision. Group members more readily accept new ideas and new work methods when they are given opportunity to participate in decision making (Gordon, 1977). Many times a complex problem can be solved as each person in the group discovers what the others really want or, perhaps, dread. Then proposed solutions can be formulated to meet the goals and protect the concerns of all involved.

Better decisions are made with a cool head and a warm heart (Johnson, 1992). Johnson suggests asking oneself if the decision helps meet the *real* need. Real needs are based on reality, not illusion or wishful thinking. Co-educators should ask, Did we have enough information to create options we may not have realized before this? Have we thought through the consequences of each option? Have we *really* thought through all the options? Taking time to ask all the necessary questions is a key to the decision-making process. Asking many questions helps make options and choices obvious.

Effective consultants facilitate problem solving in such a way that all members of the group feel their needs are being satisfied, and an equitable social and professional relationship is being maintained (Gordon, 1977). Members of the problem-solving team work together to evaluate all the suggestions made, with each presenting disadvantages and merits of the suggestions from their own perspectives. Agreement is not necessary at this point, because the barriers and merits important to each person are taken into account. Honest and open communication, using good listening skills, and an appropriate level of assertiveness are vital at this step.

Following Through and Following Up.   After sorting through data, scheduling and arranging meetings, planning agenda, facilitating and participating in the meeting, it is tempting to breathe a sigh of relief when the agreed-on plan is ready for implementation and go on to other things. But collaborators, busy as they are, must follow through on the progress of the plan and follow up with co-educators who are carrying it out and students for whom the plan was made. If the follow-up process suggests no progress has been made or unexpected problems have surfaced, the problem-solving activity should be repeated.

Problem-Solving Roles

In collaborative problem solving, the role of the consultant is to facilitate interaction and teamwork with understanding, skill, objectivity, and self-confidence. Collaborative school consultation encourages collective thinking for creative and imaginative alternatives and allows all who are involved to have their feelings and ideas heard and their goals addressed in practical ways. The ultimate goal is to provide the best learning opportunities possible for students with special needs. At this point it may be helpful to review the descriptions of consultation, collaboration, and teamwork as personified through several examples differentiating these three interactive processes.

Problem Solving through Consultation.   A preschool teacher is concerned about a child in the group who is not fluent in speech. So the teacher asks the speech pathologist to help determine what to do about it. The speech pathologist consults with the teacher and the child's family, getting more information about the observed behavior, and makes additional observations. The consultant then uses his expertise in speech pathology to address the questions and concerns of the teacher and the family.

In another instance, a physical therapist provides individual therapy for a preschool child who has cerebral palsy. The therapist wants to know about the child's social development as well as performance in preacademic skills such as letter recognition and sound discrimination. The therapist asks the teacher to serve as a consultant regarding this issue, and the preschool teacher provides the information requested.

Problem Solving through Collaboration. The kindergarten teacher and the music teacher are both concerned about a child's tendency to masturbate during group time while sitting on the rug. The two teachers meet to discuss their mutual concern. Both parties discuss their observations and engage in problem-solving activities to identify the problem clearly and select possible actions. Both parties agree to make some changes in their respective settings to address the problem. If the solutions do not work, they are committed to try other possibilities, including consultation with the child's parents. the school psychologist, and the health nurse.

In another situation, a teacher of students with behavioral disorders, along with the school counselor, three classroom teachers, and a student's parents, meet to discuss the behavior of that student. The individuals involved in the meeting engage in collaborative problem solving to formulate a plan for addressing the problem. Each individual has a role to play in defining the problem, generating possible actions, and implementing the plan.

Problem Solving through Teamwork. A special education teacher and a general classroom teacher engage in co-teaching, a form of teamwork unique to classroom settings. The teachers meet weekly to engage in co-planning. During the co-planning they decide when, where, and how to share responsibilities for meeting the instructional needs of all students in the classroom during a specified class period each day. Each teacher uses his or her areas of expertise and strength whenever feasible. The co-teachers come to consensus on evaluation systems and assign grades for all students by mutual agreement. They no longer speak of "my students" or "your students" and instead they speak of, plan for, and teach "our students."

In another situation, a team of professionals provides services for infants and toddlers with severe or profound disabilities. Each professional has an area of expertise and responsibility. The social worker has the leadership role because she is responsible for most family contacts and often goes into homes to provide additional assistance for families. The nurse takes responsibility for monitoring the physical well being of each child and keeps in close contact with other medical personnel and families. The speech pathologist works with the children to develop speech and language skills. The occupational therapist is responsible for teaching the children self-help skills. The physical therapist follows through with the medical doctor's prescribed physical therapy. Special education teachers provide language stimulation and modeling, coordinate schedules, and facilitate communication among the team that meets twice weekly to discuss individual cases.

TEN-STEP PROCESS FOR COLLABORATIVE PROBLEM SOLVING

Now that the fundamentals of a typical problem-solving process have been discussed, and distinctions have been made among (1) problem solving with a major focus on consultation, (2) problem solving that emphasizes collaboration, and (3) problem solving as a team, a ten-step process for collaborative school consultation will be introduced. This process,

FIGURE 5.3   The Ten-Step Process for Collaborative School Consultation

1. *Prepare for the consultation.*
   1.1 Focus on major topic or area of concern.
   1.2 Prepare and organize materials.
   1.3 Prepare several possible actions or strategies.
   1.4 Arrange for a comfortable, convenient meeting place.

2. *Initiate the consultation.*
   2.1 Establish rapport.
   2.2 Identify the agenda.
   2.3 Focus on the tentatively defined concern.
   2.4 Express interest in the needs of all.

3. *Collect and organize relevant information.*
   3.1 Make notes of data, soliciting from all.
   3.2 Combine and summarize the data.
   3.3 Assess data to focus on areas needing more information.
   3.4 Summarize the information.

4. *Isolate the problem.*
   4.1 Focus on need.
   4.2 State what the problem is.
   4.3 State what it is not.
   4.4 Propose desirable circumstances.

5. *Identify concerns and realities about the problem.*
   5.1 Encourage all to listen to each concern.
   5.2 Identify issues, avoiding jargon.
   5.3 Encourage ventilation of frustrations and concerns.
   5.4 Keep focusing on the pertinent issues and needs.
   5.5 Check for agreement.

6. *Generate solutions.*
   6.1 Engage in collaborative problem-solving.
   6.2 Generate several possible options and alternatives.
   6.3 Suggest examples of appropriate classroom modifications.
   6.4 Review options, discussing consequences of each.
   6.5 Select the most reasonable alternatives.

7. *Formulate a plan.*
   7.1 Designate those who will be involved, and how.
   7.2 Set goals.
   7.3 Establish responsibilities.
   7.4 Generate evaluation criteria and methods.
   7.5 Agree on a date for reviewing progress.
   7.6 Follow through on all commitments.

8. *Evaluate progress and process.*
   8.1 Conduct a review session at a specified time.
   8.2 Review data and analyze the results.
   8.3 Keep products as evidence of progress.
   8.4 Make positive, supportive comments.
   8.5 Assess contribution of the collaboration.

9. *Follow through and follow up on the consultation about the situation.*
   9.1 Reassess periodically to assure maintenance.
   9.2 Provide positive reinforcement.
   9.3 Plan further action or continue the plan.
   9.4 Adjust the plan if there are problems.
   9.5 Initiate further consultation if needed.
   9.6 Bring closure if goals have been met.
   9.7 Support effort and reinforce results.
   9.8 Share information where it is wanted.
   9.9 Enjoy the pleasure of having the communication.

10. *Repeat or continue consultation as appropriate.*

outlined in Figure 5.3, will help consultants and consultees communicate effectively and coordinate their efforts efficiently so that they can identify educational problems and design programs for students' needs.

Step 1: Preparing for the Collaborative Consultation.   As consultants plan and prepare for consultation and collaboration, they focus on the major areas of concern. They prepare helpful materials and organize them in order to use collaborative time efficiently. It is useful to distribute information beforehand so that valuable interaction time is not consumed reading new material. But they must take care to present that material as tentative and still open to discussion. It is not always expedient to plan in great detail prior to consultations.

Sometimes consultations happen informally and without notice—between classes, during lunch periods, or on playgrounds. While educators usually will want to accommodate colleagues on these occasions, they also need to look beyond them for opportunities to engage in more in-depth sessions.

Consultants need to give each collaborator enough advance notice and time to prepare. They will want to provide convenient and comfortable settings for the interaction, arranging seating so there is a collegial atmosphere with no phone or drop-by interruptions, and privacy is ensured. Serving coffee and tea can help set congenial, collegial climates for meetings. (See Figure 5.3.)

Step 2: Initiating the Collaborative Interaction. Consultants need to make a significant effort in this phase. When resistance to consulting is high, or the teaching staff has been particularly reluctant to collaborate, it is difficult to establish first contacts. This is the time to begin with the most receptive staff members in order to build in success for the consulting program. Rapport is established by addressing every consultee as special and expressing interest in what each one is doing and feeling. Teachers should be encouraged to talk about their successes. The consultant needs to display sensitivity to teachers' needs and make each one feel important. The key is to *listen.*

The consultant will want to identify the agenda and keep focusing on the concern. It is helpful to have participants write down their concerns before the meeting and bring them along. Then the consultant can check quickly for congruence and major disagreements. (Again, and with the remaining eight steps, consult Figure 5.3.)

Step 3: Collecting and Organizing Information. The data should be relevant to the issue of focus. However, data that might seem irrelevant to one person may be the very information needed to identify the real problem. So the consultant must be astute in selecting appropriate data that include many possibilities but do not waste time or resources. This becomes easier with experience, but for new consultants, having too much information is probably better than having too little. However, time is limited and must be used judiciously.

Since problem identification seems to be the most significant factor in planning for special needs, it is wise to gather sufficient data from multiple sources. A case study method of determining data sources and soliciting information is particularly effective in planning for students who have special learning and behavior needs. Refer again to Figure 5.1 for identifying up to sixteen data sources of information for problem solving to address a student's needs. The more of the sixteen that are tapped, the more easily and clearly the need is understood.

Step 4: Isolating the Problem. As discussed earlier, the most critical aspect of problem solving involves identifying and defining the problem at hand by focusing on the need, not the handy solution. Without problem identification, problem solving cannot occur (Bergan, 1995; Bergan & Tombari, 1976). The most common problem-solving error is to short-circuit the problem definition step and hasten to traditional solutions rather than developing individually tailored solutions (Conoley, 1989, p. 248). Henning-Stout (1994) notes that less experienced consultants in particular tend to spend insufficient time with the consultee on the nature of the problem and proceed too quickly to developing "the plan."

Step 5: Identifying Concerns and Stating Realities Relevant to the Problem.   All concerns and viewpoints related to the problem should be aired and shared by each participant. A different viewpoint is not better or worse, just different. An effective consultant keeps participants focusing on student needs by listening and encouraging everyone to respond. However, a certain amount of venting and frustration is to be expected and accepted. Teachers and parents will demonstrate less resistance when they know they are free to express their feelings without retaliation or judgment. Consultants should remain nonjudgmental and ensure confidentiality, always talking and listening in consultees' language.

As information is shared, the consultant will want to make notes. It is good to have everyone look over the recorded information from time to time during the consultation as a demonstration of trust and parity, as well as a check on accuracy. (A log format for recording information and documenting the consultation will be provided in Figure 6.8, on p. 199.)

Step 6: Generating Options.   Now is the time for creative problem solving. If ideas do not come freely, or if participants are blocking productive thinking, the consultant might lead the group in trying one or more of the techniques described later in the chapter. A problem-solving technique not only unleashes ideas, it also sends a message about the kind of behavior that is needed to solve the problem. Straw votes can be taken periodically if that helps the group keep moving toward solutions. Thinking outside the box and combining ideas are desirable processes at this stage. Two productive activities are to have brief discussions focusing on benefits and on concerns. These two sharing periods should be initiated with the word stems such as "I like. . ." (where the benefits are shared), and "I wish. . ." or "How to. . ." (where the concerns are shared). At this stage the group should modify, dismiss, or problem-solve for each concern.

Step 7: Formulating the Plan.   After options have been generated, wishes and concerns aired, and modifications made, the revised option is ready to be formulated into a plan. Participants must remain on-task. They need to be reinforced positively for their contributions. Consultants will want to be ready to make suggestions, but they should defer presenting them so long as others are suggesting and volunteering. They must avoid offering ideas prematurely or addressing too many issues at one time. Other unhelpful behaviors are assuming the supervisor/expert role, introducing one's own biases, and making suggestions that conflict with existing values in the school context.

As the plan develops, the consultant must make clear just who will do what, and when, and where. Evaluation criteria and methods that are congruent with the goals and plan should be developed at this time, and arrangements made for assessment and collection of data on student progress. A vital element to success in collaborative problem solving will be the commitment by *all* participants to follow through with the plan, an activity that will appear as Step 9.

Step 8: Evaluating Progress and Process.   This step and the final two steps frequently are overlooked. Consultation and collaborative decision making should be followed by assessment of student progress resulting from the collaborative plan, and also by evaluation of the collaborative consultation process itself. (Several figures in Chapter 6 are useful for this purpose.)

The consultant will want to make positive, supportive comments while drawing closure to the interaction, and at that time can informally evaluate the consultation with consultee help, being careful to record the information for later analysis, or formally evaluate by asking for brief written responses. This is also a good time to plan for future collaboration.

Step 9: Following Through and Following Up.   Of all ten steps, this may be the most neglected. Unsuccessful consultation outcomes often result from lack of follow-up service. It is in the best interest of the client, consultee, consultant, and future opportunities for consultation to reassess the situation periodically. Participants will want to adjust the student's program if necessary, and initiate further consultation if the situation seems to require it. Informal conversations with consultees at this point are very reinforcing. During the follow-up, consultants have opportunities to make consultees feel good about themselves. They can make a point of noting improved student behaviors and performance, as well as positive effects that result from the collaboration. Also, they may volunteer to help if things are not going as smoothly as anticipated, or if consultees have further needs. The sweetest words a consultee can hear are, "What can I do to help you?" However, this question *must* be framed in the spirit of: "What can I do to help you *that you do not have the time and resources to do?*" and *not* implied as, "What can I do for you that you do not have the skill and expertise to accomplish?" Consultants should follow through immediately on all promises of materials, information, action, or further consultation, and take special steps to reinforce things that are going well. Figure 5.4 is an example of a form that could be used.

Step 10: Repeating Collaborative Consultation If Needed.   Further consultation and collaboration may be needed if the plan is not working, or if one or more parties believe the problem was not identified appropriately. On the other hand, consultation also may be repeated and extended when things are going well. The obvious rationale here is that if one interaction helped, more will help further. This is very reinforcing for processes of consultation, collaboration, and teamwork. It encourages others to participate in consultation and collaboration processes.

The ten-step consultation procedure, committed to memory or stapled into one's plan book, is a good organizational tool and a reassuring resource for every co-educator, particularly for those engaging in their first consultations. When implemented, the scenario might go something like Scenario 5.B that follows.

FIGURE 5.4   Memo to Follow Through on Collaborative Consultation/Teamwork

From: _____ to _____
        (consultant)   (consultee/s)

Date: _____ Re: _____

I am eager to follow through on the plan which we developed on the date above, and also to assist in other ways that may have occurred to you since then.

How do you feel things have progressed since that time? Please be forthright.

_____

_____

What else may I do to help?

_____

_____

                                            (List here any times, descriptions, etc., that would
                                            help me respond specifically to your needs.)

_____   Information   _____

_____   Resources   _____

_____   Meet again   _____

_____   Classroom visit   _____

_____   Conference with: _____

Thank you so much! I enjoy working with you to serve our students and schools.

SCENARIO 5.B

A special education teacher asks to meet with the classroom teacher of a student with hearing impairment. Implementation of instructional strategies and curricular adaptations made to address the student's IEP goals are going well. However, she believes more could be done in the school environment beyond cognitive development to help this student fit in socially, emotionally, and physically. In a quick "one-legged" conference during hall supervision with the student's classroom teacher, she senses that he has some concerns as well, and she suggests a meeting before contacting the parents to see if adjustments to the IEP are warranted.

She prepares for their meeting with an agenda and a summary of ideas and examples for adaptations. She asks to meet in the classroom on the teacher's "turf." This promises to be a very amiable collaboration, but as a novice teacher she wants to use her most polished collaborative consultation skills with this veteran teacher. She knows that as an intuitive thinker with her problem-solving style she has a tendency to gloss over facts and move too hastily to looking at ideas for solutions. This is something she has been working on and that awareness will serve her well today because she has observed that her co-worker has an opposite style of stating problems, issues, and factual data succinctly. These differences can work to their advantage, and the ultimate benefit for the student.

During the interaction she listens and waits appropriately. She uses verbals such as "we" and "How can I assist you in addressing the student's needs?" She asks the teacher about his concerns and uses reflective listening until the teacher concludes. She suggests items from her prepared list of ideas for modifications and accommodations. They review the student's IEP and then they begin to brainstorm based on both teachers' concerns and suggestions as a launch pad. This is where the novice teacher can shine. Next they generate a description of modifications that first focus on the areas of student need, and then outline what would be each teacher's responsibilities. Each shares expertise in how these modifications can be integrated into general curriculum and other parts of the student's school day. This includes more thoughtful placement in the music room, in assemblies, at lunch, and in playground games, to target the needs that go beyond academics into social, emotional, and sensorimotor areas.

The two teachers work out the details of the plan and they include an early conference with the student's family members to present the plan and be sure all facets are in compliance with their student's IEP and have their support. They make a special note to solicit additional ideas from input by the family members. They also plan the means by which they will engage support from other personnel including music teacher, physical education teacher, bus driver, cafeteria personnel, and school nurse.

This meeting carries the joint consultation through Steps 1–7 of the problem-solving process. Steps 8–10, namely evaluation, following up/following through and repeating if necessary, will have to wait until after discussing their ideas with the family members. But both co-educators leave the meeting on this day feeling very good about their collaborative effort and the event was a special boost to the first-year teacher's confidence. (See Figure 5.5.)

What to Say during the Consultation

Of course, the consultant does not want to parrot points from an outline as though reading from a manual for programming a video machine. But by practicing verbal responses that are helpful at each step, it will become more natural and automatic to use facilitative phrases when the need arises. Each number for the phrase sets below corresponds to a numbered step of the ten-step consultation process outlined earlier.

1. *When planning the consultation.* (Comments in this step are made to oneself.)

   (What styles of communication and interaction can I expect with these consultees?)
   (Have I had previous consultations with them and if so, how did these go?)

FIGURE 5.5   First, Identify the Problem

(Do I have any perceptions at this point about client needs? If so, can I keep them under wraps while soliciting responses from others?)

(What kinds of information might help with this situation?)

2. *When initiating the consultation.* (In this step and the rest of the steps, say to the consultee—)

You're saying that. . . .

The need seems to be. . . .

May we work together along these lines . . . ?

So the situation is. . . .

I am aware that . . .

What can we do in regard to your request/situation . . . ?

3. *When collecting information.*

Tell me about that. . . .

Uh-huh. . . .

What do you see as the effects of . . . ?

Let's see now, your views/perceptions about this are. . . .

Tell me more about the background of. . . .
Sounds tough. . . .
To summarize our basic information then. . . .

4. *When isolating the problem.*

The major factors we have brought out seem to be. . . .
Are we asking the right questions?
What do you perceive is the greatest need for . . . ?
What circumstances have you noted that may apply . . . ?
Are there other parts to the need that we have not considered?
So to summarize our perceptions at this point. . . .
Are we in agreement that the major part of this issue is . . . ?

5. *When identifying the concerns and stating the realities.*

You say the major concern is. . . .
How do you feel about this?
But I also hear your concern about. . . .
You'd like this situation changed so that. . . .
How does this affect your day/load/responsibility . . . ?
You are concerned about other students in your room. . . .
What are some ways to get at . . . ?
You're feeling . . . because of. . . .
This problem seems formidable. Perhaps we can isolate part of it. . . .
Would you say that . . . ?
Perhaps we can't be sure about that. . . .
The major factors we have brought out seem to be. . . .
If you could change one thing, what would you change first?

6. *When generating possibilities.*

How does this affect the students/schedule/parents . . . ?
Do we have a good handle on the nature of this situation?
We need to define what we want to happen. . . .
How would you like things to be?
What has been tried so far?
What happened then?
Is this the best way to get it done? The only way?
How could we do this more easily?
Could we try something new such as . . . ?
Could you add to what has been said?
What limitations fall on things we might suggest?
Let's try to develop some ideas to meet the need. . . .
Your idea of . . . also makes me think of. . . .

7. *When formulating a plan.*

Let's list the goals and ideas we have come up with.
So, in trying . . . you'll be changing your approach of. . . .
To implement these ideas, we would have to. . . .

We have considered every possibility brought forth, so which shall it be?

The actions in this situation would be different, because. . . .

We've discussed all of the alternatives carefully and now it's time to choose.

We need to break down the plan into steps. What should come first? Next?

When is the best time to start with the first step?

8. *When evaluating progress.*

Have we got a solid plan?

One way to measure progress toward the goals would be. . . .

Some positive things have been happening. . . .

How can we build upon these gains?

Now we can decide where to go from here. . . .

In what ways did our getting together help?

I can see [the student] progress every day. . . .

You're accomplishing so much with. . . .

How could I serve you and your students better?

9. *When following up and interacting with colleagues.*

How do you feel about the way things are going?

We had set a time to get back together. Is that time still OK, or should we make it sooner?

I'm interested in the progress you have observed.

I'm following up on that material/action I promised.

I just stopped by. . . .

I wondered how things have been going for you.

How are things in your corner of the world these days?

I'm glad you've hung in there with this problem.

You've accomplished a lot that may not be apparent when you're with it every day.

You know, progress like this makes teachers look very good!

10. *If repeating the consultation.*

Should we have another go at discussing . . . ?

Perhaps we overlooked some information that would help. . . .

We got so much accomplished last time. How about getting together again to. . . ?

That's a great progress report. Would another plan session produce even more of these fine results?

APPLICATION 5.1
USING THE 10-STEP CONSULTING PROCESS

Select one or more of the following situations and simulate a school consultation experience, using the ten-step process and any of the "What to Say" phrases that seem appropriate:

Situation A: A middle school student is vision-impaired. Her IEP includes modifications of paper-and-pencil tests. What are the ramifications of this for classroom teacher preparations, grading issues, and NCLB-mandated testing?

Situation B: It is the first week of school. A high school student new to the area has Tourette's syndrome and even though he has medication that keeps the syndrome under control, he has asked if he may speak briefly to his classmates during class to explain his condition "just in case." He believes that few in the public know much about the condition and one of his causes is to spread awareness. Who should meet about this and what should their agenda be?

Situation C: A ninth-grade student is considered lazy by former teachers, has failed several courses, and cannot grasp math concepts. He has difficulty locating information but can read and understand most material at his grade level. He is never prepared for class, seldom has pencil and paper, and loses his assignments. Yet he is pleasant, seemingly eager to please, and will try things in a one-to-one situation. His classroom teachers say he will not pass, and you have all decided to meet about this. How will you, the learning disabilities consulting teacher, address the situation?

Situation D: You are attending an IEP meeting on behalf of a third-grade student who is emotionally disturbed and classified as having borderline educable mental retardation. You believe she should be placed in a general classroom with supportive counseling service and reevaluated in a year. The other staff participants feel she should have been in special education placement with mainstreaming into music, art, and physical education. The mother is confused about the lack of agreement among school personnel. How will you address the concerns of all in this situation, particularly the mother?

Situation E: A sixth-grade student's mother is known as a perfectionist. Her son, who has been identified for the gifted program, did not receive all As on the last report card, and she has requested a conference with you as the classroom teacher, the principal, and the school psychologist. How will you address this situation?

Situation F: A first-year kindergarten teacher has learned that one of her students will be a child with cerebral palsy. Although the child's history to date has included continuous evaluation, home teaching, group socialization experiences, special examinations, and therapy sessions as well as family counseling for three years, the teacher is nervous about her responsibilities with this child. As the speech pathologist, how will you build her confidence in caring for the kindergartner's language needs, and her skill in helping the little girl to develop her potential?

Situation G: The special education director and middle school building administrator have been asked by a group of general education teachers and special education teachers to meet with them. The director and the principal sense that this group has been chosen informally by the entire teaching staff to be their spokespersons. They know that these teachers and their colleagues are caring and conscientious educators. The representative group wants to discuss the grave concerns they have about including all students with special needs in the high-stakes standardized tests to be given in a few weeks. As they voice the concerns, ask how best to prepare the students for these tests, and question what is to be done with the results of the tests, how might the special education director and building administrator react and respond?

What to Consider If Group Problem Solving Is Not Successful

There is no universal agreement on what makes consultation effective, and little empirical support exists to guide consultants as to what should be said and done in consultation (Gresham & Kendell, 1987; Heron & Kimball, 1988). However, the ten steps outlined above have worked well for many consultants and consulting teachers. If this method of ten steps does not work, consultants should ask several questions.

- Were feelings addressed?
- Was the problem defined accurately?
- Did all parties practice good listening skills?
- Were the nitty-gritty details worked out?
- Were any hidden agendas brought to light and handled?
- Were all participants appropriately assertive?
- Was the consultation process evaluated and then discussed?
- Could any other problem-solving tools facilitate the process?
- Was there follow-up to the consultation?
- Should we convene in groups to practice problem-solving techniques?

APPLICATION 5.2
FOR A FURTHER CHALLENGE

As a team effort in a group with several colleagues who share your grade level and subject area, construct a scenario to demonstrate the ten-step collaborative school consultation process at your teaching level and in your content area(s). Role play it for other groups, stopping at key points—for example, after problem identification, and again after formulating the plan, and then perhaps just before following through—to ask the observing group what they might do at that point. If several promising alternatives are suggested, try each one and follow it to its conclusion, in the manner of the choose-an-adventure books that children like to read.

What techniques worked best? How did individual differences influence the consultation? Were these individual differences used constructively, and if not, what could have been done instead? Did participants become better collaborators as they tried more scenarios?

TOOLS FOR GROUP PROBLEM SOLVING

The collaborative format of working together and drawing on collective expertise to solve problems is widely practiced in the business and professional world. In their efforts to use the best ideas of bright, innovative minds, astute leaders employ a number of group problem-solving techniques. These techniques allow individuals to extend their own productive thinking powers and enhance those of their colleagues by participating in structured group problem-solving activities. However, such techniques are yet to be relied on to much extent for adults in educational settings, where autonomy and self-sufficiency have traditionally been more convenient than collaboration and teamwork.

One of the most frequently occurring activities of problem-finding and problem-solving in schools is the IEP process. The shared thinking in which the interactive IEP team engages is a collaborative method of finding solutions to problems (Clark, 2000). So simulated IEP conferences can be used as development tools for enhancing consultation and collaboration skills of co-educators. A group could be assigned to develop an IEP for a graduate student colleague who wants to do an advanced, independent study on the subject of autism and then will share the information with other students and instructors. Her colleagues could collaborate in assigned roles—student, facilitator for the study, representative of school administration, instructor for the subject area (autism in this case), and "parent" (that could be her spouse who had to leave work to attend). It would be illuminating to have the student *not* participate in the meeting so as to simulate the reality of most IEP scenarios in which students are not present for their own IEP planning. As the group prepares a statement of level of performance (citing the student's capability and motivation toward completing the program while working full-time), justification for placement (ability and need to do an independent study), annual measurable goals, due dates with persons responsible for facilitation and support, and evaluation methods, they would be collaborating as a co-educator team. IEP development for very capable students who are doing independent studies typically do involve the student; however, by conducting the simulation without her participation, the team could experience the feelings that young students have when IEPs are developed *for* them rather than *with* them.

Too many general educators have expressed dissatisfaction with the IEP development process, citing terms, forms, and paperwork as factors, and also concern that student input was not valued. As noted by Menlove, Hudson, and Suter (2001), dissatisfaction was higher for secondary teachers than for elementary teachers. Reasons given included team disconnect, time and preparation involved, training needed for pertinent knowledge and skills, and IEP relevance to their school context. General educators had the view that the IEP meeting is a special education teacher's meeting, not a team meeting, and when parents were present they did not like to push issues. But on the positive side, general education teachers have been seeing improvement. Potential solutions speak to the issues of time, information, communication, and preparation. This is a promising area in which both IEP participatory skills and collaborative skills can be improved simultaneously through well-targeted training programs.

Another instructive simulation as a group is rubric development for a specific purpose, such as learning and behavior expectations for a class trip, or procedures and assessment for a cooperative learning activity. Development of rubrics might lead to setting up a portfolio system in the classroom.

Yet another exercise could be problem solving collaboratively to use technology for developing differentiated curriculum plans for exceptional learning needs. After generating lists of technological tools, the group could evaluate the lists using the Plus-Minus-Interesting technique described later in this chapter.

A great number of easy-to-use problem-solving techniques suitable for group participation are available. These include, but certainly are not limited to, brainstorming, lateral thinking, Six Thinking Hats thinking, concept mapping, idea checklists, and metaphorical thinking. Others are jigsaw, reciprocal teaching, compare-and-contrast, SCAMPER, Plus-Minus-Interesting, role play, TalkWalk, and more. Some teachers have often incorporated these kinds of group problem-solving activities into their curriculum-planning for students, but have overlooked the potential that the techniques have for collaborating with adults more effectively and pleasurably. Here are a few brief descriptions and application activities.

Brainstorming

Brainstorming is a mainstay of creative problem-solving methodology. It facilitates generating many unique ideas. When a group is brainstorming, participants should be relaxed and having fun. There are no right or wrong responses during the process, because problems seldom have only one right approach. No one may critique an idea during the brainstorming process. All ideas are accepted as plausible and regarded as potentially valuable. Each idea is shared and recorded. In large-group sessions, it is most efficient to have a leader for managing the oral responses, and a recorder for getting them down on a board or chart visible to all.

The five well-known rules developed by Osborn (1963) for brainstorming are:

1. Do not criticize any ideas at this time.
2. The more wild and zany the ideas, the better.
3. Think up as many ideas as possible.
4. Try to combine two or more ideas into new ones.
5. Hitch-hike (piggyback) on another's idea. A person with a hitchhike idea should be called on before those who have unrelated ideas.

Note that when coaching others (children in particular) in brainstorming techniques, it is good to introduce them to the "humanitarian principle" before the very first session. This means that no idea will be accepted if it is obviously harmful to others. So, a response to "What are new ways to use old bricks?" that came out as "To drown kittens," (typically accompanied by its contributor with a pause for chuckles or shocked expressions from peers along with quick glances to observe teacher reaction), would be answered by a brief but firm "Sorry, but as you know, we abide by the humanitarian principle here." Then the teacher could move quickly on without accepting that idea, and yet would remain true to rules 1 and 2 of a brainstorm activity.

Brainstorming is useful when a group wishes to explore as many alternatives as possible and defer evaluation of the ideas until the options have been exhausted. People who cannot resist the urge to critique ideas during brainstorming must be reminded that evaluation comes later. Leaders should call on volunteers quickly.

When the flow of ideas slows, it is good to persevere a while longer. Often the second wave of thoughts will contain the most innovative suggestions. Each participant should be encouraged to contribute, but allowed to pass if wished.

Individual brainstorming can be a very productive precursor to group brainstorming. Recall that personal preferences often have effects on instruction in unexpected ways, and this is one example. Some people like to brainstorm privately, rather like an incubation process, before joining in a group effort. Others enjoy just getting right to it. If an agenda that states topics to be discussed is provided ahead of meeting time, with the "heads-up" suggestion that brainstorming might be used as a tool for gathering ideas, those who wish to reflect on the matter will be better prepared to contribute enthusiastically.

Reverse brainstorming is an unusual technique that sometimes proves helpful if the group is stuck and needs to find another approach. With this technique, participants propose what would be considered the opposites of good ideas, such as, "If someone wanted to *increase* bullying and extortion on the school grounds, how would that be best accomplished?" Or, "If we *didn't* want Jaime to contribute to the cooperative learning group, how would we discourage him from doing so?" On a cautionary note, participants need to know exactly what the purpose of this technique is, and bring closure to the activity in a positive way by agreeing that "these are things we must avoid having happen in the instances for which we brainstormed." Any eavesdroppers on this activity would need to be informed forthwith about the purpose of this exercise.

Using the Brainstorm Technique.   A brainstorming session would be appropriate for this situation: A first-grade student has read just about every book in the small, rural school. The first-grade teacher and gifted program facilitator brainstorm possibilities for enhancing this student's reading options and augmenting the school's resources as well.

Lateral Thinking

The conventional method of thinking is vertical thinking, in which one moves forward mentally by sequential and justifiable steps. Vertical thinking is logical and single-purposed, digging down more deeply into the same mental hole or rising along the same line of thought. Lateral thinking, on the other hand, digs a "thinking hole" in a different place. It moves out at an angle, so to speak, from vertical thinking to change direction, attitude, or approach so that the problem can be examined in a different, unique, perhaps even bizarre, way (deBono, 1986).

   Lateral thinking should not replace vertical thinking, but complement it. While many educators emphasize vertical thinking at the expense of more divergent production, both are useful to arrive at creative solutions for complex problems. The ability to use a lateral thinking mode by suspending judgments and generating alternatives should be cultivated by school personnel.

Using the Lateral Thinking Technique.   Lateral thinking could be helpful in this situation. A high school student with learning disabilities has a serious reading problem, but teachers in several classes are not willing to make adjustments. The teachers have not discussed any problems with you, the resource teacher, recently but the student has. How might you as consultant, and student as consultee, think of ways to approach the situation and modify classroom practices to help this student succeed? To think laterally, the consultant might regard the teachers as clients, and consult with the student about ways of reinforcing teachers when they *do* make things easier. The student would be modifying the behavior of teachers, in contrast to a vertical thinking tactic of asking teachers to modify student behavior. Recall the earlier comment that students sometimes are curriculum-disabled.

Six Thinking Hats

This thinking tool also was developed by deBono as a nonargumentative and creative way to think through issues (deBono, 1985). Six colored hats—white, yellow, black, red, green, and blue, are "put on" as a way to encourage helpful kinds of thinking about a problem from many different angles. With the white hat on, participants gather information. The yellow hat is for looking at positives, values, and benefits. The red hat allows sharing of emotions and feelings about the issue. With the green hat, one can think outside the box for new possibilities. The blue hat is a management and procedures reminder. Finally, the black hat provides a devil's advocate perspective.

Thinking with Six Hats.   In a group, co-educators explore all sides of a problem, for example, the pros and cons of the NCLB legislation, or the use of a particular technology with students who have disabilities, using the Six Thinking Hats approach. They make paper hats to wear or simply hold up colored sheets of paper to make a point when the leader calls for a particular hat-color perspective.

The hats are assembled into a bulletin board collage for display as a reminder to maximize different styles of thinking and responding to issues. This is another practical example of the constructive use of adults' individual differences.

Concept Mapping

Concept mapping (referred to by some as mind-mapping, semantic mapping, webbing, or trees of knowledge or information) is a tool for identifying concepts, showing relationships among them, and reflecting on the degree of generality and inclusiveness that envelopes them (Wesley &Wesley, 1990). The technique allows users to display ideas, link them together, elaborate on them, add new information as it surfaces, and review the formulation of the ideas. The process begins with one word, or issue, written on paper or the chalkboard and enclosed in a circle. Then other circles of subtopics, ideas, words, and concepts are added to that central theme by lines or spokes that connect and interconnect where the concepts relate and interrelate. More and more possibilities and new areas open up as the webbing grows. Relationships and interrelationships that can help verbalize problems and interventions are recorded for all participants to see. If the concept map is left on display, the process can go on and on as more ideas are generated and added.

Concept mapping is being taught to students for purposes such as reading comprehension at all grade levels. Buzan (1983) offers strategies for mind-mapping in which learning techniques such as note-taking can be structured to show interrelationships easily. Many students in gifted programs have been introduced to the concept of webbing to focus on a problem of interest and plan an independent study. Sometimes college students are encouraged to try mind-mapping by combining lecture notes and text reading to study for exams. Concept-mapping is a powerful tool for enhancing individual learning. It also can lead to more meaningful and productive staff development (Bocchino, 1991).

Using Concept Mapping.   A classroom teacher has agreed to work with a student new to the district who has been diagnosed with Asperger's syndrome. The student has acceptable social skills in some instances, and is friendly and cooperative. But he also requires individual instruction, is working about two years below grade level, and makes threats impulsively to other students. During previous visits the teacher had indicated to the special education teacher that things were going well. Now, in the middle of November, she asks for a consultation immediately. She is upset, saying things such as, "It just isn't working," and "I've tried so hard," but she has not really described the problem. How might concept-mapping or webbing help in this situation? What word or phrase could go into the center to begin the webbing?

Idea Checklist

Checklists to help identify problems and determine ways to solve them can be created from sources such as college texts, teaching manuals, and instructional media manuals. More unusual checklists include referral agency listings, gift catalog descriptions, instructional resource center guides, and even Yellow Pages sections of various directories. By asking a question such as, "How can we help Shawn improve in math proficiency?" and scanning a Yellow Pages section or an off-level teaching manual, new ideas may emerge.

Using the Idea Checklist.   A high school sophomore, seventeen years old and in the educable mental retardation program, is ready for a vocational training program. The EMR resource teacher believes the Vocational Rehabilitation Unit's four-month job training program would be the most appropriate program for the student. However, the parents feel very protective of their son and are concerned that the environment will be non-caring. They resist suggestions that he leave their home. How might an idea-checklist process help during this consultation?

Synectics, Metaphors, and Janusian Thinking

As an example of synectics, one secondary teacher of students with developmental delay listened with much interest and an open mind when his colleagues for the school's gifted program voiced their perspectives on incorporating complex thinking skills into curriculum for all students in the general classroom. The EMR teacher began processing this with the facts and his feelings—making the familiar strange ("What if my students could take this perspective and run with it?") and making the strange familiar ("What if I take something that's appropriate for very bright, unchallenged students and design it for my students?") After much thought, planning, trial and error, revision, and preparation of a procedural plan, he set up a catering system in which his students provided snacks at first, then full-fledged meals after the plan was going well, for special events in the schools. The results for students' academic skills, social skills, practical skills in running the business, and feelings of self-confidence and self-esteem were immeasurable and the program became the talk of not only the school but also the entire community.

Metaphors are mental maps that permit the connection of different meanings through some shared similarity. They appear often in spoken and written communication. For example, the sentences "Life is a loom," "The fog swallowed the ship," and "Last June my flower garden was a paint box of colors" are metaphorical. They connect in order to explain. Many creative people in various fields have broken with conventional thinking by engaging in metaphorical thinking.

The metaphor uses one subject to strengthen and deepen the understanding of another. Metaphors can guide groups for activating change processes. They are useful to generate new ideas and teach new concepts (Garmston, 1994). Pollio (1987) suggests that some of the most important scientific, philosophical, and technical insights were conceived from an imaginative image. One of his examples is Einstein seeing himself as a passenger on a light ray and holding a mirror in front of him, an image that helped him form the theory of relativity. People use metaphors to sort out their perceptions and reflect on the meanings of things. Einstein broke with old facts and feelings related to Euclidian geometry to create metaphors that became his theory of relativity. In art, Picasso broke with familiar metaphors of looking and painting to show the world a new way of seeing. In similar, but perhaps more subtle fashion, educators can use metaphors to connect two different viewpoints so one idea can be understood by means of the other.

APPLICATION 5.3
EXPLORING THE POWER OF METAPHORICAL THINKING

With a group of your colleagues generate free-association responses to open-ended phrases such as, "Life is a _____" (e.g., zoo, journey, pressure cooker, bank, car lot, battle, or party) and "School is a _____" (e.g., prison, twelve-act play, family, game). A second part of the activity is to continue on from that image, e.g., "If life is a *zoo,* then teachers are _____, and students are _____" "If school is a twelve-act play, students are _____, teachers are _____, principals are _____." Open-ended phrases then could move to topics such as, "Team teaching is like _____, and teachers are the _____." "Inservice days are a _____ (battery charge?) and teachers are the (dead batteries now all charged up?)." (Metaphors can be served as tart lessons sweetened with humor and a twist of wry!)

Janusian thinking was recognized by Rothenberg & Hausman (1976) who studied the Eugene O'Neill play *The Iceman Cometh.* The term for the concept was coined from the Roman god Janus who looks backward into the old year and forward into the new (January). The process involves using two or more contradictory or opposite ideas *simultaneously*—for example, sweet and salty. This simultaneous consideration of opposites creates tension that can spark original thought. As an example, Mozart told aspiring musicians that the rests in between the notes are as important, if not more so, than the notes themselves. Frank Lloyd Wright valued the concept of Janusian thinking because architects need to conceptualize the inside and outside of a building simultaneously. The key element in the process is simultaneity; thus, convex outer shapes must be reconciled with concave inner shapes in order for the architect to conceptualize the structure.

APPLICATION 5.4
EXPLORING THE POWER OF JANUSIAN THINKING

With colleagues, use the technique of group brainstorming, permitting no judging of the ideas, and having a disposition in which the strange becomes familiar, such as in Sweet Tarts, dry ice, jumbo shrimp, and snow blanket, to generate more examples of Janusian thought. Then shift to a socially focused mode and try for ideas such as win/win, and friendly fire. After thinking of several clever product-type examples, the power of the process becomes evident. But that is the easy task! Now strive for new, Janusian-based concepts that can help students, such as creative homework, innovative drill, elementary/secondary student mentorships, and more. Not so many years ago some considered collaborative consultation to be a Janusian phrase, but no more.

More Techniques for Collaborative Problem Solving

A number of other collaborative activities that are used to nurture creative thinking can be employed to facilitate exchanging information and generating ideas among co-educators for the ultimate benefit of their students. Many of them can be retrieved at Web sites under their descriptive names or under key words such as creative problem solving, creative thinking, and even creative collaboration. These include: reciprocal teaching, random word technique, In What Ways Might We? (IWWMW), visualization, and attribute listing. A brief summary of just a few follows.

Jigsaw. Participants in this learning method developed by Aronson (1978) undertake independent, collaborative research on a topic of mutual interest. A school faculty, school district staff, or other group of teachers and area specialists seek out background material in small groups and bring it back to share with the full group in order to agree on possible solutions to academic and behavioral problems. The whole group begins by deciding on the central theme(s) of the issue and several subtopics. Then the group divides into smaller groups. Each small group conducts research on one subtopic and shares that knowledge by teaching it to others. In this way all have a part in the problem solving. Time and energy of busy professionals are used to maximum benefit. Redundancy of effort is minimized. Most importantly, a collaborative synergism[1] develops that improves their ability to problem-solve in other situations.

One topic for a jigsaw procedure could be how to construct differentiated learning plans for the inclusive classroom. Others might be how to ensure appropriate behavior and decorum on school buses, or how to provide safety of equipment and student activity on school playgrounds, or making plans to deal with potential acts of violence or the aftermath of a student suicide.

A particularly useful and too often neglected area for developing educational awareness and expertise is school law. This deep and wide topic would focus on careful examination of numerous issues in the state and local school context, such as privacy of confidential information, accountability of school personnel in supervisory matters, use of corporal punishment, intervention and referral procedures, safety in the classroom or field environment, and much more. It is obvious that these jigsaw-based problem-solving experiences should include all school personnel and related and support personnel such as social workers, parents, and perhaps on occasion and for some topics, student participation as well.

Reciprocal Teaching. In reciprocal teaching, six or so participants form a group and each member takes a turn leading a discussion about an article, video, position paper, staff development presentation, or other material they have read and want to understand more fully. The leader begins with a question and summarizes the discussion at the end. Clarification for understanding and predictions about content for the future can be requested by the leader when appropriate (Brown, 1994). With this technique, group cooperation helps ensure understanding by all members, with the less well-informed learning from those who are more knowledgeable.

---

[1]Interaction of elements that when combined produce a total effect greater than the sum of the parts (*Webster's College Dictionary*, 1996).

One example of using reciprocal teaching could be to have a team of teachers read relevant material and then explore possibilities for adapting classroom settings to accommodate students with attention deficit and hyperactivity disorder or perhaps those with obsessive compulsive disorder. The synergistic discussion may open new avenues for addressing this complex concern.

Compare and Contrast.   Each small group identifies terms and phrases that define differing perspectives of an issue—for example, reading methods, math methods, tracking or mainstreaming, inclusion or pull-out programs, graded or ungraded systems. One compare-and-contrast session might draw out aspects of the two-part item, "what general classroom teachers don't know about special ed curriculum, and what special ed teachers don't know about general curriculum." An organization of the results completes the exchange, with all participants leaving the session more informed and reflective about the issues. A technique such as brainstorming or POCS could be employed during a later staff development event to make use of compare-and-contrast findings.

SCAMPER.   The SCAMPER technique was developed by Eberle (1984) as a built-in mnemonic device to brainstorm in practical situations. For example, using SCAMPER to preplan a transition program for a teen with mental retardation from school into a work area could create a number of possibilities: S, what can be substituted?; C, what can be combined?; A, what adaptations?; M, how modified, magnified, multiplied, or minified?; P, how put to other uses or purposes?; E, what could be eliminated?; and R, how could things be rearranged or interchanged?

Plus-Minus-Interesting.   This simple process can be completed in a half-hour or so, often stimulating rearrangement of perspectives and sometimes recasting values placed on those perspectives. As an example, in a school considering the use of active senior citizens as reading aides, the collaborative team would generate a three-part list of the pluses, the minuses, and things that are interesting and that the team would like to investigate further before making a decision. It is not necessary that the pluses exceed the minuses, and sometimes the interesting feature may ultimately be determined as the most promising. The discussion which PMI instigates can assist problem solving (deBono, 1973).

Role Play.   A fundamental purpose of role play as a problem-solving practice is to produce new perspectives. For example, in a teacher-parent conflict, the teacher would take the role of the parent, and the parent that of the teacher. Participants have specific parts to play. At a critical part in the interaction the leader stops the players and has the whole group explore options that would be possible from that point. Then new solutions may emerge (Torrance & Safter, 1999). In role-playing the convener must be skilled and facilitative, so that the players participate intently without self-consciousness.

Concentric Circle or Fishbowl.   A small circle of participants discusses an issue while a larger circle on the outside of that one listens and then discusses. This technique encourages participation by members usually reticent to respond, and stimulates lively discussion. Issues must be well-chosen and articulated clearly to the group.

In-Basket Techniques.   These are simulations of situations that may come to the consulting teacher's mailbox or message board. The basket contains requests or questions that need action. Because there are typically no right or wrong answers, the technique is good for engaging in a multiperspective discussion in which the teacher describes the situation and invites input. This technique could be one option offered during a staff development day when teachers choose the sessions they want to attend. In that case, some "teaser" topics should be provided in the promotional material as examples so participants would know what to expect. General issues that do not require confidentiality would be most suitable for this approach.

Case Studies.   Problems gleaned from professional literature or composed by participants are given to the group. Members react to the question "What seems to be going on here?" and then prepare individual plans or one group plan for next steps. One member coordinates discussion of the various plans to enhance the group's flexibility in problem solving. This is another promising activity for a professional development session.

Role Rotation.   Here the participants have the opportunity to consider the issue in question from a completely different perspective. For example, a classroom teacher might participate as an administrator. A learning disabilities consultant could take the role of a parent. Figure 1.2 and relevant discussion in Chapter 1 could be useful for role rotation.

TalkWalk.   In this unique form of small-group interaction the participants engage in collegial dialogue focused on instructional and curricular issues while they walk together in an open environment (Caro & Robbins, 1991). The fresh air, physical and mental exercise, and exploration of ideas lead to free thinking and expression. This technique can be used as part of a workshop or simply as an informal arrangement among colleagues.

Caro and Robbins suggest that groups of two or three work best. TalkWalk provides educators with 4 Es for problem solving—*expertise* from collective experience; *enrichment* to improve sense of self-worth and problem-solving capacity; *expediency* to obtain rapid solutions through assistance; *exercise* to bring a fresh attitude and perspective to the problem. One walk, for example, might focus on the group's vision for students who are in transition from school to work and independent living. Another might be to join preschool teachers and primary teachers in a TalkWalk to discuss that transition period for very young children. An outcome of such talks just might be a plan that will help make the vision become real.

Use of Multiple Intelligences

One unique way to generate many perspectives and perhaps arrive at some clever solutions for problems is to frame the questions in terms of Gardner's (1993) well-known multiple intelligence categories. For example, to build interest, rapport, and skills for team teaching among staff with no experience doing it, these questions could help with planning efforts:

Linguistic: How can we use words and stories to describe team teaching?

Logical–mathematical: How might we measure the benefits and drawbacks of a team-teaching approach in our school?

Musical: Should we create a team song or cheer?

Spatial: Should we make a physical map of where everything will be and what more, or less, we should include in the spaces we will share?

Interpersonal: What kinds of differences in interests, preferences, values, and personal habits would be important to discuss before embarking on a team-teaching mission?

Intrapersonal: How would I describe my feelings about giving up some of my professional autonomy, and sharing many of my ideas and techniques?

Bodily–kinesthetic: How can we move throughout the room, arrange materials, and get students' attention when we are teaching together in the same spaces?

Naturalistic: Will our school environment accommodate this team teaching so that students are comfortable, parents are satisfied, and teachers are positive about the experience?

Interaction Formats

Collaborating consultants will want to know how to set up a variety of group formats for stimulating interaction among professionals. (See Figure 5.6.) Some of the most useful ones are as follows:

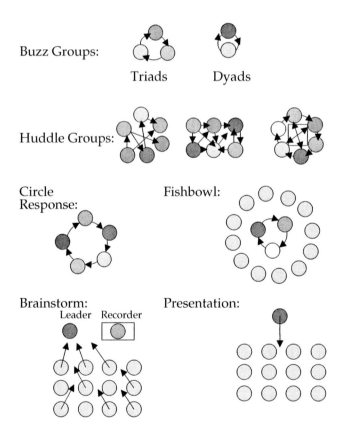

FIGURE 5.6   Interaction Structures

Buzz groups.   Buzz groups work well in a group of 50 or fewer. This format ensures total participation and is easy to set up. The leader presents a topic or problem, provides minimal directions for subgrouping by twos or threes, and invites everyone to consider all aspects of the problem in the time allowed. The main disadvantage is a high noise level if the physical space is small.

Huddles.   Huddles work best with groups of five or six discussants. The leader arranges the groups, defines the topic, announces the time limit (six minutes works well), and gives a two-minute warning that time is expiring. Each group designates its own reporter. The leader usually passes from group to group facilitating and encouraging if needed. In this structure the participants tend to build on colleagues' contributions. The reporting process can vary, from a simple "most important points" to ranking of major points, to a written summary that is collected by the leader. Some know this technique as the 6-6 method (Kohm, 2002) or the "Six Points of View" method.

Circle Response.   Small groups of collaborators sit in a circle. The designated leader begins by stating or reiterating the topic. The response pattern moves to the left, with each taking a turn or saying "I pass." At the end of a stipulated time, the leader summarizes the ideas and integrated thinking of the group.

Others.   An enterprising consultant also could consider structured role play, a structured or unstructured interview forum, reader's theater, research-and-report, round-robin (Kohm, 2002), and a film talk-back session as ways of encouraging interaction and information exchange among educators.

INTERFERENCES AND HURDLES TO OVERCOME

Co-educators must examine their own perspectives and preferences to identify any potential aspects that will impede their abilities to consult and collaborate on behalf of the student. A lack of four major aspects of teaching, as suggested by Caplan's (1995) four interfering themes, can reduce co-educators' ability to be divergent thinkers and problem solvers (Sandoval, 1996). These aspects are:

1. *Knowledge and understanding* needed to address student needs and related factors helpfully
2. Right *skills* to approach the problem in appropriate ways; for example, a teacher may not have the skills or resources needed to deal with student problems
3. *Self-confidence* needed to deal with the problem in spite of inexperience, self-doubt, or even fatigue or illness
4. *Objectivity* in approaching the problem, that keeps consultants from turning away inappropriately or from becoming too personally involved

A collaborative problem-solving process is a viable arena in which to address these four themes that threaten to interfere with the educator's ability to serve student needs. For example, some teachers might show lack of knowledge by over- or under-identifying students for special education because of stereotypical thinking. Others may show lack of skill by failing to modify curriculum for those with disabilities, or by inappropriately using a strategy such as cooperative learning. Lack of objectivity is evident when educators equate student situations to another situation in their own lives or to former students and their situations. Lack of confidence can generate resistance to new plans and inflexibility toward new ideas.

When collaborating, consultants should use every opportunity to reinforce the efforts and successes of classroom teachers and also to convey a desire to learn from them and their experiences. Too often classroom teachers, as ones occupying a non-specialist role among specialists, and parents, who know their child best, can be somewhat removed from the school setting and overlooked when ideas for addressing learning and behavior problems are explored.

When communicating and cooperating with consultees to identify the learning or behavior need, it is important that consultants avoid sending messages intimating that classroom teachers and parents are deficient in skills that only special education teachers can provide (Friend & Cook, 1990; Huefner, 1988). Communication skills and cooperative attitudes will encourage feelings of parity and voluntarism among all school personnel and parents during the problem-solving process.

Students assigned to resource settings in other schools for part of the week or school day may have teachers there who never communicate about them and their work. This is a serious drawback of some cluster group arrangements where students travel from one school to another with no planned interaction among school personnel taking place. Coordination of collaborative effort is vital.

Special education teachers who cannot identify basal reading curriculum used in various levels, and classroom teachers who cannot identify the nature of instruction taking place in the resource room, make problem identification more difficult (Idol, West, & Lloyd, 1988). Their lack of shared knowledge may even intensify the problem. All parties must think about their own roles in the problem situation, and endeavor to learn from each other by interacting, deferring judgment, and coordinating their services.

A team approach is a productive way to assess the context, conditions, interfering themes, and circumstances surrounding the student's needs and the school programs designed to meet those needs. It has been noted that astronomers from all parts of the world collaborate often because there is no one place from which every part of their "work area," the sky, can be observed. This analogy applies to educators and parents as they address each child's total needs in the cognitive, affective, physical, and social domains to develop learning and behavior goals.

Those goals become building blocks for decision making. Without goals, decision making is like a hammer without nails. Educators have long-range and short-term goals. Students have IEPs with yearly goals and short-term goals. Schools have mission statements and educational aims. Both school aims and student goals should be used for making decisions in educational environments. A goal motivates action and provides direction for that action. Reviewing goals helps educators stay focused and sort out the things that are important from those that are not.

Educators with experience as consultants describe several problems that can interfere with the success of consultation, collaboration, or teamwork among educators. By recognizing them as possibility but not necessarily expecting them to occur, consulting teachers can be ready to sidestep or step over potential hurdles such as:

- Loss of touch with the students when not in direct service with them
- Uncertainty about what and how to communicate with those who resist or resent collaboration
- Being regarded as a teacher's aide, "gofer," or quick-fix expert
- Having consultation regarded as a tutorial for students
- Territoriality of school personnel
- Rigid curriculum and assessment procedures
- Unrealistic expectations (either too high or too low) toward the role
- Not having enough information or appropriate materials to share
- Being perceived as a show-off, or a bossy expert, or an interloper
- Running into veils of professional politeness that shield consultees from genuine commitment
- Difficulty managing time and resources, which often happens
- Lack of training for the role
- An excessive caseload that short-circuits effectiveness
- Too many "hats" to wear in the role
- Most of all, resistance of colleagues toward change of any kind

Knowing potential hurdles can help educators keep them from becoming insurmountable barriers by ensuring that there is role delineation, a consultation framework, adequate evaluation of the process, and careful preparation to develop the necessary skills. Some of the mystique surrounding special education and support services is reduced when classroom teachers become familiar with the techniques and are led to appreciate and understand special education roles.

Positive and Not-So-Positive Consultations

Some collaborative consultations are more successful than others. In a few instances, they turn out rather discouragingly. Collaborators have reported positive outcomes in the following situations:

- "Primary-level teachers and I sat down and discussed what materials they thought would be good to order and place in the resource room, for their use as well as mine. Everyone had a chance to share needs, express opinions, and make recommendations."

- "An undergraduate asked me about my student teaching and substituting days. She was feeling very down and unsure of her teaching abilities. I reassured her by telling of some things that had happened to me, and why. I encouraged her to find a dependable support system, and gave her some ideas and things to think about."

- "One of the teachers I have spent several weeks with stopped me in the hall yesterday to ask for an idea to use in her class that next hour. Before she finished putting her question into words, she had thought of an idea herself, but she still thanked me!"

■ "I participated in a parent conference in which the parent wanted to kick the daughter out of the house and into a boarding school. It ended with the daughter agreeing to do more work at home, and the mother agreeing to spend one special hour of togetherness a week with just her daughter."

And now some not-so-positive situations:

■ "A kindergarten child was staffed into my program, but the teacher wouldn't let me take her out of 'her' class time. So I arranged to keep the child after school. The first night I was late coming to fetch the child, and the teacher blew up about it."
■ "The music teacher asks students who cannot read well to stand up in class and read, and then pokes fun at them. I approached the teacher about the situation, but the teacher wanted nothing to do with me, and after that made things even worse for the students."
■ "In visiting with the principal about alternatives in altering classroom assignments, it ended with his speaking harshly and suggesting that I was finding fault with the school staff, which I had not done."
■ "I give a sticker every day to a student who has learning disabilities if he attends and does his work in the resource room. His classroom teacher complained to the principal about it because 'other students work hard and don't get stickers.'"

ETHICS FOR COLLABORATIVE AND CONSULTATIVE PROBLEM SOLVING

An ethical climate and impeccably ethical behavior are keenly important in special education. Howe and Miramontes (1992) remind us that the actions of special educators have lifelong ramifications and must be taken very seriously. Many of the proposed actions require judgment to deal with potential consequences. As an example, consider the dilemma of a church-school teacher alone in her room preparing for class when a student entered the room and grabbed her from behind in an inappropriate and forceful way. After backing him off and calming him down, to whom should the teacher go first? She was virtually certain that the parents' harsh and peculiar child-rearing practices were the root of his alarming behavior. Should she report to social services, the school administrator, or the church pastor? As Kaufmann (1993) notes, teachers have little training in thorny issues such as these. But, as co-educators in inclusive settings with joint responsibility for students, they must pool their expertise and collaboratively make decisions for the welfare of the student and others.

When groups of co-educators gather (and in some IEP conferences the number of adults in attendance may be as many as a dozen), there is more risk in handling confidential material. A collaborative ethic guides such groups in discussing sensitive matters calmly, objectively, and respectfully. It empowers the professionals to support and motivate each other toward best instructional and management practices. Collegial problem solving must be valued and promoted as a tool to help students who need to succeed (Phillips & McCullough, 1990).

Collaborative consultants must not assume that all colleagues have the necessary information and skills to collaborate successfully. They need to be watchful for negative outcomes resulting from "groupthink," in which incompleteness, bias, failure to examine risks of proposed choices, and failure to work out plans carefully can result in quite negative outcomes (Murray, 1994). They must respect the right of every individual to hear and be heard, and they must also resolve to be responsive, accountable, and vigilant toward recognizing and refraining from unethical practices.

TIPS FOR PROBLEM SOLVING THROUGH COLLABORATIVE CONSULTATION

1. Have materials and thoughts organized before consultations and develop a list of questions that will help ferret out the real problem.
2. Be prepared for the meeting with a checklist of information typically needed. Do not be reluctant to say that you do not have *the* answer. If it is something you should know, find out when you can and get back to the person who asked.
3. Have strategies and materials in mind that may be helpful to the situation, but do not try to have all the answers. This discourages involvement by others.
4. Do not offer solutions too readily, and try not to address too much or too many topics at once.
5. Avoid jargon, and shun suggestions that conflict with policies or favored teacher practices.
6. Make it a habit to look for something positive about the teacher, the class, and the student, and comment on those things. Use feedback as a vehicle that can provide *positive* information, not just negative comments.
7. Don't try to "fix it" if it is not "broken."
8. Don't wait for the consultee to make the first move. But do not expect that teachers will be enthused or flattered to have questions asked about their classrooms and teaching methods.
9. When a teacher asks for advice about a student, first ask what the teacher has already observed. This gets the teacher involved in the problem and encourages ownership in serving the student's special need. Whenever possible, use the terms *we* and *us,* not *I* and *you.*
10. Know how to interpret test results and how to discuss those results with educators, parents, and students.
11. When possible, provide parents with samples of the child's schoolwork to discuss during the conference. Refrain from talking while they peruse the materials. Have a list of resources ready to share with parents for help with homework, reinforcements, and study tips. When providing materials, explain or demonstrate their use, and then keep in touch so that no problems develop.
12. Maintain contact with teachers during the year. You may find that the teacher has detected an improvement that is directly related to your work, and this reinforcement will be valuable for you and your own morale.
13. Remember that minds, like parachutes, work best when they are open.

CHAPTER REVIEW

1. Fundamental components of problem solving, practiced in fields as diverse as business, industry, science, entertainment, health care, education, and more, include gathering data, finding and defining the problem, generating ideas for action, making a plan, implementing the plan, and following up on success of the plan.

2. Problem identification is the most critical phase of problem solving. Information from multiple sources and collaborative input by a team of educators will help identify the real problem and facilitate its solution.

3. There are ten important steps in a problem-solving consultation: planning, initiating the consultation, collecting information, identifying the problem, generating options and alternatives, formulating a plan, evaluating progress and process, following through and following up, interacting informally, and repeating if necessary.

4. Collaborative consultants will benefit from practicing active listening and formulating key phrases to use during each phase of the consultation. They should monitor their own skills for rapport building, onedownsmanship, appropriate body language, avoidance of jargon, and active listening.

5. Divergent production of ideas during problem solving can be enhanced by the use of techniques and tools such as brainstorming, idea checklists, lateral thinking, Six-Hat thinking, concept mapping, idea checklists, synectics, metaphorical thinking, and Janusian thinking. Other tools for interaction include jigsaw, reciprocal teaching, compare-and-contrast, role play, TalkWalk, and more. Teachers may have used these techniques with students from time to time, but in too many cases have overlooked their potential for enhancing professional interactions. Collegiality and collaboration are cultivated by the use of a variety of interaction formats such as buzz groups, huddle groups, circle responses, role play, panels, and interviews.

6. Many of the interferences and hurdles to circumvent and overcome when collaborating and consulting emanate from the "lack of" themes identified by Caplan (1995)—lack of knowledge about general and special education and other education roles; lack of skills in applying differentiated curriculum, interventions, and adaptations; lack of objectivity by becoming too involved or not involved enough; and lack of self-confidence in managing special needs situations.

TO DO AND THINK ABOUT

1. When consultants introduce themselves to consultees, what are four or five things they can mention about themselves in order to develop rapport?

2. Discuss at least five things a consultant does *not* want to happen while consulting and collaborating, along with the conditions that might cause these unwanted events, and how the conditions might be avoided or overcome. Who has the most control over whether these unwanted events will or will not happen?

3. For a challenging assignment, select a school issue or student problem and create a method for engaging in consultation by designating a system, perspective, approach, prototype, mode, and model, as discussed in Chapter 3. Carry out the consultation as a role play or simulation, using the ten steps and verbal responses provided in this chapter. In a "debriefing" session with your colleagues, discuss which parts of the consultation process were most difficult, some possible reasons, and what could be done to make the consultation successful.

4. Choose a TV program that shows meetings—for example, committees for congressional hearings or locally televised school board meetings. Note the body language exhibited during meetings and make some inferences about possible effects this can have on progress and outcomes of the meeting. Examples would be fiddling with a pencil, looking at a watch or clock, crossing arms, pulling corners of mouth apart, leaning back, talking with hands, writing notes while spoken to, looking sideways without a focus, and so forth. Monitor your own personal body language and make efforts to modify anything you found disconcerting by others during the observation exercise.

5. As coordinator for a meeting to discuss a particularly sensitive educational issue, identify preparations that should be made for efficient, effective communication among all participants.

6. Complete the following partial statements with a variety of possible responses. Then generate ideas for developing mutual understanding of roles and responsibilities and eliminating these potential impediments to collaborative activity,

- Special education teachers often are not able to _____.

- General education teachers often are not able to _____.

ADDITIONAL READING AND RESOURCES

Clark, S. G. (2000). The IEP process as a tool for collaboration. *Teaching Exceptional Children, 33*(2), 56–66.

DeBoer, A. (1997). *Working together: The art of consulting and communicating.* Longmont, CO: Sopris West.

DeBoer, A., & Fister, S. (1998). *Working together: Tools for collaborative teaching.* Longmont, CO: Sopris West.

deBono, E. (1973). *Lateral thinking: Creativity step by step.* New York: Harper & Row.

deBono, E. (1985). *Six thinking hats.* Boston: Little, Brown.

Gardner, H. (1993). *Multiple intelligences: The theory in practice.* New York: Harper Collins.

Giangreco, M. F. (1993). Using creative problem-solving methods to include students with severe disabilities in general classroom activities. *Journal of Educational and Psychological Consultation, 4*(2), 113–135.
   Provides specific examples of using the Osborn-Parnes Creative Problem-Solving process for instructional inclusion relevant to students with intensive educational needs.

Haynes, M. E. (1988). *Effective meeting skills: A practical guide to more productive meetings.* Los Altos, CA: Crisp.

Hobbs, T., & Westling, D. L. (1998). Promoting successful inclusion through collaborative problem solving. *TEACHING Exceptional Children,* Sept./Oct. 1998.
   Presents five key components of a structured problem-solving process and a number of professional practices to maximize success of the process.

Menlove, R. R., Hudson, P. J., & Suter, D. (2001). A field of IEP dreams: Increasing general education teacher participation in the IEP process. *Teaching Exceptional Children, 33*(5), 28–33.

Mills, G. E., & Duff-Mallams, K. (2000). Special education mediation: A formula for success. *Teaching Exceptional Children, 32*(4), 72–78.

Morris, A. (1999). *Teamwork.* New York: Lothrop, Lee, & Shepard.
   A delightful children's book describing teamwork as a group from any culture or walk of life that works together and plays together. Photos from fifteen different countries and descriptions of activities as diverse as college students laying sandbags to contain a river in the United States, to whitewashing a temple roof in Thailand. The book could be a useful prelude to a group problem-solving meeting, or with students to explain the concept of team-teaching when it is introduced into their classroom.

Osborn, A. F. (1963). *Applied imagination: Principles and procedures of creative problem-solving.* New York: Scribner.

Starko, A. (2001). *Creativity in the classroom: Schools of curious delight* (2nd ed.). Mahwah, NJ: Erlbaum.

CHAPTER EIGHT

CONTENT:
Family
Partnerships

Working Together with Families and Communities

Education must be a shared responsibility. Education of the whole child requires solid, well-functioning partnerships among school, community, and family. In a 2003 Delta Kappa-Gallup poll of attitudes toward public schools, 94 percent of respondents declared that home life, parent involvement in education, student interest in education, and the community environment are crucial to improving student achievement (Blank, 2004).

Family members are a child's first and most influential teachers. The nature of education makes families and schools partners in educating children with special needs. Too often the conventional pattern of relationships between schools and parents is limited to having parents as donors, classroom volunteers, or passive recipients of information. This pattern should be altered by joining family members and community members in partnerships to prepare students for their future. Cultivating home-school collaboration allows school educators and home educators to fulfill their commitments toward developing each child's potential.

FOCUSING QUESTIONS

1. How does involvement by families in home-school partnerships benefit students, their families, teachers, their schools, and communities?

2. What legislation has mandated parent involvement and supported family empowerment in schools?

3. In what ways has family involvement matured into family partnership and collaboration?

4. What are barriers to home-school collaborative partnerships?

5. How can educators examine their values and attitudes toward families in order to build collaborative relationships?

6. How can school personnel initiate and individualize partnerships with families and involve students in planning for their own learning?

From Chapter 8 of *Collaboration, Consultation, and Teamwork for Students with Special Needs*, 6/e. Peggy Dettmer. Linda P. Thurston. Ann Knackendoffel. Norma J. Dyck. Copyright © 2009 by Pearson Merrill. All rights reserved.

KEY TERMS

cultural and linguistic
    diversity (CLD)
empowerment
equal partnerships model

family-focused collaboration
home-school collaboration
Individualized Family Service
    Plan (IFSP)

parent involvement
parent partnerships

SCENARIO 8.A

The setting is a junior high school. The learning disabilities teacher has just arrived at the building, hoping to make some contacts with classroom teachers before classes begin, when the principal walks out of her office briskly, with a harried look.

Principal: Oh, I'm glad you're here. I believe Barry is part of your caseload this year, right? His mother is in my office. She's crying, and says that everybody's picking on her son.

LD Consultant: What happened?

Principal: He got into an argument with his English teacher yesterday, and she sent him to me. After he cooled down and we had a talk, it was time for classes to change, so I sent him on to his next class. But he skipped out. The secretary called and left word with the babysitter to inform the mother about his absence. He must have really unloaded on her, because she's here, quite upset, and saying that the teachers do not care about her son and his problems. Could you join us for a talk?

LD Consultant: OK, sure. (Enters the principal's office and greets Barry's mother.)

Mother: I am just about at my wit's end. It's not been a good week at home, but we've made an effort to keep track of Barry's work. Now this problem with his English teacher has him refusing to come to school. Sometimes I feel that we're at cross purposes—us at home and you at school.

LD Consultant: We certainly don't want this to happen. I'd like to hear more about your concerns, and the problems Barry and his teachers are having. Is this a good time, or can we arrange for one that is more convenient for you?

Mother: The sooner, the better. I don't want Barry missing school, but with the attitude he has right now, it wouldn't do him any good to be here.

LD Consultant: Sounds like you are eager to work on this! I would like us to move into the conference room and talk about Barry's problems here at school. We may want to involve others in our discussions later. Would that be OK with you? We are all concerned about Barry, and we need for him to know that.

MANDATES FOR FAMILY INVOLVEMENT

School partners need to be aware of several legislated mandates intended to ensure and strengthen educational partnerships between home and school. The Education for All Handicapped Children Act of 1975 (P.L. 94-142) prescribes several rights for families of children with disabilities. Succeeding amendments have extended those rights and responsibilities.

Legislation mandating family involvement is part of EACHA, the Handicapped Children's Protection Act, Early Intervention for Infants and Toddlers (Part H of P.L. 99-457), and the Individuals with Disabilities Education Act (IDEA, P.L. 101-476). Passage of P.L. 94-142 in 1975 guaranteed families the right to due process, prior notice and consent, access to records, and participation in decision-making. To these basic rights the 1986 Handicapped Children's Protection Act added collections of attorney's fees for parents who prevail in due process hearings or court suits. The Early Intervention Amendment was part of the reauthorized and amended P.L. 94-142. Passed in 1986, it provides important provisions for children from birth through five years and their families. Part H addresses infants and toddlers with disabilities or who are at-risk for developmental delays. Procedural safeguards for families were continued and participation in the Individualized Family Service Plan (IFSP) was added.

The IFSP is developed by a multidisciplinary team with family members as active participants. Part B, Section 691, mandates service to all children with disabilities from ages three to five, and permits noncategorical services. Children may be served according to the needs of their families, allowing a wide range of services with parent training. This amendment fosters collaboration based on family-focused methods. The legislation speaks of families in a broad sense, not just a mother and father pair as the family unit. Families' choices are considered in all decisions.

The 1990 amendments under P.L. 101-476 increased participation by children and adults with disabilities and their families. An example is the formation of community transition councils with active participation of parents in the groups. Subsequent court decisions and statutory amendments have clarified and strengthened parent rights (Martin, 1991). The spirit of the law is met when educators develop positive, collaborative relationships with families.

The Individuals with Disabilities Education Act (IDEA) Amendments of 1997 were signed into law in June of 1997 after two years of analysis, hearings, and discussion. This reauthorization of IDEA, as Public Law 105-17, brought many changes to P.L. 94-142. Parent participation in eligibility and placement decisions, and mediation as a means of resolving parent-school controversies are two critically important areas of change. P.L. 105-17 strengthens the involvement of parents in all decision making involving their children (National Information Center for Children and Youth with Disabilities, 1997).

The 1997 amendments were reauthorized in 2004 as P.L. 108-446, the No Child Left Behind (NCLB) legislation. NCLB mandates that schools give parents the tools they need to support their children's learning in the home and that they communicate regularly with families about children's academic progress, provide opportunities for family workshops, and offer parents chances to engage in parent leadership activities at the school site.

EDUCATIONAL RATIONALE
FOR FAMILY INVOLVEMENT

School, family, and community provide overlapping spheres of influence on children's behavior and achievement. All spheres should be included for involvement by the collaborative team for partnerships that operate with students at the center of the model. Student development and learning at all levels of education are supported by strong home-school relationships within which they improve academic behavior and social behavior, achieving higher attendance rates and lower suspension rates.

Families make a difference in the academic and social lives of children and youth. At all phases of schooling, strong home-school relationships are critical for children's learning and development. Extensive research demonstrates that family involvement can enhance a student's chances for success in school and significantly improve achievement. Students have higher attendance rates, more pro-social behavior, better test scores, and higher homework completion rates. Level of family involvement predicts children's academic and social development as they progress from early childhood education programs through K–12 schools and into higher education (Caspe, Lopez, & Wolos, 2007).

For preschool children, family involvement means improved cognitive and social development. Frequency of parent-teacher contact and involvement at the early childhood site is associated with preschool performance (Weiss, Caspe, & Lopez, 2006). In their study of experimental research on parent involvement at the early childhood level, the Harvard Family Research Project found that participation in school activities is associated with child language, self-help, social, motor, adaptive, and basic school skills (Weiss et al., 2006).

Home-school relationships have positive short-term and long-term benefits for elementary school students, too (Caspe et al., 2007). Barnard (2004) showed that when low-income African American families maintained continuously high rates of parent participation in elementary school, children were more likely to complete high school. Dearing, Krieder, Simpkins, and Weiss (2006) conducted a longitudinal study that showed consistent family involvement was predictive of gains in children's literacy performance. In a meta-analysis of studies examining the relationship of parent involvement with student academic achievement in urban elementary schools, Jeynes (2005) discovered that continuous and consistent parent involvement shields and protects children from the negative influences of poverty; it may be one approach to reducing the achievement gap between white and nonwhite students.

At the middle and high school levels, family involvement is a powerful predictor of various positive academic and social outcomes. Because of the adolescent's increasing desire for autonomy and changes in school structure, family involvement in education tends to decrease in middle and high school (Kreider, Caspe, Kennedy, & Weiss, 2007). However, family involvement in learning remains important in the adolescent years. Parents can monitor their children's academic and social progress and acquire information they need to make decisions about their children's future, then engage in positive relationships with school staff (Hill & Taylor, 2004). They also have the opportunity to learn skills that help with their child's needs, such as behavior management techniques and communication strategies.

As parents work with teachers, they can provide input about their children's histories and experiences and express their own wisdom about their children's interests and needs. Teachers learn more about students' backgrounds and receive support from family members who can provide encouragement to their children as they study and learn.

School systems benefit from home-school collaboration through improved attitudes toward schools and advocacy for school programs. A positive home-school relationship helps others in the schools and the community. Family involvement increases positive communication among all who are involved on the education team.

All in all, substantial research supports family involvement, and a growing body of intervention evaluations demonstrates that family involvement can be strengthened with positive results for children and youth (Caspe & Lopez, 2006). Therefore, it is crucial for encouraging optimal outcomes by students.

Family Empowerment

A significant goal of family and community involvement with education is empowerment of families. The old way of working with families of children with disabilities often meant "helping them into helplessness." Well-intentioned educators and other professional helpers provided services and solved problems, and families were deprived of the experience of learning to solve their own problems. But families are the constant in children's lives and family members need the knowledge, skills, and motivation to become advocates for themselves and their children. Empowerment means that family members take action to reach goals for their children, satisfying their wants and needs and building on their strengths. Empowered people have the means and knowledge to act; they know what they want and take action to get it (Turnbull, Turnbull, Erwin, & Soodak, 2006).

True educational partnerships support empowerment of families. Educators should provide families with some of the means they need to become empowered. Turnbull and Turnbull et al. (2006) describe an empowerment model of collaboration. In their empowerment framework, family resources, professional resources, and education context resources are all involved in collaborating for empowerment. Family resources include motivation, expectation, energy, and persistence. Families often need additional skills and knowledge to become empowered as strong advocates for their children and partners with their children's teachers. This knowledge includes information, problem solving, life management strategies, and communication skills. Teachers can use their resources to empower parents and support development of their skills. Providing this support for parents, families, and siblings of children with exceptionalities also means fostering community support and advocacy (Fiedler, Simpson, & Clark, 2007). Resources for studying the interests and needs of siblings of people with special health and developmental needs are available online at Web sites such as www.siblingsupport.org.

Several program attributes can help assure consultants that school-home-community programming will result in family empowerment. Those listed here are based on principles of Family Support America (Dunst, 2002):

- Educators and families work together in relationships based on equality and respect.
- Educators enhance families' capacities to support growth and development in all family members.
- Families are recognized as resources to their own members, to other families, to programs, and to communities.
- Schools affirm and strengthen families' cultural, racial, and linguistic identities and enhance their ability to function in a multicultural society.
- Educators and communities advocate for services and systems that are fair, responsible, and accountable to the families served.
- School personnel work with families to mobilize formal and informal resources to support family development.
- Programs are flexible and responsive to emerging family and community issues.

Broadened Conceptualization of Family

Changing times and changing families require new ideas, new languages, and new models. The first step in these changes is to think in terms of family rather than parent. Many children do not live with both parents, or with either biological parent. Part H and Section of 619 of IDEA refer to families rather than parents. Consultants who are collaborating with adults for development and well-being of children with special needs should have a broad, inclusive definition of *family*.

This new, inclusive definition for family was suggested to the Office of Special Education and Rehabilitation Services (OSERS) by the Second Family Leadership Conference:

> A family is a group of people who are important to each other and offer each other love and support, especially in times of crisis. In order to be sensitive to the wide range of lifestyles, living arrangements, and cultural variations that exist today, family . . . can no longer be limited to just parent/child relationships. Family involvement . . . must reach out to include mothers, fathers, grandparents, sisters, brothers, neighbors, and other persons who have important roles in the lives of people with disabilities. (Family Integration Resources, 1991, p. 37)

Consultants need to help school personnel accommodate differences in families—families of children with disabilities, poverty-level families, CLD families—and recognize that they are not homogeneous groups. Educators need to respond in individually relevant ways rather than to make assumptions about families based on their language, ethnicity, or background. Educators need to learn more about full-service models and collaborate actively with related service providers and community networks. If they become knowledgeable about services and advocate for broader services and access, collaborative efforts with parents will be more successful, to the benefit of students, families, and school personnel.

MOVING FROM PARENT INVOLVEMENT TO PARTNERSHIPS WITH FAMILIES

Educational consultants and their colleagues must be aware of the realities and new legislation facing today's families. Increases are evident in poverty levels, births to unwed adolescent parents, and the rise of nonbiological parents as primary caretakers (foster care, grandmothers, extended family, adoptive parents, and so on). In addition, there are increasing numbers of families with cultural minority backgrounds, single-parent families, parents with disabilities, gay and lesbian parents, and blended and extended families.

Many families are overwhelmed by family crises and normal life events. Others face multiple stressors such as long work hours, illness and disability, and overwhelming responsibilities. Many are discouraged and burned out. Such situations make family collaboration a challenge for collaborative consultants and many families. Educational legislation and social reality result in an inclusive school context that gives educators the opportunity and flexibility to work collaboratively with persons who may be helpful and supportive of the child's success in school.

It is possible for families to be involved in the school life of their children but not be collaborative. Collaboration goes beyond involvement. Educators may provide families

with information, parenting classes, and advocacy groups. However, this kind of involvement does not ensure that family needs and interests are being heard and understood. It
does not signify that educators are setting program goals based on family members' concerns and input. It might involve parents in a narrow sense, but not in the larger sense of
working together to form a home-school partnership.

It is important to distinguish between parent involvement and family collaboration in
two ways:

1. Parent involvement is parent participation in activities that are part of their children's
   education—for example, conferences, meetings, newsletters, tutoring, and volunteer
   services.
2. Family collaboration is the development and maintenance of positive, respectful,
   egalitarian relationships between home and school. It includes mutual problem solving with shared decision making and goal setting for students' needs.

Values Inherent in Home-School Collaboration

Collaboration with families adds a dimension to home-school relationships. Not only
should family members be involved with schools, educators must be involved with families. Metaphorically speaking, a one-way street becomes a two-way boulevard to provide
an easier road to "Success City" for students. Family-focused home-school collaboration is
based on these principles:

- Families are a constant in children's lives and must be equal partners in all decisions
  affecting the child's educational program.
- Family involvement includes a wide range of family structures.
- Diversity and individual differences among people are to be valued and respected.
- All families have strengths and coping skills that can be identified and enhanced.
- Families are sources of wisdom and knowledge about their children.

Central to family-centeredness is the respect for family concerns and priorities,
issues of family competence and assets, and utilization of family and community resources
and supports. Hammond (1999) lists other characteristics of family-centered programs:
flexible programming, individualizing services for families, communication, developing
and maintaining relationships, building family-staff collaboration, and respecting the family's expertise and strengths. This is a tall order for educational consultants, but new,
empowering relationships and better outcomes for students depend on this shared sense of
respect and care.

BARRIERS TO COLLABORATION WITH FAMILIES

Changing family structures make traditional methods of recruiting parent participation
somewhat problematic. Historical, attitudinal, or perceptual factors in regard to work, transportation, and child care can influence family participation. Major changes in immigration

patterns and in the diversity of the U.S. population add to the complexity of collaboration with families (see Berger, 2008; Lynch & Hanson, 1998; and Chapter 9 in this book). Collaborative consultants who recognize potential barriers to home-school partnerships will be better prepared to use successful and appropriate strategies in bridging the gap between home and school.

Most educational consultants recognize the importance of family involvement, but going beyond the "what can parents do for the school" presents a barrier to some educators. Christie (2005) believes it is often easier to talk about what parents can do for the school than it is to listen to parents about what they know their children need to be successful. Sometimes when parents appear not to care, Christie says, it is because they know that what they have to say probably will not be heard.

The success of family collaboration activities is based on partnerships developed and maintained by using the relationship and communication skills such as those described in Chapter 4. However, other barriers overshadow the need for effective communication. They surface as formidable challenges to educators even before lines of communication are established. Examples of such barriers are time limitations, anticipation of negative or punishing interactions, denial of problems, blaming, or a personal sense of failure in parenting and teaching.

Parents of children with learning and behavior problems can be effective change agents for their children; therefore, the question is not whether to involve them, but *how* to do it (Bauer & Shea, 2003). Although family members may want very much to play a key role in encouraging their children to succeed in school, they may be inhibited by their own attitudes or circumstances. Many parents, while very concerned about their child's education, are fearful and suspicious of schools, teachers, and education in general (Hansen et al., 1990). They may fear or mistrust school personnel because of their own negative experiences as students. Or they may have experienced an unfortunate history of unpleasant experiences with other professionals, so that current school personnel fall heir to that history.

Parents of children with special needs face many economic and personal hardships such as work schedules and health concerns. Low-income families may have difficulty with transportation and child care, making it hard to attend meetings or volunteer in school even when they would like to do so (Thurston & Navarette, 1996). Also, families stressed by poverty or substance abuse will be less available to consult and collaborate with school personnel.

The single parent, already burdened with great responsibilities, is particularly stressed in parenting a child with special needs. The role can be overwhelming at times. For collaborative efforts to produce results, the interaction must fit the single parent's time and energy level. When working with the single parent, school personnel will need to tailor their requests for conferences and home interventions, and to provide additional emotional support when needed (Conoley, 1989).

The two-parent, two-home student also struggles with repercussions from family strife leading to the divorce, breakup of the family, and passage back and forth between parents, oftentimes with stepparents and new brothers and sisters in the mix. Educators at school and at home must organize a cooperative and collaborative team for managing the academic and emotional needs of the students. As just one example, homework assignments can be problematic for the child who will be with one parent for only a short time. Teachers need to partner with the noncustodial parent to integrate homework and other school activities into visitation periods (Frieman, 1997). School counselors, support personnel from community mental health centers, and social workers should be included as part of the team for assisting the student torn between two or more homes.

The same can be said for children in foster care, who often fall behind academically, fail classes, neglect homework, or are truant. Some students do not know how to ask their foster family for help with homework or other school problems. Many have low self-esteem and associate school with fear and anxiety, so validating self-esteem through small successes and acquiring problem-solving skills can be first steps toward succeeding in school (Noble, 1997).

Many types of disability are very expensive for families, and the impact on the family budget created by the special needs of a child may produce formidable hardships. Sometimes families arrive at the point where they feel their other children are being neglected by all the attention to the child with exceptional learning needs. This adds to their frustration and stress. In addition, children with special needs and their families are vulnerable to stereotypes of society about disabilities. The ways in which families cope with the frustrations and stress influence their interaction with school personnel. Providing support networks can help them cope with the situation (Dunst, 2002; Turnbull et al., 2006).

Family members may avoid school interactions because they fear being blamed as the cause of their children's problems. Sometimes teachers do blame parents for exacerbating learning and behavior problems—"I can't do anything here at school because it gets undone when they go home!" But blaming does not facilitate development of mutually supportive relationships. Family members are very sensitive to blaming words and attitudes from school personnel. A teacher who is part of a therapeutic foster family reported that he felt "blame and shame" after a school conference about the child with emotional and behavior problems who had been his foster child for two months.

Judging attitudes, stereotypes, false expectations, and basic differences in values also act as barriers and diminish the collaborative efforts among teachers and families. It is difficult to feel comfortable with people who have very different attitudes and values. Families and teachers should make every effort not to reproach each other, but to work together as partners on the child's team. Educators, including teachers and parents, must abandon any posture of blaming or criticism, and move on to collaboration and problem solving. It is important to remember that it does not matter where a "fault" lies. What matters is who steps up to address the problem.

Culturally and Linguistically Diverse Families

Active parent and community involvement in educational programs for culturally and linguistically diverse (CLD) students is essential. Yet the growing differences among cultural and linguistic backgrounds of school personnel and their students makes home-school collaboration a challenge. The unfortunate portrayal of CLD families as deficient in skills necessary to ready children for school is a huge barrier to active parent participation. Misconceptions about parental concern for their children's schooling are all too prevalent among school personnel (deValenzuela, Torres, & Chavez, 1998).

Too often programs for parent involvement are based on middle-class values. Effective collaborative consultants recognize that sometimes there are differing views between home and school educators about the involvement of families in education of their children and varying levels of visibility for that involvement. August and Hakuta (1997) researched patterns of parental involvement (parent behaviors that support education) among Puerto Rican families, Chinese American families, and Mexican American families and found that parent behaviors nurturing child learning may not always be visible to school personnel or recognized as such.

Classrooms today have increasing numbers of students from culturally and linguistically diverse backgrounds. It is important to note that the concept of *disability* is culturally and socially constructed. Each society's culture defines the parameters of what is considered normal, with some cultures having a broader or different definition of disability from that in U.S. schools (Linan-Thompson & Jean, 1997). This may be one reason ethnically diverse parents tend to be less involved and less informed about their child's school life than mainstream parents. It is important to learn from family members how their beliefs and practices will affect programs for children with special needs. Educational consultants who work with families must be aware of the family's perceptions of disability. Linan-Thompson and Jean (1997) suggest taking time to learn about family perceptions of special needs, carefully and thoroughly explaining the whole special education process, using informal assessments in addition to formal assessment tools (which helps explain the disability on other than formal terms), and discovering and using parents' preferred forms of communication (written, informal meetings, video- or audiotapes).

Collaborative consultants need to help other school personnel accommodate differences in families—families of children with disabilities, poverty-level families, CLD families—and consider that they are not homogeneous groups. Educators should respond in individually relevant ways rather than make assumptions about families based on language, ethnicity, or background. Educators need to learn more about full-service models and collaborate actively with related service providers and community networks. If they become knowledgeable about services and advocate for broader services and more access, collaborative efforts with parents will be successful to the benefit of students, families, and school personnel.

Traditional approaches to reaching out to families are not always appropriate for families from cultural and other minority groups. Educators must develop cultural competence that demonstrates acceptance and respect for cultural diversity and differences (Cross, 1996; Lynch & Hanson, 1998). This allows individualization of educational programs for students and individualization of parent interactions to be done in a manner that respects the family's culture. Cross (1996) recommends that educators learn about cultures they serve by observing healthy and strong members of different groups. Other recommendations include spending time with people of that culture, identifying a cultural guide, reading the literature (professional as well as fiction) by and for persons of the culture, attending relevant cultural events, and asking questions in sensitive ways.

Bruns and Fowler (1999) recommend that educators give special recognition to cultural preferences in transition planning. Traditional parental roles of teacher, information source, decision maker, and advocate for transition planning may not be appropriate for or sensitive to all families. They suggest transforming these roles to be that of guide, information specialist, decision maker, and ally. They also recommend inviting extended family members, friends, and community members to take part in education-related decisions as a way to meet diverse values and traditions of cultural groups. As educators develop cross-cultural competencies and increasingly collaborate with families culturally or linguistically different from themselves, they need to remember that one approach does not fit all ranges of diversity (Parette & Petch-Hogan, 2000).

The following ten strategies are helpful when collaborating with families from diverse cultural groups:

1. Acknowledge cultural differences and become aware of how they affect parent-teacher interactions.
2. Examine your personal culture, such as how you define family, and your desired life goals and perceived problems.
3. Recognize the dynamics of group interactions such as etiquette and patterns of communication.
4. Go out into the community and meet the families on their own turf.
5. Adjust collaboration to legitimize and include culturally specific activities.
6. Learn about the families. Where are they from and when did they arrive? What cultural beliefs and practices surround child rearing, health and healing, and disability and causation?
7. Recognize that some families may be surprised by the extent of home-school collaboration expected in the United States.
8. Learn and use words and forms of greetings in the families' languages.
9. Work with cultural mediators or guides from the families' cultures to learn more about the culture and facilitate communication between school and home. Examples are relatives, church members, neighbors, or older siblings.
10. Ask for help in structuring the child's school program to match home life, such as learning key words and phrases used at home.

Well-publicized policies at the district level encouraging home-school collaboration are vital in providing opportunities for minority family members to become full partners with teachers. Traditional methods of parent involvement such as PTA meetings, open house, or newsletters seldom permit true collaboration, constructing instead a "territory" of education that many parents are hesitant to invade. Concern, awareness, and commitment on the part of individuals in the educational system are beginning steps in challenging the limitations that inhibit collaboration between teachers and families who have language, cultural, or other basic differences.

BRIDGE BUILDING FOR SUCCESSFUL HOME-SCHOOL COLLABORATION

Friendly, positive relationships and honest, respectful communication can help bridge the barriers that might exist to home-school collaboration. The goal of collaboration is to promote the education and development of children by strengthening and supporting families.

Keeping this in mind, consultants will remember that collaboration is not the goal but the means to the end. Strategies that have proved to be sturdy bridges to circumvent barriers are building trust, focusing on family strengths, using appropriate communication skills, and promoting positive roles for family members.

Focusing on Family Strengths

Family-focused services and collaboration emphasize an empowerment approach rather than focusing on what is going wrong. Instead of focusing on a child or family's problem, collaborators focus on family members and the strength of their experiences. An effective partner-educator provides support and reinforcement for family members in their family roles. In addition to listening to family members and acknowledging their expertise, it is crucial to empower families by giving them positive feedback about their efforts to support their child's education. Families often get very little reinforcement for parenting, particularly for the extra efforts they expend in caring for children with special needs. They should be encouraged and commended for providing three types of parental engagement at home that are consistently associated with student performance at school (Finn, 1998):

1. Organizing and monitoring the student's time
2. Helping with homework
3. Discussing school matters with their child

Too few families hear positive comments about their children. They may feel guilty or confused because of their children's problems. Examples of support and reinforcement that teachers can use include thank-you notes for helping with field trips; VIP (very important parent) buttons for classroom volunteers; supporting phone calls when homework has been turned in; and Happygrams when a class project is completed.

Using Appropriate Communication Skills

Bridges to circumvent language and communication barriers are difficult to construct. Chapter 4 describes communication skills that are important in building and maintaining collaborative relationships with adults in the lives of students with special needs. Consultants will want to use rapport-building skills to build trust and confidence in the collaborative relationship, and to recognize and reduce their own language and communication barriers. Those who communicate with family members should use these guidelines:

- Be aware of voice tone and body language.
- Be honest and specific.
- Give your point of view as information, not the absolute truth.
- Be direct about what is wanted and expected.
- Do not monopolize the conversation.
- Listen at least as much as talk.
- Do not assume your message is clear.

- Avoid educational or psychological jargon.
- Attack the problem, not the person.
- Focus on positive or informational aspects of the problem.
- Have five positive contacts for every negative one.
- Always be honest; do not soft-pedal reality.
- Attend to cultural differences in verbal and nonverbal communication.

Providing Social Support

Families rely on informal and formal social support networks for information and guidance they need to carry out responsibilities for child rearing, children's learning, and child development. Schools can provide a rich array of child, parent, and family support in the form of information and environmental experiences to strengthen family and child competence and influence student outcomes. Parenting supports include information and advice that can strengthen existing parenting knowledge and skills and facilitate acquisition of new competencies (Dunst, 2000).

For families of children with disabilities, supports are a crucial aspect of family-focused collaboration. Workshops, newsletters, informational meetings, provision of emotional support, and multigenerational gatherings are examples of formal supports needed by families. Schools are also instrumental in promoting informal support systems for families. According to extensive research by Dunst (2000) and his colleagues, informal support demonstrates a stronger relationship to many child, parent, and family outcomes than does formal support. Fiedler, Simpson, and Clark (2007) suggest that providing support for all family members and siblings also benefits children with special needs, as does fostering community advocacy and support. Thus, consultants should encourage activities that help families develop informal support networks such as parent-to-parent groups and informal multiple-family gatherings.

Promoting Positive Roles for Family Members

Family members play a range of roles from purveyor of knowledge about the child to advocates for political action. No matter what role is taken by individual family members, educational consultants should remember that families are:

- Partners in setting goals and finding solutions
- The best advocates and case managers for the child with special needs
- Individuals with initiative, strengths, and important experiences
- The best information resource about the child, the family, and their culture

Within any role along the wide continuum of family members, the consultant must respect and support the courage and commitment of family members to struggle with the challenges of daily living faced by all families. Recognizing, supporting, and reinforcing interventions on behalf of the child with special needs will promote an increased sense of competency and help create a safe, nurturing environment for children, while maintaining

FIGURE 8.1   Suggestions for Building Bridges to Successful Home-School Collaboration

- Keep in mind that the family usually has concerns and issues that have nothing to do with you personally and that you may not know about.
- Be sensitive to the language levels, vocabularies, and background of the family and adjust your language, but be yourself.
- Get enough information, but not more than you need. You don't want to appear "nosy."
- Focus discussions on factors you can control.
- Find out what has been tried before.
- Listen so that you are completely clear about the family's concerns.
- Honor confidentiality.
- Remain open to new approaches and suggestions. Each family is different.
- Set concrete, measurable goals. Communication is clearer and measures of success are built in and promote collaboration.
- Wait until the family asks for help or until a good relationship is established before making suggestions.
- Help families solve their own problems and allow them to become, or develop the skills to become, their child's own case manager.

Source: Adapted from PEATC. (1991). *Partnership series.* Alexandria, VA: Parent Educational Advocacy Training Center.

the unique cultural and ethnic characteristics of their family unit (Barbour, Barbour, & Scully, 2008; Caspe & Lopez, 2006; Turnbull et al., 2006).

Supporting and reinforcing families in their chosen roles is not always easy. Members in multiproblem families often are viewed as having defective or faulty notions of parenting, no problem-solving skills, and mental health problems. Even for families having different values and expectations, and risk factors such as poverty mental illness or drug/alcohol involvement, focusing on strengths and providing positive supports is the best approach for collaborators. Figure 8.1 lists other suggestions for developing bridges to overcome potential or real barriers in collaboration.

DEVELOPING HOME-SCHOOL PARTNERSHIPS

There is great variation in individual practices for home-school collaboration. Effective collaboration efforts depend on attitude of teachers, their beliefs about the family roles and the efficacy of family involvement, and their comfort level and communication skills. When school personnel collaborate with family members, they nurture and maintain partnerships that facilitate shared efforts to promote student achievement. As families and teachers plan together and implement plans of action, they find that working as a team is more effective than working alone. Each can be assured that the other is doing the best for the child and each can support the other, thus producing positive educational outcomes for children with special needs. Families that are stressed by poverty or substance abuse will be less readily available to consult and collaborate with school personnel, so educators must be resourceful in developing strategies for encouraging their participation.

Family involvement is usually conceptualized from family member perspectives (Wanat, 1997). In her study with fifty-seven parents, Wanat (1997) found that parents did not distinguish between involvement at school and at home and they had specific ideas about what constituted meaningful involvement. One parent summarized legitimate parent involvement as "everything you do with the child because education involves a lot more than just sitting at school." It would be good for education consultants to remember this statement when they work collaboratively with parents.

APPLICATION 8.1
READING CENTER FOR FAMILIES

Visit a school library, or revisit your own school library, and find a corner that could be outfitted as a "Parent/Family Reading Center." (Try to find a quiet, pleasant place but not *too* out-of-the-way.) Display an attractive painting, a plant, perhaps a snapshot display of recent school events, along with a small table, comfortable chairs, and, of course, books and periodicals. These should be focused on interests and needs of families, parents, day care providers, grandparents, and home-school projects. Promote the center at parent-teacher meetings and parent conferences. Perhaps meet with a group of parents there on a nonconfidential matter (planning the yearly social event, initiating a coupon drive for playground equipment, and so forth.) Work into the plan the school personnel who would be responsible for upkeep, checkout and returns, and materials acquisition. Some of this might even be accomplished by students.

Five Steps for Collaborating with Families

Five basic steps will assist school personnel in developing successful home-school partnerships:

Step 1: Examining personal values
Step 2: Building collaborative relationships
Step 3: Initiating home-school interactions
Step 4: Individualizing for parents
Step 5: Evaluating home-school collaboration

Step 1: Examining Personal Values.   Value systems are individualistic and complex. They are the result of nature and the impact of experiences on nature. People need to apply information and logic to situations that present values different from their own. Kroth (1985) provides an example. He notes that a significant amount of research indicates a positive effect on children's academic and social growth when teachers use a daily or weekly report card system to communicate with parents or guardians. This information provides logical support for interaction among teachers and family members on a regular, planned basis.

School personnel must guard against valuing teacher knowledge and experience over family knowledge and experience. As stated earlier, it is vital to recognize that parents are the experts when it comes to knowing about their children, no matter how many tests educators have administered to students, or how many hours they have observed them in the classroom. If professional educators are perceived as *the* experts, and the *only* experts, false expectations may create unrealistic pressure on them. Some family members find it difficult to relate to experts. So a beautiful "boulevard of progress" becomes a one-way street of judging, advising, and sending solutions.

The first step in collaborating with families is to examine one's own values. Figure 8.2 is a checklist for examining one's values and attitudes toward parents and other family members.

Communicating messages of equality, flexibility, and a sharing attitude will facilitate effective home-school collaboration. The message that should be given to parents of students with special needs is, "I know a lot about this, and *you* know a lot about that. Let's put our information and ideas together to help the child."

The checklist in Figure 8.3 on page 290 serves as a brief self-assessment to test congruency of attitudes and perceptions with the two-way family collaboration discussed earlier. Inventorying and adjusting one's own attitudes and perceptions about families are the hardest parts of consulting with them. Attitudes and perceptions about families and their roles in partnerships greatly influence implementation of the consulting process.

School personnel also must keep in mind that family members are not a homogeneous group; therefore, experiences with one family member cannot be generalized to all other parents and families. Resources for examining values and for increasing cultural sensitivity are found in the Additional Readings and Resources section of this chapter and in Chapter 9.

Step 2: Building Collaborative Relationships.   The second step in collaborating with families is building collaborative relationships. As emphasized in Chapter 4, basic communication and rapport-building skills are essential for establishing healthy, successful relationships with family members. To briefly review, these are the most important skills for educators in interacting with families:

- Responsive listening
- Assertive responding
- Mutual problem solving

Prudent teachers avoid words and phrases that may give the impression that a disability or a person with a disability is undesirable. They listen for the messages given by parents and respond to their verbal and nonverbal cues.

In communicating with families, school personnel must avoid jargon that can be misunderstood or misinterpreted. Parents often feel alienated by professional educators and one common cause is words (*program, site*) and acronyms (IFSP, ITBS) that pepper the conversation without explanation of their meaning (Soodak & Erwin, 1995). Some professional educators seem unable, or unwilling, to use jargon-free language when they communicate with laypeople (Schuck, 1979). Choices of words can ease, or inhibit, communication with parents, and professional educators must respect language variations created by differences in culture, education, occupation, age, and place of origin (Morsink et al., 1991).

Teachers and administrators often find that one of the most important, but difficult, aspects of developing relationships with parents is listening to them. The challenge lies in

FIGURE 8.2   Examining Own Values

Instructions: Rate belief or comfort level, from 1 (very comfortable or very strong) to 5 (very uncomfortable or not strong at all).

How comfortable do you feel with each?

_____ Parents or others who are overly protective

_____ Teachers who think they are never wrong

_____ Families who send their children to school without breakfast

_____ Teachers who get emotional at conferences

_____ Teachers who do not want mainstreamed students

_____ Open discussions at family meetings

_____ Parents who have lost control of their children

_____ Volunteers in the classroom

_____ Conflict

_____ Being invited to students' homes

_____ Using grades as a behavior management tool

_____ Family members who call every day

_____ Teachers who do not follow through

_____ Students attending conferences

_____ Principals attending conferences

_____ Parents who do not allow their children to be tested

_____ Different racial or ethnic groups

_____ Family members who do not speak English

_____ Others who think special needs children should be kept in self-contained classrooms

_____ Teachers who think modifying curriculum materials or tests is watering down the lessons

_____ Family members who drink excessively or use drugs

_____ Administrators who do not know your name

_____ Criticism

How strongly do you believe the following?

_____ Family members should be able to call you at home.

_____ Newsletters are an important communication tool.

_____ Family members should volunteer in the classroom.

_____ General classroom teachers can teach students with special needs.

_____ All children can learn.

_____ Family members should come to conferences.

_____ Resistance is normal and to be expected in educational settings.

_____ Children in divorced families have special problems.

_____ Family resistance is often justified.

_____ Teacher resistance is often justified.

_____ Family influence is more important than school influence.

_____ Medical treatment should never be withheld from children.

_____ Children with severe disabilities are part of a supreme being's plan.

_____ Sometimes consultants should just tell others the best thing to do.

_____ Consultants are advocates for children.

_____ Teachers should modify their classrooms for children with special needs.

_____ It is a teacher's fault when children fail.

_____ Consultants are experts in educating special needs children.

_____ Some people do not want children with special needs to succeed.

Do you think all teachers, administrators, counselors, psychologists, parents, grandparents, social workers, and students would have responded as you did? What happens when members of the same educator team have different views?

FIGURE 8.3   Self-Assessment of Attitudes and Perceptions Concerning Families and Family Collaboration

Rate yourself on the following, from 1 (very little) to 5 (always).

1. I understand the importance of parent involvement.	1 2 3 4 5
2. I recognize the concerns parents may have about working with me.	1 2 3 4 5
3. I recognize that parents of students with special needs may have emotional and social needs I may not understand.	1 2 3 4 5
4. I recognize and respect the expertise of families.	1 2 3 4 5
5. I feel comfortable working with families whose values and attitudes differ from mine.	1 2 3 4 5
6. I am persistent and patient as I develop relationships with families.	1 2 3 4 5
7. I am comfortable with my skills for communicating with families.	1 2 3 4 5
8. I am realistic about the barriers for me in working with families.	1 2 3 4 5
9. I find it difficult to understand why some families have the attitudes they have.	1 2 3 4 5
10. I recognize that some family members will have problems interacting with me because of their experience with other teachers.	1 2 3 4 5

listening to parents' messages even though they might disagree strongly with family members, and their attitudes and values might differ significantly from those of the families. Although the quality of the interaction should be a primary focus in parent relationships, the numbers and variety of initiated communications are important as well. Phone calls, introductory and welcoming letters, newsletters, teacher-to-parent calendars, and notepads with identifying logos all have been used effectively by educators to initiate partnerships. Each note, phone call, conversation, or conference, whether taking place in a formal setting or on the spur of the moment at the grocery store, should reflect the willingness and commitment of school personnel to work with parents as they face immense responsibilities in providing for the special needs of their child.

It is important for teachers to arrange and encourage more regular, informal contacts with parents. Family members often report being put off by the formality inherent in some scheduled conferences, particularly when they are limited to ten minutes, as they often are, with another child's family waiting just outside. (Lindle, 1989). Ask parents for preferred modes of communication. Phone calls are appropriate for positive reports, but should not be used to discuss weighty concerns. Notes sent home can promote consistency in expectations and help teachers and family members develop a common language (Bos, Nahmias, & Urban, 1999). Some consultants have found e-mail and school Web site access an effective way to communicate with families. However, many families do not have access to this technology. Chapter 4 has important recommendations for using e-mail in collaborative efforts.

Step 3: Initiating Home-School Interactions.   Parents want their children to be successful in school. Even parents who are considered "hard to reach," such as nontraditional, low-income, and low-status families, usually want to be more involved (Davies, 1988). Most, however, wait to be invited before becoming involved as a partner in their child's education. Unfortunately, many have to wait for years before someone opens the door and provides them the *opportunity* to become a team member with others who care about the educational and social successes of their children. Parent satisfaction with their involvement is directly related to perceived opportunities for involvement (Salisbury & Evans, 1988). They are more motivated to carry on when they are aware that the results of their time and energy are helping their child learn. School personnel who are in a position to observe these results can provide the kind of reinforcement that parents need so much.

When parents are welcome in schools and classrooms, and their child's work and experiences are meaningful to them, parents often experience new aspirations for themselves and for their children (St. John, Griffith, & Allen-Hayes, 1997).

Step 4: Individualizing for Families.   Special education professionals are trained to be competent at individualizing educational programs for students' needs. Nevertheless, they may assume that all family members have the same strengths and needs, thereby overlooking the need to individualize family involvement programs (Turnbull et al., 2006). By using the assessments discussed earlier, and taking care to avoid stereotypes and judgments, they will be more successful in involving parents as partners in their child's learning program. Another helpful instrument is the checklist for determining family interests in Figure 8.4 on the next page.

Successful work with parents calls for establishing respectful and trusting relationships, as well as responding to the needs of all partners. The degree to which parents are placed in an egalitarian role, with a sense of choice, empowerment, and ownership in the education process, is a crucial variable in successful collaboration.

Step 5: Evaluating Home-School Collaboration.   Evaluation of efforts to provide opportunities for collaboration in schools can indicate whether or not families' needs are being met and their strengths are being utilized. Evaluation also shows whether needs and strengths of educational personnel are being met. Assessment tools used after a workshop, conference, or at the conclusion of the school year allow school personnel to ask parents, "How did we do in facilitating your learning of the new information or accessing the new services?" Some teachers use a quick questionnaire, to be completed anonymously, to see if the activity or program fulfilled the goals of the home-school collaboration. If data show that the activity gave families the information they needed, provided them with the resources they wanted, and offered them the opportunities they requested, educators know whether or not to continue with the program or modify it.

Educators also should evaluate their own involvement with families. This means assessing the use of family strengths and skills to facilitate educational programs with children who have special needs. Did teachers get the information they needed from families? How many volunteer hours did parents contribute? What were the results of home tutoring on the achievement of the resource room students? What changes in family attitudes about the school district were measured? Chapter 6 contains information about procedures for evaluating collaboration efforts. Note again that the purpose of family collaboration is to utilize the unique and vital partnership on behalf of their children.

FIGURE 8.4   Ascertaining Family Interests

Families! We want to learn more about you so that we can work together helping your child learn. Please take a few minutes to respond to these questions so your voice can be heard. It will help the Home-School Advisory Team develop programs for families, teachers, and children.

Check those items you are most interested in.

____   1. Family resource libraries or information centers
____   2. Helping my child learn
____   3. Support programs for my child's siblings
____   4. Talking with my child about sex
____   5. Helping with language and social skills
____   6. Mental health services
____   7. Talking with another parent about common problems
____   8. Respite care or babysitters
____   9. My role as a parent
____   10. Classes about managing behavior problems
____   11. Making my child happy
____   12. Managing my time and resources
____   13. Making toys and educational materials
____   14. Reducing time spent watching television
____   15. What happens when my child grows up
____   16. Recreation and camps for my child
____   17. State wide meetings for families
____   18. Vocational opportunities for my child
____   19. Talking to my child's teacher
____   20. Talking with other families
____   21. Learning about child development
____   22. Things families can do to support teachers
____   23. Home activities that support school learning
____   24. Information about the school and my child's classes
____   25. Helping my child become more independent
____   26. Others?

_____

_____

_____

Thanks for your help!

Name of family member responding to this form:

_____

Child's name: _____

APPLICATION 8.2

First, meet in groups of four or five teachers to discuss the situation below:

A fifth-grade girl is having difficulty with her schoolwork, especially math and spelling. Family members try hard to help, but they and the child become frustrated and little progress is made. Tension within the family is palpable. The mother feels her daughter needs more instructional attention at school to relieve strain on the family at home. She has requested a conference with the girl's teachers and related services personnel.

As you discuss this, make a list of things you would *not* want to have happen during any ensuing home-school conference. Make another list of things that you would want to have happen. Then combine and arrange all lists into overall "Do and Don't" help sheets for home-school involvement in students' learning programs and study strategies. Embellish with illustrations if appropriate. Find practical uses for these help sheets.

Family Partners in IEP, ITP, and IFSP Planning

The Individualized Education Plan (IEP), Individualized Family Service Plan (IFSP), or Individualized Transition Planning (ITP) conference can be a productive time or a frustrating experience. Parents may be emotional about their child's problems, and teachers can be apprehensive about meeting with the parents in emotion-laden situations. A number of researchers have found that too little parent involvement in team decision making, particularly relating to IEP, IFSP, and ITP development, is a major problem in special education programs (Boone, 1989).

School consultants will improve school-home collaboration in these areas if they provide family members with information for the meeting. Consultants can communicate with family members by phone, letter, or informal interview to inform them about names and roles of staff members who will attend; typical procedure for meetings; ways they can prepare for the meeting; contributions they will be encouraged to make; and ways in which follow-up to the meeting will be provided.

Turnbull and Turnbull (2006) list eight components that an IFSP/IEP conference should include:

1. Preparing in advance
2. Connecting and getting started
3. Sharing visions and great expectations
4. Reviewing formal evaluation and current levels of performance
5. Sharing resources, priorities, and concerns
6. Developing goals and objectives (or outcomes)
7. Specifying placement and related services
8. Summarizing and concluding

Figure 8.6 (Dettmer, 1994) to be presented later in this chapter outlines specific ways parents can be involved in IEP, ITP, or IFSP development and implementation before, during, and after the IEP conference. These lists could be printed in the school handbook.

When parents and teachers work together as equals, they have more opportunities to express their own knowledge and can come to respect each other's wisdom. Siblings need information about disabilities, opportunities to talk about their feelings, time to hear about the experiences of other siblings of children with disabilities, people with whom to share their feelings of pride and joy, and ways to plan for the future (Cramer, Erzkus, Mayweather, Pope, Roeder, & Tone, 1997; Fiedler, et al., 2007).

Equal Partnership Model

Parents have much to communicate to school personnel about their children—the "curriculum of the home," and the "curriculum of the community" (Barbour et al., 2008). This information can include parent-child conversation topics, how leisure reading is encouraged, deferral of immediate gratifications, long-term goals, how homework is assisted and assessed, what TV is watched and how it is monitored, and how affections and interests in the child's accomplishments are demonstrated. If school personnel do not understand (or attempt to understand) the curriculum of the home and the community, equal partnerships are difficult to establish. Educators can use checklists, conversations, home visits, and community involvement to learn about the strengths, interests, and needs of parents and the communities in which the families live. If school personnel offer workshops and materials that are not based on family interests and needs, a message is communicated that educators know more about their needs than they do; and then the family involvement is not a true partnership. An example of a needs and interests assessment is included in Figure 8.5.

The equal partnership model stresses not only respect for the curriculum of the child's home and community, but also the importance of providing opportunities for family members to use their strengths, commitment, and skills to contribute to the formal education of their children. This relationship is not based on a deficit model of blame and inequality. Families appreciate having their special efforts recognized, just as teachers do. Multiyear research by St. John and colleagues (1997) showed mixed results when parents were not treated as full partners in the education of their children.

Tools for assessing parent strengths are similar to those for assessing needs. Interviews and checklists are useful in determining what types of contributions families can bring to the partnership. These assets can be conceptualized along four levels of involvement (Kroth, 1985), from strengths that all family members have, to skills that only a few family members are willing and able to contribute. For example, all parents have information about their children that schools need. At more intensive levels of collaboration, some family members are willing and able to tutor their children at home, come to meetings, help make bulletin boards, and volunteer to help at school. At the highest level of collaboration, only a few parents can be expected to lobby for special education, serve on advisory boards, or conduct parent-to-parent programs. A number of parent advocates of children with learning and behavior disorders have made impressive gains in recent decades toward state and national focus on the rights of children with special needs. They have formed organizations, identified needs, encouraged legislation, spoken for improved facilities, and supported each other through crises. In many instances they have involved pediatricians, community agency leaders, and businesses in special projects for children with special needs.

FIGURE 8.5   Family Member Participation Checklist

Families! We need your help. Many of you have asked how you can help provide a high-quality educational program for your children. You have many talents, interests, and skills you can contribute to help children learn better and enjoy school more. Please let us know what you are interested in doing.

_____   1. I would like to volunteer in school.
_____   2. I would like to help with special events or projects.
_____   3. I have a hobby or talent I could share with the class.
_____   4. I would be glad to talk about travel or jobs, or interesting experiences that I have had.
_____   5. I could teach the class how to _____.
_____   6. I could help with bulletin boards and art projects.
_____   7. I could read to children.
_____   8. I would like to help my child at home.
_____   9. I would like to tutor a child.
_____   10. I would like to work on a buddy or parent-to-parent system with other parents whose children have problems.
_____   11. I would like to teach a workshop.
_____   12. I can do typing, word processing, phoning, making materials, or preparing resources at home.
_____   13. I would like to assist with student clubs.
_____   14. I would like to help organize a parent group.
_____   15. I want to help organize and plan parent partnership programs.
_____   16. I would like to help with these kinds of activities:

At school _____

At home _____

In the community _____

Your comments, concerns, and questions are welcome. THANKS!

Name: _____

Child's Name: _____

How to Reach You: _____

By considering family member strengths as well as needs and interests, educators will be focusing on the collaborative nature of parent involvement. An example of a strengths assessment form is provided in Figure 8.6.

Utilizing the strengths and interests of family and community members to engage them with the education of infants and toddlers, preschool and kindergarten students, primary, middle, and secondary students can be approached in many creative ways. Teachers Involve Parents in Schoolwork (TIPS), developed by the National Network of Partnership Schools (Van Voorhis, 2003) as an interactive process for encouraging homework, used strength and motivation of middle school families to help sixth- through eighth-graders

FIGURE 8.6 Checklist for Families in Developing IEPs

Throughout the year:

Read about educational issues and concerns.

Learn about the structure of the local school system.

Observe your child, noting work habits, play patterns, and social interactions.

Record information regarding special interests, talents, and accomplishments, as well as areas of concern.

Before the conference:

Visit the child's school.

Discuss school life with the child.

Talk with other families who have participated in conferences to find out what goes on during the conference.

Write down questions and points you would like to address.

Review notes from any previous conferences with school staff.

Prepare a summary file of information, observations, and products that would further explain the child's needs.

Arrange to take along any other persons that you feel would be helpful in planning the child's educational program.

During the conference:

Be an active participant.

Ask questions about anything that is unclear.

Insist that educational jargon and "alphabet soup" acronyms be avoided.

Contribute information, ideas, and recommendations.

Let the school personnel know about the positive things school has provided.

Ask for a copy of the IEP if it is not offered.

Ask to have a follow-up contact time to compare notes about progress.

After the conference:

Discuss the conference proceedings with the child.

Continue to monitor the child's progress and follow up as agreed on.

Reinforce school staff for positive effects of the planned program.

Keep adding to the notebook of information.

Be active in efforts to improve schools.

Say supportive things about the schools whenever possible.

complete more accurate homework and get better grades. At the early childhood level, Mayer, Ferede and Hou (2006) used storybooks to successfully promote family involvement. The online Family Involvement Storybook Corner promotes awareness and practice of family involvement through storybooks (www.gse.harvard.edu/hfrp/projects/fine/resources/storybook/index.html). Another example is the Raising a Reader Program, based on the work of Judith K. Bernhard (www.ryerson.ca/~bernhard/early.html). She and her colleagues built their Early Programs on parents' strengths to benefit children by giving parents a prominent role as their children's literacy teachers. Raising a Reader is a nonprofit organization in California whose purpose is engaging parents in a routine of daily "book cuddling" with their children birth through age five (www.pcf.org/raising_reader/research.html).

As stated earlier, involvement is not synonymous with collaboration. Developing a workshop on discipline or a volunteer program without assessing strengths, needs, and goals demonstrates failure to respect the partnership between school and home. True partnership features mutual collaboration and respect for the expertise of all parties.

STUDENT PARTICIPATION IN CONFERENCES

The student has the greatest investment and most important involvement in constructing an individual education plan for learning. Indeed, it is counterproductive to formulate goals and objectives without involving students in their conferences as a member of the planning team.

Having students help plan a student-led conference with family members will give them a sense of ownership in their own learning process. Students and their teachers should talk beforehand about the purpose of their conference and then set some goals for the meeting. Teachers should convey to students that family members like this kind of parent-teacher conference and it will be fun.

The student will want to decide which samples of work to show and what learning activities to describe. Developing a sample rubric to evaluate the conference after it takes place will add to the learning process. The classroom teacher or special education teacher, or both, may want to have a brief practice session so the process feels familiar and comfortable when the conference takes place. See the summarized ten-step process on page 298.

Teachers should prepare family members for the student-led conference with a phone call or a brief letter, focusing on the contributions it can make to their child's confidence and pride in achievement.

Parent partnerships can be particularly difficult to cultivate at the secondary level. Much of the difficulty stems from attitudes of teenage students who would just "die" of humiliation if their parents were seen at school by their peers. Other teens might head off a teacher's efforts to have involved family members with "Go ahead, but they won't care/come/participate," "They have to work," "They don't care," and so on. Parents pick up on these attitudes and acquiesce to them, and teachers are hard-pressed to find time for and ways of addressing them (McGrew-Zoubi, 1998).

In some middle school settings where traditional parent-teacher interactions and conferences have been perceived as more problematic than problem-solving, an innovative student-centered model for conferencing has been developed and tried. In this model, a structure is created by which students are helped to prepare for their own conferences. The new format is communicated to parents and colleagues and procedural operations are developed (Countryman & Schroeder, 1996). In the planning, development, and evaluation phases of this new approach, teachers find that students should have more participation in preparing conference scripts. They need a log to help them organize their products, and they must not overlook bringing to the discussion such classes as art, family and consumer science, and modern languages or those subjects will not get discussed. Students reasonably express the need to see how teachers have evaluated them before it is revealed at the conference.

Hanna and Dettmer (2004) provide a detailed, ten-step plan for getting students ready to guide their parent-student-teacher conference. Student and teacher should discuss these steps and prepare for them, even rehearse them, in advance of the scheduled conference:

1. Determine the purpose(s) of the conference.
2. Formulate goals for the conference and prepare the invitation to family members. In the invitation, family members should be clued as to what to expect and ways to contribute.
3. Develop an agenda and determine location, seating plan, format for introductions, and possible opening and closing remarks.
4. Select samples of work and pertinent information that focus on accomplishments, interests, and any major concerns. Anticipate questions or concerns parents might bring up and think of responses to give.
5. Rehearse a simulated conference.
6. At conference time, explore ideas for further learning and achievement.
7. Set reasonable goals.
8. Adhere to the time schedule, summarize, and close on a positive note.
9. Determine follow-up and follow-through procedures for attaining the planned goals.
10. Have all participants evaluate the event with rubrics designed specifically for the purpose.

A student-guided conference must not be hurried. A thirty-minute segment of time might be reasonable. Busy teachers, particularly those at the secondary level with dozens of students, will need strong administrator support and innovative scheduling ideas to make student-guided conferences effective. But for a courageous, energetic school staff, student-guided parent conferences can promote meaningful ownership by students in their own learning. Students and other participants also can benefit from an assessment of conference outcomes by using a rubric designed for the purpose. (See Figure 8.7.)

Benefits from having students participate in conferences for their individualized programs include receiving information about their progress, feeling involved in their own education, being motivated to improve, and having awareness that both parents and teachers are interested in working collaboratively on their behalf.

MAINTAINING HOME-SCHOOL COLLABORATION AND PARTNERSHIP

Home-school collaboration is mandated, it is challenging, and it is rewarding. Educators have two choices in collaborating with families—to see school as a battleground with an emphasis on conflict between families and school personnel, or to see school as a "homeland" environment that invites power sharing and mutual respect, with collaboration on activities that foster student learning and development (Epstein, 1995). The goal for educators and their partners is to integrate family involvement as part of the school instructional strategy, that is, as part of the curriculum rather than added on to school activities. Successful models for home-school-community partnerships are those that:

FIGURE 8.7   Rating Form, Student-Led Conference on Portfolio Achievement

Name: _____

Criterion	Needs Improvement		Fair	Good	Outstanding
1. Was prepared for the conference	0	1	2	3	4
2. Participated enthusiastically	0	1	2	3	4
3. Presented material in organized way	0	1	2	3	4
4. Explained learning process effectively	0	1	2	3	4
5. Assessed achievement realistically	0	1	2	3	4
6. Submitted ideas for next work/studies	0	1	2	3	4
7. Credited resources accurately	0	1	2	3	4
8. Involved all participants in discussion	0	1	2	3	4

Total: ___ of 32

Areas of strengths:

Areas which need more work:

- Respect the family as the child's first teacher
- Empower families and communities to support and advocate for all students
- Understand learning as a lifelong endeavor involving families and communities
- Recognize that all families want the best for their children and can have a positive, significant impact on their children's education

Students, schools, and families are strengthened by appropriate outreach efforts and partnership activities that are based on values and practices of a family-focused approach. Educators who empower and support families of their students recognize that they are part of a powerful partnership and the work they do with parents is part of the educational legacy they leave with the student and with the family. (See Figure 8.8.)

RESOURCES FOR SCHOOL EDUCATORS AND FAMILIES

The library and Internet are excellent sources of information about successful home-school-community collaborative efforts. Many state and national organizations are dedicated to providing helpful information about disabilities, special education, legal issues, and successful parent-as-partner strategies. For example every state has least one parent center that is funded by the U.S. Department of Education (www.taalliance.org). Most states have a Parent Training and Information Center and a Community Parent Resource Center; they provide training and information to families of children and young adults from birth to age twenty-two who have physical, cognitive, emotional, or learning disabilities. They help families obtain

FIGURE 8.8   Good Meeting of Home and School Educators

appropriate education and services for children with disabilities and function to improve education results for all children. They train and inform parents and professionals on a variety of topics, resolve problems between families and schools or other agencies, and connect children with disabilities to community resources that address their needs. Other resources include:

National Association for the Education of Young Children (www.naeyc.org)

Harvard Family Research project (www.hfrp.org)

National Network of Partnership Schools and the Center on School, Family, and Community Partnerships (www.csos.jhu.edu/P2000/center.htm)

National Dissemination Center for Children with Disabilities (NICHCY; www.nichcy.org)

Children, youth and families education and research network (CYFERNet; www.cyfernet.org)

Most of these resources have both Spanish and English versions of their Web sites and are excellent resources for both parents and educators.

ETHICS FOR WORKING TOGETHER
WITH FAMILY AND COMMUNITIES

In an ethical climate for home-school collaboration, educators will demonstrate keen awareness of realities facing today's families. Challenges in working with families today are very different from those of past decades due to significant changes in society. Many families are overwhelmed by specific family crises as well as everyday life events. And many face multiple and prolonged stressors such as poverty, long work hours or multiple jobs, health issues without insurance, and bi- or multilingual communication between home and school. Families might include a single parent, a blended family, gay or lesbian parents, unwed adolescent parents, nonbiological parents serving as primary caregivers, foster care, grandparents, extended families, and adoptive parents.

Collaborative consultants must avoid judging attitudes, overtones of blaming, stereotyping, holding false expectations, and dwelling on basic differences in values. They must be tolerant if parents want to obtain second or even third opinions. It is important to have empathy with families with the awareness that parents may be having considerable difficulty in coming to terms with their child's disability or disabilities. Confidentiality of information and privacy pertaining to family matters must be honored and preserved.

In an ethical climate families and school personnel will make every effort not to reproach each other, but work together as partners on the child's team. They will be honest with each other and willing to listen and empathize, acknowledging anger and disappointment with patience and calmness. In potentially explosive situations the teacher will want to include the principal, remain calm and open-minded, and listen to learn exactly what the family members' views are. Teachers who find out that they are wrong should acknowledge that before stating their views. They will want to stress that all parties have the welfare of the child in mind. Teachers and administrators will want to keep in mind that most families are doing the best they can; parents of students do not start out the morning saying, "I think today I will be a poor parent." Collaboration will not require total agreement in values or educational method, but school personnel and families must focus on needs and interests of children and their families.

TIPS FOR HOME AND SCHOOL COLLABORATION

1. Establish rapport with families early in the year. Call right away, before problems develop, so that the first family contact is a positive one.
2. Invite families in to talk about their traditions, experiences, hobbies, or occupations.
3. Send home "up slips," putting them in a different format from the "down slips" that families sometimes receive, and have conferences with families because the student is performing *well* in the classroom.
4. When sharing information with families, "sandwich" any necessary comments about problems or deficits between two very positive ones.
5. During interaction with families, notice how your actions are received, and adapt to that.
6. When interacting with families, never assume anything.

7. When several staff members will be meeting with family members, make sure each one's role and purpose for being included in the meeting will be understood by the parents.
8. Introduce families to all support personnel working with the child.
9. Build interpersonal "bank accounts" with frequent deposits of good will to families. The "interest earned" will be better outcomes for students.
10. Send out monthly newsletters describing the kinds of things the class is doing, and school news or events coming up. Attach articles families would be interested in. Have a Family Corner occasionally, for which families provide comments or ideas.
11. Encourage volunteering in the classroom to read stories, help with art lessons, listen to book reports, or give a lesson on an area of expertise such as a job or hobby.
12. Ask families about their educational expectations for their children. Develop a climate of high expectations in the home, school, and community.
13. Send follow-up notes after meetings. Put out a pamphlet about home-school collaboration in IEP planning conferences.
14. Provide classroom teachers with handouts that can be useful during conferences.
15. Have a Home Book notebook of pictures, activities, and stories about class that students take turns sharing at home.
16. Put a Family Board at the entrance of the building for posting ideas of interest to families, examples of class activities, and pictures.
17. Involve parents and siblings, babysitters, and grandparents to all class parties.
18. Write the right notes. Say thanks, confirm plans, ask for opinions, praise work, give good news, give advance notice of special events and classroom needs.
19. Have families from other countries or culture groups talk to students about their customs and culture.
20. Ask families what their family goals are, and respond with how those goals are being met by the classroom curriculum.

CHAPTER REVIEW

1. The variable with the most significant effect on children's development is family involvement in the child's learning. Educational professionals are integral parts of children's lives, but families are the link of continuity for most of them. Parents and other family members and caregivers are the decision makers for their children, whose futures are largely dependent on the continued ability of their parents to advocate for them. Numerous mandates and passages of legislation have recognized this relationship and provided for involvement by families in the educational programs of students who have special learning and behavioral needs. Educators must be partners with families of students with special needs. This is a demanding and challenging responsibility; however, educators are committed to such a partnership because it fulfills a legal right of families.

2. Legislation codifies the benefits of the partnership for children, families, and schools. Important mandates include P.L. 99-457, P.L. 101-476, P.L. 94-142, and P.L. 105-17.

3. Educational consultants have begun to focus successfully on family strengths by broadening the concept of parent involvement to parent partnership, by using appropriate communication skills, and by promoting positive

roles for family members. These enhanced perceptions recognize family needs and promote family competence.

4. Educators and families encounter numerous barriers to home-school collaboration, including underutilization of services, lack of organizational cultural competency, and differing attitudes, history, values, culture, and language. Examining their own culture and values as potential barriers to understanding will enable them to address the diversity they experience during collaboration.

5. Educators must clarify their own values in order to respect the values of others. Check-

lists, structured value-clarification activities, or thoughtful consideration help educators identify their specific values about education, school, and home-school collaboration.

6. Educators should provide a variety of opportunities for families to become involved with the school. These opportunities should be based on family strengths, expertise, and needs. Family strengths represent contributions that they can make to the partnership. The needs of parents are those interests and needs they have concerning their families.

TO DO AND THINK ABOUT

1. Put yourself in the place of a parent of a student with a disability. Reflect on:

   ■ What you would expect to find in a climate of family partnership at your child's school
   ■ What you would want in terms of knowledge about services and opportunities to be involved in the educational process
   ■ What questions you would have for your child's teacher(s)
   ■ What kinds of school environment or teacher behavior would encourage you to engage in partnership with the school and teachers

   Then summarize these thoughts into a set of do's and don'ts for family school partnership.

2. Brainstorm to identify family characteristics or strengths that would be encouraging to a consultant or teacher who has students with learning or behavior disorders. Then develop a set of guidelines for interaction and involvement between school educators and home educators that would cultivate those characteristics.

3. Plan a booklet that could be used by consultants to improve home-school communication and collaboration. Determine who would compose it, how it could be distributed and used, and how it would be helpful for involving families as collaborative partners in their child's education. In the booklet include either the do's and don'ts of #1 above, or the guidelines from #2, or both.

ADDITIONAL READINGS AND RESOURCES

Berger, E. H. (2008). *Parents as partners in education: Families and schools working together* (7th ed.). Upper Saddle River, NJ: Prentice Hall.

Caspe, M., & Lopez, M. E. (2006). *Lessons from family-strengthening interventions: Learning from evidence-based practice.* Cambridge, MA: Harvard Family Research Project. Available at www.gse.harvard.edu/hfrp.html

Caspe, M., Lopez, M. E., & Wolos, C. (2007). *Family Involvement in elementary school children's*

education. Cambridge, MA: Harvard Family Research Project. Available at www.gse.harvard.edu/hfrp.html

Fiedler, C. R., Simpson, R. L., & Clark, D. M. (2007). *Parents and families of children with disabilities: Effective school-based support services.* Upper Saddle River, NJ: Prentice Hall.

Harry, B., Kalyanpur, M., & Day, M. (1999). *Building cultural reciprocity with families: Case studies in special education.* Baltimore: Paul H. Brookes.

Hildebrand, V., Phenice, L. A., Gray, M. M., & Hines, R. P. (2000). *Knowing and serving diverse families*. Upper Saddle River, NJ: Merrill.

Kreider, H., Caspe, M., Kennedy, S., & Weiss, H. (2007). *Family Involvement in middle and high school students' education*. Cambridge, MA: Harvard Family Research Project. Available at www.gse.harvard.edu/hfrp.html

Soodak, L. C., & Erwin, E. J. (1995). Parents, professionals, and inclusive education: A call for collaboration. *Journal of Educational and Psychological Consultation, 6*(3), 257–276.

Researchers found that parents want more meaningful collaboration with educators because they do not necessarily support the goals of the schools' philosophy and practices in special education.

Turnbull, A., Turnbull, R., Erwin, E. J., & Soodak, L. C. (2006). *Families, professionals, and exceptionality: Positive outcomes through partnership and trust* (5th ed.). Upper Saddle River, NJ: Pearson.

Weiss, H., Caspe, M., & Lopez, M. E. (2006). *Family Involvement in early childhood education*. Cambridge, MA: Harvard Family Research Project. Available at www.gse.harvard.edu/hfrp.html